From Folklore
to Fiction

Recent Titles in
Contributions in Afro-American and African Studies
Series Advisers: John W. Blassingame and Henry Louis Gates, Jr.

From Folklore to Fiction

A STUDY OF FOLK HEROES AND RITUALS IN THE BLACK AMERICAN NOVEL

H. Nigel Thomas

Contributions in Afro-American and African Studies,
Number 118

Greenwood Press
New York ● Westport, Connecticut ● London

Library of Congress Cataloging-in-Publication Data

Thomas, H. Nigel, 1947–
    From folklore to fiction : a study of folk heroes and rituals in
the Black American novel / H. Nigel Thomas.
        p.   cm. — (Contributions in Afro–American and African
studies, ISSN 0069–9624 ; no. 118)
    Bibliography: p.
    Includes index.
    ISBN 0–313–26224–1 (lib. bdg. : alk. paper)
    1. American fiction—Afro–American authors—History and criticism.
2. Afro–Americans in literature.   3. Folklore in literature.
4. Heroes in literature.   5. Rites and ceremonies in literature.
6. Afro–Americans—Folklore.   I. Title.   II. Series.
PS153.N5T47 1988
813′.009′896073—dc19   88–15491

British Library Cataloguing in Publication Data is available.

Library of Congress Catalog Card Number: 88–15491
ISBN: 0–313–26224–1
ISSN: 0069–9624

First published in 1988

Greenwood Press, Inc.
88 Post Road West, Westport, Connecticut 06881

Printed in the United States of America

The paper used in this book complies with the
Permanent Paper Standard issued by the National
Information Standards Organization (Z39.48–1984).

10 9 8 7 6 5 4 3 2

Contents

Contents

"Learn It to the Younguns": Passing on Folk Wisdom

Daryl Cumber Dance

This is the book I had been planning to write for the past fifteen years, it was inevitable that if I kept procrastinating, someone would more expeditiously respond to the obvious void. Finally H. Nigel Thomas has provided the kind of exploration and explication of the use, influence, and impact of Black folklore on literature that I perceived was so much needed. Despite the numerous published commentaries on the influence of Afro–American folklore on individual works and specific authors, and the occasional consideration of its influence on a particular genre or a limited period (such as Keith Byerman's focus on ten contemporary writers in *Fingering the Jagged Grain*), nothing approaching the scope of this study has appeared. Thus I welcome *From Folklore to Fiction: A Study of Folk Heroes and Rituals in the Black American Novel*, at the same time I upbraid myself for dallying while Thomas forged ahead.

Black writers have long acknowledged the significance of their folk heritage to their development as writers. A heritage that influences the subject matter, the themes, the motifs, the characters, the symbolism, the tone, the value system, the language and the style of their writing. Ralph Ellison acknowledges that "Negro American folk tradition constitutes a valuable source for literature," and frequently comments on his use of his folk heritage (Ellison 1964, 59). Langston Hughes acclaimed the Black folk community that "furnish[es] a wealth of colorful, distinctive material for any artist" (Ellison 1964, 693). Richard Wright maintained that "Negro folklore [is] the Negro writer's most powerful weapon" (1937 [1971], 8). Noting that one of her early efforts at writing began with an idea from her mother's oral tales and a consequent interest in exploring voodoo, Alice Walker informs us that with its completion she experienced that "wonderful feeling...of being with...ancient spirits, all very happy to see me consulting and acknowledging them" (Walker 1983, 9–13); her continuing sense of herself as a medium, recording and transmitting folk experience, wisdom, and magic, is reinforced with her ending to her latest novel, *The Color Purple*:

I thank everybody in this book for coming.

A. W., author and *medium* (italics mine)

Paule Marshall frequently lauds those "poets in the kitchen" who passed on to her "the rich legacy of language and culture" (Marshall 1983, 30). Toni Cade Bambara asserts when asked what her mother tongue is: "The language of Langston Hughes, the language of Grandma, the language of 'mama say'" (Bambara 1980, 48); elsewhere she declares, "the voice of my work is bop" (Tate 1983, 29). Similarly, Gayl Jones credits the "'speech community' in which I lived" as being one of the "most important influence[s] on my storytelling writing style" (Tate 1983, 94). And thus, ad infinitum, from Paul Laurence Dunbar and Charles Chesnutt through Sterling Brown and Zora Neale Hurston on to Ishmael Reed and Toni Morrison, Black writers have maintained that they are inspired and shaped by Black folk culture.

H. Nigel Thomas begins this important study by introducing the principal forms of Afro-American folklore, tracing their African roots and considering their function in the folk community. He then proceeds to review the major folk heroes, including the Preacher, the Bad Nigger, the Black Moses, and that most popular of all the heroes—the Trickster. He goes on to introduce the rituals, including religious rituals, blues, dozens, and jive. This important review not only provides a useful introduction to Black folklore, its origins, role, and significance in Black culture, but it also serves as a valuable bibliographical study since Thomas offers a comprehensive survey of major folklore studies and collections.

Having laid a firm foundation, Thomas proceeds to explore the appearance of these folk heroes and rituals in the literature, focusing on selected, relevant works by James Baldwin, Hal Bennett, Arna Bontemps, Cecil A. Brown, Charles W. Chesnutt, Alice Childress, Countee Cullen, Paul Laurence Dunbar, Ralph Ellison, Leon Forrest, Ernest J. Gaines, Langston Hughes, Zora Neale Hurston, James Weldon Johnson, John Oliver Killens, Paule Marshall, Toni Morrison, Ishmael Reed, Margaret Walker, and Richard Wright. In addition to the intensive consideration of these authors he mentions specific instances of particular heroes and rituals in the works of such authors as Claude Brown, Martin Delaney, Lorenz Graham, Gayl Jones, Louise Meriwether, Albert Murray, Ntozake Shange, Mildred Taylor, Alice Walker, and Walter White, thereby providing a basis for expanding the exploration that he begins here. His discussion of the literature reviews significant prior scholarship and offers interesting new and often provocative readings of a number of the works.

Looking over the whole body of Black American literature that incorporates folklore, Thomas concludes that while earlier writers were "somewhat clumsy" in their integration of folklore into their fiction (partly because of publishers' demands and reader expectations), most writers from the thirties on have been selective of materials that can be truly integrated into their work. Thus the folklore and rituals used do not remain a thing apart, interesting for their quaintness only, but rather become an integral part of the quest of the characters and the revelation of the plot. He notes also that what the writer does with the folk material "is largely determined by a folk tradition, in the main African-derived, that demands that black artists minister to their society (176)." This conclusion is sanctioned by a number of Black writers, most notably Toni Morrison, who insists that the Black novelist must assume the duty of the ancestors, the "timeless people whose relationships to the characters are benevolent, instructive, and protective, and they provide a certain kind of wisdom" (Morrison 1984, 343). Theirs is the wisdom that Ralph Ellison has the Invisible Man's grandfather pass on to him on his death bed, where he reveals the traditional ways in which the Black man has appeased, misled, and thus overcome his enemy. Then with his last breath he whispers fiercely, "Learn it to the younguns" (Ellison 1952, 20). Countless contemporary authors are about the business of studying their past, preserving the wisdom of their ancestors, and dedicating their work to "learn[ing] it to the younguns."

Finally, Thomas observes interesting new and innovative trends occurring in the more recent works of Toni Morrison, Ishmael Reed, Toni Cade Bambara, and Paule Marshall, but concludes that this "requires a study of its own" (177). Ending on this provocative note, Thomas inspires the possibility that, though he has given a comprehensive overview, he has not exhausted this brainchild I cherished so long as my own; thus there may *perhaps* be a second volume that I shall attempt. If indeed I (or some less procrastinating scholar out there) attempt this sequel, I (or he/she) shall certainly profit from the groundwork that Thomas has laid out in this pioneering effort at defining, identifying and assessing the use, incorporation, and impact of folk materials in the full range of American literature.

REFERENCES

Bambara, Toni Cade. "Searching for the Mother Tongue." An Interview with Kalamu ya Salaam. *First World* 2 (1980): 48–53.

Byerman, Keith E. *Fingering the Jagged Grain: Tradition and Form in Recent Black Fiction.* Athens, Ga.: The University of Georgia Press, 1986.

Ellison, Ralph. *Invisible Man*. New York: Random House, 1952.

——. *Shadow and Act*. New York: Random House, 1964.

Marshall, Paule. "From the Poets in the Kitchen." *Callaloo* 6 (Spring-Summer, 1983): 23–30.

Morrison, Toni. "Rootedness: The Ancestor as Foundation." In *Black Women Writers (1950–1980): A Critical Evaluation*, edited by Mari Evans. New York: Anchor Press, 1984.

Tate, Claudia, ed. *Black Women Writers at Work*. New York: Continuum, 1983.

Walker, Alice. *The Color Purple*. New York: Harcourt Brace Jovanovich, 1982.

———. *In Search of Our Mothers' Gardens*. New York: Harcourt Brace Jovanovich, 1983.

Wright, Richard. "Blueprint for Negro Literature." In *Amistad 2*, edited by John A. Williams and Charles F. Harris. New York: Vintage, 1971.

Preface

When Toni Morrison's *Tar Baby* (1981) was published, I became convinced that Morrison had added a new dimension to the rhetorical use of folklore in black American literature. Three years later I decided to analyze that contribution, to add it to other studies that I was sure existed on the subject. I was dismayed by the absence of scholarship that compared black American writers' use of folklore. I decided to turn my attention in that direction, and the present study is largely the result of that decision.

Several people have provided me with invaluable assistance in making this study a reality. Professor Jay Bochner of the English department of l'Université de Montréal stands foremost among them. His perceptive comments, made after numerous hours of reading an earlier version of this manuscript, have resulted in greater clarity and better organization of the ideas expressed here. Ms. Shirley Small, a friend and colleague, listened to and commented on many of the ideas expressed here. Doctor Daniel Kabasele and I talked for long periods about the presence of African beliefs in the African diaspora. The professors of the English department of l'Université de Montréal showed an interest in my work through its varying stages, especially Professor Richard Robillard with whom I discussed many of the works analyzed here. Special thanks go to Professor Daryl Dance of the English department of Virginia Commonwealth University for her very insightful criticism of this manuscript and her very valuable suggestions.

It is my hope that this study will spur others into exploring the asset that black folklore is to black writers and into creating a body of scholarship for future scholars and creative writers to draw on.

Introduction

This study focuses on the transposition of Afro–American folk heroes and rituals from folklore to literature. There exists enough material on folk heroes and rituals for either to be a full-length study. But the one telescopes into the other; the folk hero is a part of ritual creation and is usually best understood in his ritual context. Before proceeding, it is important that folklore be defined—if only because many people claim not to understand what the term means. Folklore is the dramatization of the psychic essences that bind a people. It is therefore the sum total of the rituals, practices, and behaviors undertaken with community sanction to reinforce the beliefs, the values, and the attitudes of a community. Thus, all culturally recognizable codes constitute a part of that culture's folklore. The more homogenous a culture is, the more effective is its folklore.

Identifying whether there exists a tradition for the treatment of black American folk heroes and rituals in the black American novel and examining their function within the black American novel are the principal reasons for this study. It is postulated on the fact that Afro–American novelists utilize folklore because it embodies certain truths or attitudes that they wish their work to reflect or analyze. With few exceptions, the novelists we shall encounter here have as their principal goal a clearer understanding of the role that folklore plays in black American survival.

Aware that many readers of this study may be ignorant of the principal forms of Afro–American folklore, their origins and functions, I intend the first chapter to express precisely that. There one will see, where such can be proved, a tracing of such forms back to Africa, either through an examination of analogous forms in present day West Africa or of similar forms among blacks of the diaspora. My other concern in the first chapter is to analyze the functions of these folk forms, a necessary task since the value of the lore is of predominant interest for the novelist and very little scholarship that interprets the lore exists.

Chapter two deals with major folk heroes who nonetheless appear infrequently as major figures in the novel. This chapter is concerned with how and why the authors incorporate these heroes in their work. In this category of heroes we shall first examine the black preacher of folklore—Dunbar's Parker, Hurston's Pearson, and Bennett's Titus and Cobb—for their similarities to the preacher of black popular imagination; Baldwin's Gabriel we shall analyze as a contrast to the foregoing. We shall next look at defiant heroes—Killen's John Henry; Bontemps' Gabriel, and Morrison's Shadrack as Black Moses; and Wright's Bigger Thomas and Gaines' Marcus as Bad Niggers.

By focusing on the trickster, the most popular character in Afro–American folklore and fiction, the third chapter continues the examination of folk heroes. The chapter begins with a commentary on the various trickster traditions that have influenced the Afro-American version. Thereafter various tricksters are examined for what each author reveals about his function. These include Chesnutt's Uncle Julius, Dunbar's Buford, Scatters, and Ruggles, Cullen's Sam, Ellison's Bledsoe, Rhinehart, and Invisible Man, Wright's Tyree, Cecil Brown's George Washington, Leon Forrest's Ford, Hughes' Laura, and Childress' Mountain Seeley.

The techniques and reasons for incorporating Afro–American rituals in the black American novel are the chief concerns of chapter four. The number of rituals discussed vary according to the novelist and the value accorded the ritual in question. By far the most frequently appearing are those of the black church—the folk sermon, the singing of the spirituals, and the ecstasy that derives from these. The blues are next in importance, followed by the dozens and jive. The rituals are discussed on a novel by novel basis, for the first concern of this study is the individual artist's use of his material. The works to be covered are Johnson's *The Autobiography of an Ex-Colored Man*, Hughes's *Not Without Laughter*, Wright's *Lawd Today* and *The Long Dream*, Walker's *Jubilee*, Ellison's *Invisible Man*, Baldwin's *Go Tell It on the Mountain*, Marshall's *The Chosen Place, The Timeless People*, and Forrest's *The Bloodworth Orphans*. This chapter points out the increasing adeptness at exploiting Afro–American rituals that develops with each new generation of novelists.

From chapter one to chapter four the key word is *survival*. Matters of technique aside, the discussion centers for the most part on whether the values symbolized by these folk heroes and dramatized in these rituals promote or impede Afro–American survival. The conclusion summarizes the principal findings of this study.

REVIEW OF SCHOLARSHIP

In 1982 Berndt Ostendorf wrote: "In 1969 Lawrence Levine complained that the history of black culture could not be written since there were so few documents to go by; in 1977 he is overwhelmed by the sheer mass of unanalyzed material which rests in collections of black folklore and in archives all over the United States" (3). This statement is indicative of the change of attitudes, since the 1960s, on the part of white scholars vis-à-vis Afro–American culture. Much of the credit for this change of attitude, as Albert Murray notes, belongs to those Afro–American and occasional whites who told the truth about the black experience at a time when Americans wished to see blacks as simply deviants (1970, 179).

Such a change of attitudes has resulted in an abundance of available folk material and increased scholarship devoted to interpreting those materials. Since Langston Hughes and Arna Bontemps published *The Book of Negro Folklore* (1958), several other collections have appeared. They include John Mason Brewer, *American Negro Folklore* (1968), Harold A. Courlander, *A Treasury of Afro–American Folklore* (1976), and Daryl Cumber Dance, *Shuckin' and Jivin'* (1978). These four collections complement one another, for each tends to be strongest in an area where the others are weak. They are fine for an initiation to Afro–American folklore. Another collection, Benjamin A. Botkin, *A Treasury of American Folklore* (1944), is useful for someone wishing to compare parallel black and white forms of folklore.

When we turn to specific areas of Afro–American folklore we come not only to collections but to interpretations as well. In the area of the Afro–American folktale, everyone knows of the popular "Uncle Remus" stories of Joel Chandler Harris, which are quite entertaining despite the old fool that Harris creates to tell them. But as a repertory of Afro–American trickster tales this collection is limited, for slaves never allowed whites to hear stories about the slave trickster John. For these we need to turn to Zora Neale Hurston, *Mules and Men* (1935). Hurston's collection is also superb for its "lies." John Mason Brewer, *The Word from the Brazos* (1953) is a wide collection of tales from rural Texas, especially preacher tales. Richard M. Dorson's *American Negro Folktales* (1967) is, as well, excellent. For an understanding of the ethos out of which these folktales emerged one should browse through George P. Rawick, ed., *The American Slave: A Composite Autobiography* (1972), for it is rich in accounts, anecdotes, and tales of slavery.

Among the better interpretations of the Afro–American folktale are Daryl Dance, "In the Beginning: A New View of Black American Etiological Tales" (1977), and Langston Hughes, "Fooling Our White Folks" (1956). Hughes's essay is not about tales *per se* but rather how Afro–Americans apply the cunning the tales dramatize. Bernard Wolfe's "Uncle Remus and the Malevolent Rabbit" (1949) is marred by an interpretation that promotes the stereotype of the black man existing to entertain the white. Alan Dundes, "African Tales among the North American Indians" (1965), explores the scholarship that once argued that blacks borrowed the tales from Indians. Dundes feels it was a part of the white attempt to prove that black culture is always an imitation of somebody else's culture.

The specific body of folktales in verse form that is called toasts and that Daryl Dance refers to as "Tales of the Bad Nigger" now exists principally in three collections: Seymour Fiddle, *Toasts: Images of a Victim Society* (1972), Bruce Jackson, *"Get Your Ass in the Water and Swim Like Me:" Narrative Poetry from the Black Oral Tradition* (1974), and Dennis Wepman, Ronald B. Newman, and Murray Binderman, *The Life: The Lore and Folk Poetry of the Black Hustler* (1976). Not convincing, however, is the scholarship that purports to interpret the toast: Roger D. Abrahams, *Deep down in the Jungle* (1970) and *Positively Black* (1970); Bruce Jackson, "Psychosocial Aspects of the Toast" (1972); David Evans, "The Toast in Context" (1977). Such scholarship suffers from a basic ignorance of the use of functions of Afro–American language. More to the point is Lawrence Levine, who identifies the roots of the toast in the various inverted functions of language in West Africa (1977).

Alongside the toast one should look at the dozens, which could best be defined as ritual insult. Among the publications containing these insults are Abrahams's *Deep down in the Jungle* (1970, 46–51) and H. Rap. Brown, *Die, Nigger, Die* (1969, 25–29). Regarding interpretation, Abrahams sees the dozens as functioning to liberate the young black male from the dominance of his mother. It is a theory that is generally rejected nowadays. An earlier study, John Dollard, "The Dozens: Dialectic of Insult" (1939), is excellent for its description of the ritual and sees it as a way of channeling aggression into the group rather than into the white community where such hostility could have fatal consequences for the dozens player. William Grier and Price Cobbs (1971) perceive the dozens as a black young man's initiation into the humiliation that he must endure for the rest of his life in America. None of these scholars knew that parallel forms of the ritual are widespread in Africa. Lawrence Levine, writing at a time when this information became known and benefiting from the pioneering scholarship, provides the best overall analysis of the ritual. He emphasizes the play element and the ritual bonding it fosters.

The musical forms of Afro–American folklore is the area that is best known and most widely studied. Several collections of blues lyrics exist. From earlier times there are Howard Odum, *The Negro and His Songs* (1925), and Howard Odum and Guy B. Johnson, *Negro Workaday Songs* (1926). Post-1960 collections, thematically arranged, include Kay Shirley, *Patterns of the Blues Romance* (1963); Harry Oster, *Living Country Blues* (1969); Eric S. Campbell, *The Blues Line* (1969); and Jeff Todd Titon, *Early Down Home Blues* (1977).

When it comes to blues scholarship, an interesting situation presents itself in the distinctions between scholarship by whites and scholarship by blacks. The former are preoccupied with form and history, the latter with ritual function. The most obvious place to examine the blues is in the accounts blues musicians provide about their craft. W. C. Handy, *Father of the Blues*, edited by Arna Bontemps (1941), is fascinating both for its insights into composing blues music and for its understanding of the people's need for the music. LeRoi Jones (Amiri Baraka), *Blues People* (1963) is a fine study of the blues from a historical, sociological, psychological, and political point of view. Ralph Ellison's "Blues People" in *Shadow and Act* (1964) is occasioned more by Ellison's ideological quarrel with Jones rather than any fundamental disagreement with Jones's explanation of the blues. Charles Keil, *Urban Blues* (1966) is a significant exploration of the relationship between the blues performer and his audience. The best overall work on the blues, one that comments on ritual, performance styles, and relationship of the blues to the Afro–American ethos, is Albert Murray's *Stomping the Blues* (1976). Other works, particularly valuable for close textual analysis, are Paul Oliver's *Blues Fell This Morning* (1960) and *Aspects of the Blues Tradition* (1968); and Paul Garon's *Blues and the Poetic Spirit* (1975). Robert Palmer's *Deep Blues: A Musical and Cultural History of the Mississippi Delta* (1981) is a strictly historical work via biography based on episodes in the lives of various Mississippi blues musicians.

When we discuss the spirituals we are in fact examining black American theology and an aspect of black American religious rituals. Several collections of spirituals, complete with musical notation, are available. They include William A. Fisher (ed.), *Seventy Negro Spirituals* (1926); James Weldon Johnson and J. Rosamond Johnson (eds.), *The Book of Negro Spirituals* (1925) and *The Second Book of Negro Spirituals* (1926); John Work (ed.), *American Negro Songs and Spirituals* (1940).

One of the earliest essays on the spirituals is W. E. B. DuBois' "Of the Sorrow Songs" found in *The Soul of Black Folk* (1903). It focuses on the doctrines of self-vindication and on the musical styles and influences in these songs. Alain Locke's "The Negro Spirituals" (1925) was published within the context of the Harlem Renaissance (1923–1930). It therefore focuses on what is distinctly Afro–American in the spirituals as a preliminary to finding touchstones for distinctly Afro–American art. Miles Mark Fisher's *American Negro Slave Songs* (1953) explores an aspect of the spirituals that scholars had previously ignored, i.e., their documentation of contemporary events. Fisher probes the nineteenth century spirituals and historical documents and points to the way in which the spirituals, via allegory, record the slaves' reactions to events of the time. Many of the essays on the spirituals tend to make exaggerated claims about them as political tools. D. K. Wilgus' "The Negro-White Spiritual" (1959) is mandatory reading since it outlines the major tenets of a century-old debate on whether the spirituals are imitations of white music or are in the main modified African music. Christa K. Dixon, *Negro Spirituals: From Bible to Folksong* (1976), is typical of the type of scholarship that exists on the spirituals. While the study reflects the author's thorough knowledge of the Bible and Judaeo-Christian traditions in general, she writes little beyond cliché about the psyche and traditions of the people who produced the spirituals.

In the case of the black church, much has been written about its political dimension, but not a great deal about its folklore. (Most Christians, black or white, would find it sacrilegious to have the term *folklore* applied to their beliefs and rituals, for folklore is still commonly held to mean fanciful creations and superstitions that no educated westerner presently believes.) Of those works that exist on the subject of black religion as folklore, the following are quite good: James Weldon Johnson's preface to his *God's Trombones* (1927) is an explication of the black preacher's role in the religious rituals of his flock. On the subject of the folk sermon, Bruce Rosenberg's "The Formulaic Quality of Spontaneous Folk Sermons" (1970) is a structural analysis of the folk sermon for the purpose of abstracting the formula for its composition. Grace Sims Holt, "Stylin' Outta the Black Pulpit" (1972) discusses the preacher's role as guardian of his congregation's morals and as magician-healer of its members' woes from the past week. Hortense Spillers's "Martin Luther King and the Style of the Black Folk Sermon" (1971) is a brilliant analysis of Dr. King's use of rhetorical devices inherent in the folk sermon to communicate cognitively and emotionally to all sectors of his audience. Henry H. Mitchell's *The Recovery of Preaching* (1977) is an eloquent analysis both of the preacher and of the sermon. This book argues convincingly that the attitudes and forms that characterize black American religion are essentially African. Gerald L. Davis, *I Got the Word in Me* (1985) is an excellent study that analyzes the intricate aesthetic structure of the folk sermon and that takes into account at all times the crucial role of the preacher-congregation exchange in the delivery of the sermon.

Zora Neale Hurston discusses the ritual function of "shouting" in the black church ("Shouting" [1933] 1970) and links it to the Afro–American's religious roots in Africa. Melville J. Herskovits, *The Myth of the Negro Past* (1941) traces the antecedents of black American religion to Africa, scholarship that he continued in *Dahomean Narrative* (1958). Harold A. Carter, *The Prayer Tradition of Black People* (1976) documents the African sources for the prayer patterns of Afro–Americans. On the role that visions play in the black church, Zora Neale Hurston, "Conversions and Visions" (1933), and "Religion" in *Dust Tracks on a Road* (1942), as well as John Mason Brewer's "Religious Conversion" in *American Negro Folklore* (1968) are quite informative. William Grier and Price Cobbs devote two chapters of *The Jesus Bag* (1971) to a discussion of Afro–American religious attitudes. Grier and Cobb, are ambivalent about the value of the black church; they see reinforcement of self-hate in the conversion rituals and overdependence on God to solve temporal problems, but they note that the black church has imbued many black Americans with a compensating morality that makes them as a group the only genuine reflectors of American national ideals. Sterling Plumpp's *Black Rituals* (1972) is a compelling study of various rituals of the black church and the sense of identity they forge among its members. His analysis of the "right hand of fellowship" by which the convert is initiated into the church is particularly interesting.

The above, then, is a selective overview of the sources and scholarship on the various Afro–American folk forms that are relevant to this study. Of far more value to the scholar, of course, is to witness Afro–American folklore in its ritual setting. It was quite one thing for Mahalia Jackson to record the spirituals and quite another for her to sing them as part of church fellowship.

There is very little scholarship that touches the subject of folk heroes and rituals in the black American novel *per se*. Sherley Anne Williams, *Give Birth to Brightness* (1972) gives a very detailed study of black folk attitudes regarding the hero and the carryover of those attitudes into literature. She analyzes one of the protagonists in my study, Ernest Gaines's Marcus Payne. Williams sees him as a "streetman." I see him as a Bad Nigger.

In her unpublished 1976 Ph.D. dissertation, "Modern Black Writers and the Folk Tradition," Susan L. Blake examines the folklore in the works of four black authors: Chesnutt, Hurston, Hughes, and Ellison, and concludes that it is erroneous to refer to a folk tradition in Afro–American literature. Blake further argues that every author exploits the folklore for his unique purpose, a fact that negates the existence of a tradition for folklore usage. As she sees it, the basis of black literature and black folklore is oppression.

Whether or not a tradition exists for the use of folklore in Afro–American literature depends strictly on how one defines tradition. Given the essentially creative nature of literature, reactions to, modifications of, and imitations of other writers' use of folklore could be shown to constitute a tradition. The rhetoric of folklore in black literature itself is sufficient to argue that a tradition exists for the use of folklore. The claim, however, that the foundation of black American folklore is oppression is only partially true when one considers that the germs of that folklore came, along with the slaves, from Africa.

Since the black preacher is one part of my study, Walter C. Daniel's *Images of the Black Preacher in Afro–American Literature* (1981) deserves to be mentioned. While it identifies several works that deal with the black preacher, it does little more than provide a plot synopsis of the preacher's role within the story. Wilson Jeremiah Moses, *Black Messiahs and Uncle Toms: Social and Literary Manipulations of a Religious Myth* (1982) is a well-written, well-documented work on the political and folk-created Black Moses (Joe Louis and Jack Johnson, for example) in the black American community. His literary exposition of the concept is limited to Ralph Ellison's *Invisible Man*. My focus is on Bontemps' Gabriel and Morrison's Shadrack.

Various articles and sections of books touch upon numerous aspects of folklore in the works of some of the authors included in this study. Most of them, however, are content to identify the folklore without analyzing its function within the literary text. Keith F. Byerman's *Fingering the Jagged Grain: Tradition and Form in Recent Black Fiction* (1985) is the only book-length study I know of that attempts to analyze systematically the role of folklore in black fiction. Byerman's work is only peripherally similar to mine in that the literary use of folklore is one of his several concerns. In my study it is the sole concern. Moreover it is fiction written after 1960 that claims his interest, and to these works he applies touchstones developed from Ellison's writings. In my own case the works analyzed date from as far back as 1898. There are other differences as well. Toni Cade Bambara, Ishmael Reed, and Gayl Jones, authors peripherally treated in this work, and James A. McPherson, Clarence Major, and Alice Walker, authors not included, receive detailed treatment in Byerman's study. Byerman's analysis of Forrest's *There's a Tree More Ancient than Eden* and his interpretation of Ishmael Reed's novels are to date the most thorough criticism I have read of these writers' works.

Attention should be given to the role of black literary critics in promoting or discouraging the presence of folklore in the black American novel. Neither can we ignore the literary marketplace, which was overwhelmingly white, essentially racist, and dogmatic about the manner in which it wanted to see blacks depicted. This fact, probably more than any other, caused blacks to be ambivalent about using folklore in their work, if only because editors would have wanted such folklore to reflect the prevailing prejudices. Ideally I would have preferred to offer a résumé of the various opinions on and reactions to those opinions on the subject of folklore or attitudes that encouraged or discouraged the use of folklore in black American literature. Space prohibits such an undertaking. In its place I offer a sample bibliography on the subject.

Before doing so, however, I would like to make a few comments. In the earlier part of the twentieth century, those writers who defied black middle-class opinion and employed folklore in their creations were often subjected to castigating reviews by the black press. It took a very long time, until Ellison, in fact, for black American writers to be convinced that what earlier generations of blacks and whites saw as debasement of the race in folklore was in reality sustenance and should be depicted as such. Fortunately, doubt no longer exists about the value of folklore as a tool for the black writer who wishes to explore the wellsprings of the black American soul. For this we owe a great deal to the Black Arts Movement of the 1960s and 1970s (Cultural Nationalists), who waged an unrelenting war to make black readers and writers and, indirectly, publishers understand the value of the black American experience in its numerous manifestations.

For an understanding of the problems faced by early black writers using folklore the following works are useful: Benjamin Brawley, *The Negro in Literature and Art in the United States* (1930) (this work is significant for its avoidance of serious criticism); for Chesnutt's dilemma on the subject, Helen Chesnutt, *Charles Waddell Chesnutt: Pioneer of the Color Line* (1952), is an excellent work; Dunbar's difficulties regarding dialect poetry are discussed in James Weldon Johnson, *Along this Way* (1933) and in Jay Saunders Redding, "Portrait against a Background" (1975); for opposite reasons, William Dean Howell's preface to Dunbar's *Lyrics of Lowly Life* (1898) and James Weldon Johnson's prefaces to *The Book of Negro Poetry* (1922 and 1931) are worth reading for they show what black critics were reacting against when black writers expressed themselves in the folk idiom.

The folklore debate became most acute in the late 1920s, when the Harlem Renaissance was in vogue. The reviews of this literature by W. E. B. DuBois in *The Crisis*, the most significant of which have been reproduced in Herbert Aptheker, *Book Reviews of W. E. B. DuBois* (1977); Charles S. Johnson, "New Frontage in American LIfe" (1925); Langston Hughes, "The Negro Artist and the Racial Mountain" (1926); as well as Alain Locke's initial embrace and later rejection of the movement, readily available in Jeffrey C. Stewart's *The Critical Temper of Alain Locke* (1983), contribute substantially to an understanding of the literary folklore debate.

For a continuation of the debate into the 'thirties, DuBois' and Locke's works are useful as well as Richard Wright's "Blueprint for Negro Literature" (1937). The discussion of the responses to Zora Neale Hurston's novels in Robert E. Hemenway, *Zora Neale Hurston: A Literary Biography* (1977), is essential reading in this regard.

The debate continued into the 'fifties with Baldwin's essays on Wright: "Everybody's Protest Novel" (1949) and "Many Thousands Gone" (1951) but principally in Ralph Ellison's essays, lectures, and interviews on the subject of folklore in the black novel—now compiled in *Shadow and Act* (1964).

Under its editor Hoyt Fuller, *Negro Digest* (later *Black World*), became an organ for discussing a black aesthetic that goes to the core of the black experience. These viewpoints as well as the art they encouraged became known as Cultural Nationalism. The views of Fuller himself, Carolyn Gerald, Addison Gayle, Larry Neal, Don L. Lee, Val Ferdinand, Adam David Miller, M. Ron Karenga, James Emmanuel, and others on this subject have been collected in Addison Gayle's *The Black Aesthetic* (1971) and in "Criticism," *New Black Voices*, edited by Abraham Chapman (1972). LeRoi Jones' (Amiri Baraka's) *Home* (1966) and Ed Bullins' preface to *New Plays from the Black Theater* (1969) and his preface to *The Theme is Blackness* (1973) are also indispensable reading.

Since the 1970s the criticism of Afro–American literature has moved in the direction of finding critical approaches indigenous both to the literature and the community that produces it. The following works are noteworthy for their efforts in this regard. Alvin Aubert, "Black American Poetry: Its Language, and the Folk Tradition" (1971); Chestyn Everett, "Tradition in Afro–American Literature" (1975); Houston Baker, *The Journey Back* (1980); "A Black and Crucial Enterprise" (1982); *Blues, Ideology, and Afro–American Literature: A Vernacular Theory* (1984); "Belief, Theory and Blues: Notes for a Post-Structuralist Criticism of Afro–American Literature" (1986); and "Caliban's Triple Play" (1986); Henry-Louis Gates, "Introduction: Criticism in de Jungle" (1981); " 'The Blackness of Blackness': A Critique of the Sign and 'The Signifying Monkey' " (1983); Ernest D. Mason, "Black Art and the Configurations of Experience: The Philosophy of the Black Aesthetic" (1983); Toni Morrison, "Rootedness: The Ancestor as Foundation" (1984); Joyce-Ann Joyce, "The Black Canon: Reconstructing Black Literary Criticism" (1987); and June Jordan, "Strong beyond all Definitions..." (1987).

The following anthologies provide a broad cross-section of views on the literature: Henry-Louis Gates, ed., *Black Literature and Literary Theory* (1984); Joe Weixlmann and Chester J. Fotentot ed., *Studies in Black American Literature Volume I: Black American Prose Theory* (1983); and *Volume II: Belief vs Theory in Black American Literature* (1986).

The exclusion from this list of several other critical anthologies and individual essays is due solely to the fact that here my principal concern is with literary theory rather than with author-centered criticism. The inclusion of pre-1950s author-centered criticism is attributable primarily to the fact that little else existed.

1

Afro-American Folklore: Identification and Interpretation

PRELIMINARY REMARKS

Whether it is to deal with everyday situations—such as the telling of a joke to put one's audience at ease, or the employing of witty, verbal hostility in lieu of physical combat, or the finding of refuge in myth rather than embracing the anxieties of the unknown—folklore has its momentary as well as perennial functions. Certainly the more besieged a people is by forces outside its own community, the greater is its need for a unifying and liberating folklore. Numerous examples come to mind. One is the stoning to death of Achan, reported in the Old Testament book of Joshua (chapter seven), for violating a taboo, thereby causing the Israelites to lose a battle. Another is the seven-year banishment of Okonkwo in Chinua Achebe's *Things Fall Apart* (1959) so that the clan would escape the curse deriving from Okonkwo's killing of a klansman, albeit accidentally. In both examples the community is threatened by the violations and must demonstrate its noncomplicity.

The subject of this chapter is the identification and interpretation of black American folklore as a prelude to understanding folklore's function in the black novel. As a people originating from preindustrial societies, blacks, when they were transported to the New World, brought with them, if only vestigially, many of the myths, rituals, and attitudes their ancestors had created to mediate the various phenomena affecting their lives. In America, where every attempt was made by white slavemasters to prove that blacks were only partially human, and where they were punished for revealing too much of their humanity, blacks needed to create a folklore in which they could surreptitiously assert their humanity. Sometimes, as is the case with the spirituals, it was a folklore of desperation and compensation; sometimes it was a folklore of accommodation. To study the folklore of black Americans is to examine their dreams, their aspirations, the mental curtains they designed to shut out the brutality of slave and postslave reality, the psychic wings on which they bore themselves temporarily away from oppressive pain, as well as the aesthetic objects—the blues, spirituals, folktales, toasts, etc.—they fashioned from their pain. Therefore, the study of black American folklore—as Lawrence Levine demonstrates and most scholars of black folklore imply—is essentially a study of the survival of black people in America. Furthermore, serious black American writers have expressed their commitment to exploring black American reality (Tate 1983, 11, 18, 84, 112, 129–30, 164, 203). In doing so many of these writers rely heavily on the folklore of the Afro–American community.

In this chapter I shall not devote any analysis to black folk heroes like John Henry, boxer Jack Johnson, or the legendary heroes of the slave revolts. I feel that the obvious nature of such types is easily analyzed within those works in which they are found. I shall focus instead on those aspects of black folklore that are controversial, little analyzed, or poorly known.

Establishing separate categories of black American folklore is a very artificial process, for the folklore operates more like a symphonic whole or like a huge lake fed by several streams. The categories that follow must be seen as parts of a whole and, for the most part, are meaningless outside of that whole.

RELIGIOUS FOLKLORE

The black church is the obvious category with which to begin. As it evolved in America from the time of slavery to the Great Depression, the black church involved the recasting of the rituals of the Christian religion to make them respond to the needs of blacks. During slavery, the "field hollers"—loud, plaintive cries—brought the slaves some relief from the woes of indignity and forced toil. Eventually such hollers became ritualized and incorporated into the religious worship; they became the office of those members who directed the congregation in its exorcism of pain.

Music has been an integral part of this church, and it took the form of spirituals, Methodist/Baptist tunes that were recast into the slaves' own harmonies and lyrics whose purpose was to comfort and reassure the slave in his life of abject servitude. The emphasis on the life to come, on the glory that awaited those who suffer on this earth, on the torment reserved for those who lead sumptuous lives, contrasted vividly with the quotidian reality of slavery. "The singing of the spirituals serves as a release; the fervour of the release indicates something of the confining pressure that folk Negroes know too well and have known too long" (Brown 1958, 228).

The spirituals contain much "signifying" (this term is explained later in this chapter) against the white race. "Ride on King Jesus/No man can hinder him" implies the feeling that the slavemaster's power did not extend to heaven, where real justice will be dispensed. "He never said a mumbalin' word...,"—referring to what the slaves believed to be Christ's stoic acceptance of His crucifixion—shows that they felt that the suffering of seemingly helpless people ended eventually in triumph over the oppressors.

In "My name is written on high" and "my Lord's a-writin' all the time," there are hints that not only did they feel heaven was theirs but also that their masters could not inherit it. In all these lines the slaves refer to an authority that superseded their masters', an authority that they felt would punish their masters. Lyrics like the following are good indications of the extent to which the experience of slavery and the ontological position of the slaves became the subject of their songs and of the slaves' attempts to find compensatory solace in their music:

> No more auction block for me...
> Many thousand gone

> Sometimes I feel like a motherless child...
> A long ways from home.

> Go down Moses
> Way down in Egyptland
> Tell ole Pharaoh to let my people go.

On the other hand,

> Rich man Dives, he lived so well,
> When he died he found a home in hell

and

> God gave Noah the Rainbow Sign...
> No more water but the fire next time

express a need on the part of the slaves to be avenged. Writing in 1854, an ex-slave, Charles Ball, explained this feeling of the slaves for vengeance: "Heaven will be no heaven" to the black man "if he is not to be avenged of his enemies...I learned this in the religious meetings of the slaves themselves" (82). The following stanza from "Promises of Freedom," a secular slave song, reinforces Ball's statement:

> Yes my ole masser promise me
> But his papers didn' leave me free.
> A dose of pisen helped 'im along,
> May the devil preach his fun'ral song.
> (Hughes and Bontemps 1958, 88).

In this regard Frederick Douglass' testimony regarding the purpose of the spirituals is important in the light of more than a century of controversy by white scholars over the origin and function of this folk form. Douglass writes that the spirituals told a tale of woe...they were tones loud, long, and deep; they breathed the prayer and complaint of souls boiling over with the bitterest anguish. Every tone was a testimony against slavery, and a prayer to God for deliverance from chains....

Slaves sing most when they are most unhappy. The songs of the slaves represent the sorrows of his heart; and he is relieved by them, only as an aching heart is relieved by its tears. ([1854] 1968, 31–32).

Well-meaning whites were baffled totally by the cathartic effect such singing as part of the religious worship produced:

Men stamped, groaned, shouted, clapped their hands; women shrieked and sobbed, two or three tore off their bonnets and threw them under foot, and sprang into the air....

A fog seemed to fill the church; the lights burned dimly, the air was close, almost to suffocation; an invisible power seemed to hold us [the whites] in its iron grasp; the excitement was working upon us also, and sent the blood surging in wild torrents to the brain that reeled in darkened terror from the shock (Kilham [1870] 1967, 128).

(More will be said about this seeming frenzy when the subject of African forms in black American religion is discussed.)

Margaret Just Butcher points out a frequently overlooked aspect of the spirituals: the fact that they contained the slaves' theology. Unable to read, they found it necessary to use song as a codifying medium for their religious beliefs (1956, 100). A cursory look at the biblical stories the spirituals narrate—the creation, Samson's exploits, the Exodus, the crucifixion, etc.—easily confirms that certain stories became songs primarily because of the relevance of those stories to the slaves' actual condition. To the extent that these songs are the codifications of a nonliterate people's beliefs—they are similar in intention to the moral folktales of the slaves' ancestors. In chapter four we shall analyze the fictional use that James Weldon Johnson, Langston Hughes, and Margaret Walker make of the spirituals.

Like the spirituals, the prayers of blacks, dating back to slavery, concentrated on the search for deliverance from bondage. In "Memories of Slavery" Hughes and Bontemps include a short piece whose beginning states, "Lias would pray any time, but no matter what he was doing at twelve o'clock noon, he would stop short, kneel, and pray to God. The prayer Lias prayed at this hour was a special one. 'Oh Lawd,' he would pray, 'Won't You gib us owah freedom?'" (Hughes and Bontemps, 1958, 77). Rawick reports, in *The American Slave: A Composite Autobiography I*, the following by a slave: "Massa never 'lowed us slaves to go to church; but they have big holes in the field; they gits down and prays. They done that way 'cause white folks didn't want them to pray. They used to pray for freedom" (1972, 33).

Black American poet Sterling Plumpp opines that the God black slaves prayed to was "the spirit of their ancestors...disguised as the Judaic God of

the Old Testament and Christ, the Bleeding Lamb of the New Testament"
(1972, 33). Ball's statement that the slaves believed that after death they
would return to Africa and "rejoin their former companions and friends"
gives credence to Plumpp's interpretation (Ball, 87).

Arising out of the black church is a different folk form that is attractive to
both spectators and students of black folklore alike; the black folk sermon.
The drama, versification, imagery, metaphor, and grandiose scenery
painted for the congregation and enlivened by the congregation's cries of
approval made these sermons a phenomenon hitherto unknown in the
western world. James Weldon Johnson reworked some of these sermons to
produce the seven outstanding poems comprising *God's Trombones: Seven
Negro Sermons in Verse* (1927). His preface to this collection sums up most of
what has been written since on the black folk sermon. These were sermons
he had heard throughout his childhood, in various locales, and with only
the slightest modifications. They included "The Valley of Dry Bones," based
on the thirty-seventh chapter of Ezekiel; "'The Train Sermon', in which
God and the Devil [are] pictured as running trains, one loaded with
saints...the other with sinners;...'The Heavenly March'...and an untitled
sermon that highlighted the creation, the experience of the Hebrew children, through the coming of Christ and ended with the Apocalypse" (11).

Undoubtedly these preachers were urged on by the needs of their congregations. Johnson tells us that such men were well beyond average intelligence and must have been close to genius, considering that their knowledge of the Bible came from hearing whites read it (4). He goes on to say
that the old time black preacher knew that "the secret of oratory" lay in the
"rhythmic progression of words", that his voice "could modulate from a
sepulchral whisper to a crashing thunderclap...that his tone" ranged from
"high fervency" to "colloquialism"; his imagination "bold and unfettered";
and his language "not prose but poetry" (5). In the words of one such
preacher, who was a boy at the time of emancipation, "When it comes to
handling the Bible, I knocks down verbs, breaks up prepositions, and jumps
over adjectives" (Hughes and Bontemps, 1958, 56).

An aspect of the black folk sermon that Johnson neglects but one that is
vital to the congregation is reported by Bruce Rosenburg, Henry Mitchell
and Gerald Davis in their observations of the contemporary preacher of
these sermons. They tell us that the congregation's responses are an integral part of the minister's timing. A sermon can fail or succeed depending
on the congregation's participation. "Chanting builds up the emotions of
the audience." When the emotional acme is attained, it is then that "the
spirit of God is said to be most noticeable." (Rosenburg 1970, 5)

Above all else the preacher is expected to know the members of the
congregation well and to castigate their lapses in his sermons. However,
how he addresses them is more important than the fact that he does so.
Grace Sims Holt, someone intimately familiar with the black church, states:

the preacher relates his knowledge of local happenings to the sin context, exhorting his audience, which shares his knowledge.... The preacher's beginning is slow-moving (funky) to get the audience physically involved. The preacher walks, body swaying from side to side, slightly bent, from one side of the pulpit to the other.... He waits until he gets to one side, stands up straight, and makes a statement about sin. If a husband "ain't actin' right," if he's running around with another woman, or gambling, and not bringing home his money to his wife and children, the preacher must "get on his case" with a strong use of melody and rhythm (1972, 191).

As is implied in this citation, the physical aspects of the preacher's delivery are a vital component of the sermon. Furthermore, style is of paramount importance, for its presence or absence determines whether the congregation will be repentant or offended.

In this manner the black church, even during slavery, functioned to give blacks some dignity. It created a reality, albeit a verbal one, that compensated for the bleakness of black lives. The preachers were Ezekiels, promising life from "dry bones." Denied material possessions, denied political power—even taught that they did not have a soul and that they should serve their masters rather than God—blacks since the time of slavery fashioned a religion that provided them with psychic freedom even while they were in physical bondage (Hughes and Bontemps 1958, 56). In chapter four we shall examine Johnson's, Walker's, Baldwin's, and Forrest's portrayal of the black folk sermon as both ritual and rhetoric.

The black church also had its political dimension. James Weldon Johnson states that "these scattered and often clandestine groups have grown into the strongest and richest organization among [black] Americans" (1927, 4). Catharsis, fellowship, and entertainment aside, it seems that the political aspect of the black church was its most important feature—first to fight slavery and later racism. One is led to conclude this from the numerous reports that blacks failed to exhibit the pious behavior of those who had been converted. "They go to the evening meetings, stamp, shout and have the 'power' and 'get religion' and next day fight, swear, and steal.... At the next meeting they will go through the same exercise with precisely the same results" (Kilham [1870] 1967, 132). In his work describing conditions in the seaboard states during the early 1850s, Federick Olmstead tells of a house slave who made it her habit to steal and who, when lectured by her mistress about the wickedness of stealing and lying, replied, "It's all right for us poor colored people to appropriate whatever of white folks' blessings the Lord puts in our way" (Olmstead 1856, 117). Ball affirms that this feeling was universal among the slaves (Lester, 257). Moreover, slaves whose masters underfed them could count on slaves on nearby plantations stealing food to give to them (Hughes and Bontemps 1958, 51).

Thus, while the rituals of Christianity appealed to blacks, the mores did not. The key reason for this was that black religion was essentially defiant of slavery; it was a form of protest. To the extent that it was to their ancestral spirits that they prayed, the slaves utilized Christian forms for the purpose of camouflage. Brother Zeke—the preacher in Margaret Walker's *Jubilee* (1966)—informs the slaves on numerous plantations about the progress of the abolition battle, spirits slaves out of the South via the Underground Railroad, and during the Civil War spies for the Union Army. The political aspect of the black church has continued to this day, Jesse Jackson's presidential campaign being its latest manifestation.

It is equally pertinent to note that many black Americans, even the devout believers, are able to distance themselves from the core doctrines of Christianity. Black folklorist Daryl Dance writes:

The sacrilegious tone of many [religious folktales] should not mislead the reader into assuming that the tellers are either irreligious or anti-religious. Several of the harshest anecdotes that I collected were related by sincerely devout Christians, many of whom were deacons, and by others who were unquestionably conscientious and dedicated church workers, including even an occasional minister or the minister's wife (1978, 42).

Black psychiatrist Alvin Poussaint adds that blacks in America are less affected by the puritanical mores of white America, and have retained a good deal of their African heritage, especially in their perceptions of sex, marriage, and children (1972, 191). This leads one to wonder if many black Americans view their religion as an art form, and are thus able to distance themselves from it whenever they feel the need. The fact that the black preacher, the deacon, and pious church sister are frequent figures in black satirical folklore reinforces this feeling. In the Afro-American novel a few of the portraits of the black preacher incorporate such folklore. In chapter two Dunbar's Parker, Hurston's Pearson, Baldwin's Gabriel, and Bennett's Titus and Cobb will be analyzed in this light. A somewhat similar analysis obtains for Hughes' Laura and Childress' Seeley in chapter three.

Since we have been using the term *black church*, it is worthwhile to look at what distinguishes it from its white counterpart. We have already looked at folk sermons, spirituals, and audience participation. Left to be discussed are the vestigial influences of African beliefs and forms on the religious practices and beliefs of black Americans.

Despite the writings of early missionaries and even of blacks like Richard Wright who were ignorant of African customs and beliefs and therefore misinterpreted them, Africans have always believed in a supreme being. In a 1983 interview Zambian president Dr. Kenneth Kaunda remarked that he laughs at the notion that the white man brought God to Africa (1983, 48). Those blacks who were brought to the West arrived with their concepts of God and in some instances succeeded in a smooth marriage of Christian and African concepts.

As regards specific African influences on the black American church, first, there is the identification of God's presence with ecstasy. Kilham's observation that "Men stamped, groaned, shouted, clapped..." is an example of that phenomenon. Inasmuch as such ecstacy required a particular type of music, the slaves had to create that music. This was one rationale for the birth of the spirituals. Whereas in Africa blacks used percussion instruments, particularly the drum, to obtain the desired mood for such ecstasy, in America, where the playing of drums was forbidden, they resorted to hand clapping. The argument can be made that ecstasy is certainly known among white worshippers; however, researchers, among them Melville J. Herskovits, have observed practices similar to those of western blacks in West African societies (Herskovits [1941] 1970, 124–25). The praise house, the ritual site for such ecstasy, was extremely popular in early black America. Harold A. Carter notes that the praise house has an African background. "In village after village in West Africa I found many houses erected for the specific purpose of song, dance, libations, and praise to God" (1976, 27–28). The name *praise house* is still retained in the English-speaking Caribbean by those sects for whom ecstasy is central to the manifestation of God, and communication with ancestral spirits an acceptable reality. In some islands— St. Vincent, Grenada, St. Lucia, for example—where the African-derived people comprise over 90 percent of the population, more than three-quarters of the population hold such beliefs and practices to be valid. In early America as well as in the present-day islands cited, "song and dance are alike extremely energetic, and often, when the shout lasts into the middle of the night, the monotonous thud, thud, of the feet prevents sleep within half a mile of the praise house" (Joseph Washington, 1972, 75). In most contemporary black American Baptist and Sanctified churches that have resisted "middle class muting," ecstasy is still a vital factor in the worship. We shall examine this ecstasy closely when we look at Baldwin's *Go Tell It on the Mountain* in chapter four.

One aspect of black religion that seems to have disappeared from contemporary black American society is the praying under or in the presence of a tree. This practice is as distinctly African as the Kum tree is to the Ashanti vision of reality. Esther Dagan who, as an anthropologist, has lived among many African groups and filmed many of their rituals, talks of the special relationships West Africans have with trees and of their festivities that almost always take place at the site of a tree sacred to the culture (in conversation, 1983). Furthermore, John S. Mbiti tells us that for the Ashanti individual there are spirits "that animate trees, rivers, animals" and beneath these reside those family spirits that act as guardians (1969, 87). An ex-slave reported that he usually prayed behind a big beech tree a little distance from the house, "and often during the night, when I would feel to pray, I would get out of bed and go to this tree" (Clifton Johnson 1969, 20).

Haitians have told me that in *vodun* ceremonies the loa often manifest themselves in the boughs of trees. In St. Vincent, when children used to be delivered at home rather than in a hospital, the umbilical cord and placenta were buried deeply at the root of a certain tree (My own and those of my brothers have been treated thus). This practice establishes a particular relationship between that individual and the tree; but of greater significance is that it makes the individual an inseparable part of the community. That one's "navel string" is buried in a village is the most frequently cited reminder of one's membership in the community. Such a declaration is often enough to silence hostility on the part of one's antagonist. The next best thing is that one's mother's (not father's) "navel string" is buried there too. According to David Jenkins a similar practice exists in Sierra Leone. Its function, however, is to effect a magical connection between the growth and flourishing of the tree and that of the newborn baby (1975, 228). In St. Vincent the breadfruit tree, the unofficial national emblem, has a significance beyond providing food, it has a vague religious importance. I have been told that in Haiti this same tree is the subject of many legends dealing with its magical fruitfulness rescuing the population from outright starvation. Alice Walker in *Meridian* invests the tree with an alluring power, as does Toni Morrison in *Tar Baby*.

The use of pots by slaves in their worship is another African element that long escaped students of Afro-American culture. The rationale that the slaves gave for using this device was that it muffled sounds and therefore prevented white folks from finding out about their religious activities. It has since been observed that certain West African groups, particularly in Benin, sacrificed young chicks in pots that each hold an ancestral spirit, including those in America. It is now known as well that Haitian loa are kept in pots and that in West Africa pots are associated with river spirits (Hughes and Bontemps 1958, 52; Carter 1976, 29–30).

One of the features of the early black church in America was what came to be called the *ring shout*. Blacks believed that without the ring the spirit could not enter into their midst, and the sinners among them would not be converted (Carter 1976, 28). This practice, of course, had nothing to do with Christianity but with the physical formation of people participating in religious rituals in West Africa. This circular formation is observable even in the architecture of the Shango temples in the West Indian islands where the cult is still flourishing, and is also true of the *peristyle* (*vodun* temple) found in Haiti. Esther Dagan believes that this circular formation emphasizes the value of community over individuality (personal conversation 1983). This circular pattern of worship still exists unaltered among the African derived sects of the Caribbean but has disappeared in Afro–America.

Finally, the anthropomorphic god of the folk sermons and the spirituals, the biblical characters depicted in terms of the daily activities of the community, and the concreteness given to every aspect of religious belief have their origins in the animism of West African culture, where every abstraction is given a physical dimension. This inclination is also carried over to the secular folklore, which will be discussed later.

That blacks coming to the New World could readily take to certain aspects of biblical doctrine and not to others has as much to do with the inherent parallels they found in them as it does with the solace those doctrines provided them. Their gods of fire and water (Shango and Ogun, for example), whose qualities they had already accounted for mythologically and for whom cults already existed, inclined them to biblical stories like the Flood, of which they had their own version (see Harris 1881, 31–34). The sacrament of baptism as practiced by the Baptists easily claimed blacks, for they could identify it with their own river gods. The livelier forms of worship of the Baptists and Methodists closely corresponded to the rituals of ecstasy they had known in Africa. It is worth noting that the Quakers were most exemplary in their opposition to slavery, yet blacks were never attracted to the Quaker form of worship. To this day, blacks who become Presbyterians or Anglicans are suspect of wanting to be white.

I have discussed at length the black church, for it is felt by many scholars that the verbal emphasis of black American folklore is influenced and nourished by it (Plumpp 1972, 77). At any rate black American folklore is the product of an imagination that was forced to fabricate pleasant escapes to counter the deadliness of servitude. And if we accept Sterling Plumpp's assertion that black American survival is first learned in the church, then perhaps we ought to see the church as the mother of the oral arts. Plumpp refers to black artists such as Ray Charles, Aretha Franklin, James Baldwin, and Dick Gregory, among others, as preachers in the black church (71–72). Undoubtedly Plumpp is referring to the comfort, hope, and education in the songs and writing, and, in the case of the musicians, of the unifying effect of their performances on the black audience—a recreation of the ethos of the primitive black church. Charles Keil, black blues scholar, makes a somewhat similar statement about the performances of the outstanding blues singers (1966, 15); and James Baldwin calls Aretha Franklin the black church (*A Dialogue* 1973, 79–80).

SECULAR MUSICAL LORE

What I shall call *secular folklore* has parallel functions in many instances with the religious folklore, and, insofar as verbal skills are concerned, draws heavily from it. Langston Hughes, in *Not Without Laughter* (1930), dramatizes the extent to which the singing of the blues functions as a religion. During slavery the secular and religious forms coexisted, probably indistinct from each other, because African rituals, with their tendencies to reconcile the needs of body and soul, were fresh in the minds of the newly arrived slaves. With the years came an increasing influence of the doctrines of those churches to which blacks were attracted; those influences no doubt gave rise to conflicts between the secular and religious practices. After abolition the effect of these conflicts was visible in the war the black church waged against the blues. Arna Bontemps recounts a memory that under-scores this rift: "The box (guitar)... has always been a special device of the devil's. I can remember [a] careless minstrel... wandering onto the church grounds during an intermission between services back in my childhood. The sisters of the church lit into him like a flock of mother hens attacking a garter snake..." (Hughes and Bontemps 1958, xiii–xiv).

There is little room in the rituals of the black church for satirizing America; the church could not sanction the telling of folktales, for their purpose was then and is now to give pleasure. Moreover they exalt mischief and ignore puritan mores. And while the vision of heaven made this life some-what bearable for many blacks, others for reasons of temperament, or any number of other psychological factors, had to find sustenance in other forms. Not ironically many of those forms—conjuring (to be explained later), for example—were fundamentally African. Sometimes both the religious and secular were practiced without the expected attendant guilt, especially in urban America where because of anonymity behavior was less open to censure by the community.

The blues, the secular counterpart of the spirituals along with jazz is the most studied aspect of black American folklore, and many blues scholars are from the black community.

According to John Work, the blues appeared around 1900. Bessie Smith chanced upon them while she was performing in the South. They evolved from field hollers ([1926] 1940, 32). In form the blues make use of repetition, a distinct feature of the oral tradition. Sometimes as many as three lines are repeated, sometimes two, sometimes in a stanza none at all, though some of those lines are repeated in other stanzas. This repetition is related to the actual effect the singer or composer desires. The songs are usually sung from a first-person perspective (which seduces many white critics into believing that blues lyrics are actual accounts of the singers' lives) and take the guise of informing the listener of the narrator's experience or of the narrator's giving the audience advice or both.

Tone is the most distinguishing feature of the blues. The subject matter is frequently human disappointment, but for the most part the lyrics discourage the listener from becoming oversentimental about such mishaps. Sterling Brown's essay, "The Blues as Folk Poetry," is one of the most intimate in its understanding of this folk form. Of the blues he writes, "stoicism is here as well as self-pity... rich humor as well as melancholy" (Hughes and Bontemps [1958] 1984, 372).

Metaphorically and rhythmically the blues convey the texture of Afro–American life. Ralph Ellison perceives them as "an impulse to keep the painful details of a brutal existence alive in one's consciousness, to finger its jagged grain, and transcend it, not by the consolation of philosophy but by squeezing from it a near-comic, near-tragic lyricism" ([1964] 1972, 189–90). Albert Murray notes that the blues affirm black American life "in all its complexities," its "infinite confusions," and are "a confrontation of human failure and existential absurdity. The spirit of the blues moves in the opposite direction from ashes to sackcloth, self-pity, self-hatred and suicide." Murray notes equally that the "most low down blues are not only not depressing, they function like an instantaneous aphrodisiac" (1970, 147). No profound analysis is required to see that the unfaithful woman so frequent in male blues singers' songs is a metaphor of America. The more general complaints are related to the black man's exclusion from the American dream.

On the subject of blues style and content Sterling Brown writes that "the diction of the blues is immediately connected as it should be with folk life" (Hughes and Bontemps [1958] 1984, 373). The storehouse of folk knowledge and beliefs—proverbs and superstitions especially—from which the blues lyrics draw makes them a veritable chronicler of the "souls of black folk"; the predilection for innuendo understood only within the black community puts them firmly within the African tradition (I shall expand upon this later).

In the ability of the blues to speak directly to the black audience in innuendo that frequently only the black audience and singer understand, in the spontaneity with which the audience shouts its approval and comments on the individual lines, in the blues singer's constant improvising to make his lyrics pertinent to his immediate audience—a blues concert has always functioned for black Americans as a secular form of worship—in the paradoxical manner that Ellison's and Murray's observations note. As such the blues is a member of the family of rituals black Americans employ to contain, shape, and triumph over the pain of racial oppression. In chapter four we shall examine Langston Hughes', Richard Wright's, and Leon Forrest's depictions of the blues concert.

Jazz, on the other hand, is a music of joyousness. "The true spirit of jazz is a joyous revolt from every thing that would confine the soul of man and hinder its riding free on the air" (Rogers [1925] 1975, 217). That there is much interrelationship between jazz and blues is to be seen in the facility with which the blues/jazz musician switches from one form to the other. Jazz, nevertheless, is differentiated from the blues not by the actual words of the songs but by its tempo—a rapid, rollicking, rocking rhythm. Emphasis is placed on the orchestra, especially on the clarinet, trumpet, trombone, or saxophone. The effect of the music is "the release of all the suppressed emotions, a blowing off the lid, as it were" (Rogers [1925] 1975, 217). The patently Dionysian element of jazz made it very unpopular with the black American middle class and helped to reinforce the white American stereotype of blacks as a happy, contented, and sensual people.

The origin of jazz is a subject of great dispute. It is generally accepted that it began in the South, most likely New Orleans, and traveled North, where it underwent changes as a result of pressure from the black middle class and from white audiences for a music more closely conforming to their own (Hansen, in Dundes 1973, 504 ff.). Like the spirituals and the blues, some of the most distinctive features of jazz are recognizable in African music styles (Rogers [1925] 1975, 219).

To understand the function of jazz within the life of black folk one has to return to its precursors during slavery. There is a story told in most collections of Afro–American folklore that gives some indication of the pleasures to be had from the Saturday frolics: a black man tells a white man that if he became black for one Saturday night, he would not, despite the horrors of slavery, ever wish to be white again. In his 1845 *Narrative of the Life of Frederick Douglass*, Frederick Douglass wrote disparagingly of these frolics as sapping the slaves of a moral force that should have been preserved to battle the master ([1845] 1968, 84–85). Ralph Ellison sees the jazz musician as who one learned the "best of the past" and added "to it his personal vision" so that he could with "a fluid style" reduce "the chaos of living to form." Of the player/ audience relationship he notes, "the delicate balance struck between strong individual personality and group during those early jam sessions was a marvel of social organization" (Ellison [1964] 1972, 189–90).

But in *Go Tell It on the Mountain*, Baldwin's narrator observes the maimings caused by the Saturday night frolics; and the reader is reminded that the violence that comes from thwarted aspirations is not always canalized and rendered serene by what is ostensibly a folk form designed to do just that. Jazz is usually never far from the lugubrious aspects of black American experience. Jelly Roll Morton speaks of the parades that moved to a jazz rhythm in New Orleans: the marchers were armed with sticks, knives, and baseball bats to meet the enemy—racist whites—on the way; the injuries that resulted sometimes necessitated the coming of two ambulances; and yet these parades culminated in food and drink and dancing (Hughes and Bontemps 1958, pp. 438–39).

One vital function of the jazz bands in New Orleans was to play for black funerals. This practice of having pomp and splendor at funerals appears to have been a transfer of a West African custom (Herskovits 1941, 164–67). Jelly Roll Morton recounts this practice in New Orleans:

A dead man always belonged to several organizations—secret orders and so forth— so when anybody died a big band always turned out the day he was supposed to be buried... You could hear the band coming up the street taking the gentleman for his last ride. You could hear the drums, rolling a deep slow rhythm. A few bars of that and then the snare drummer would make a hot roll on his drums and the boys in the band would just tear loose. In New Orleans they believed [in rejoicing] at death and [crying] at birth (Hughes and Bontemps 1958, 441).

In a sense, therefore, jazz was created to respond to varying needs of Afro–Americans, one of them being an attempt to overcome through pleasure the pain of prejudice, another being to continue, even if in vestigial form, West African customs that had not been totally forgotten.

Another aspect of black American music worth studying for its folkloric value is the black worksong. LeRoi Jones (Amiri Baraka) states that such songs were the progenitors of the blues and jazz forms (1963, 17). These songs, especially those of the rail liners, frequently possess an onomatopoetic quality that corresponds to the sound, rhythm, and duration of the activity. For example, in the following song the lyrics are timed to fit a particular activity; the "huh" sound probably coincides with the blow of the hammer in securing a bolt:

> Take this hammer—huh!
> To the captain—huh!
> You tell him I'm gone—huh!
> Tell him I'm gone—huh! (Hughes and Bontemps 1958, 399)

Where cranes and other mechanical lifting devices were absent, the worksong provided the rhythm necessary to coordinate the activities of as many as fifty men. I remember as a boy watching scores of men transporting walls of houses, and doing so in perfect time to the rhythm of an obscene song that included the name of the man or woman whose house they were transporting. As Lawrence Levine notes, these songs helped to ease the ennui of tedious, back-breaking labor, such as corn husking, cotton picking, hoeing, etc. (1977 208).

The following citation by Harold Courlander on the function of music in work in Haiti reflects what used to be the situation in the American South, except that there the musicians were absent. "The singing leader, called a *samba* or *simidor*, begins a song, the drummers play, the hoes begin to rise and fall in unison, and the workers join in the singing." Where the group is large it subdivides into "two or three squads, each trying to outdo the other." The men are abreast of each other, their hoes rise and fall in unison as they sing their various parts. "The *samba* beats on his hoe blade with a stone to keep time for his song." The songs sung by the "*coumbite* are a newspaper of the affairs of the people. The news is personalized, editorialized and replete with comic vignettes" (1960, 117–118). The practice of using song to set the pace of work is visible wherever there are large concentrations of people of African ancestry. As in Africa these songs lend themselves to social commentary.

SECULAR SPOKEN LORE

The black American folktale overshadows all the other forms of spoken lore. Most popular are the tales in which Brer Rabbit stars, these having been widely circulated in Joel Chandler Harris' *Uncle Remus* stories. The black folktale in the United States is quite diverse, and the canon grows from year to year.

At least subconsciously early white collectors of black folklore were aware of the subterfuge implicit in black folktales, a subterfuge blacks employed to preserve their humanity in oppression. The defensive posture of the first white collectors is evident in the mindless, groveling, worshipful-of-whites, mimicking black narrators they created to tell the lore. One sees, for example, a glaring contrast between the survival cunning dramatized in the lore in which Brer Rabbit is chiefly protagonist and the fictive, benign, buffoon narrator, Uncle Remus.

No area of life, no subject, segment of society, or activity is considered too sacrosanct to escape interpretation or satirical treatment in the black folktale. Daryl Dance, whose 1978 collection of contemporary black American folklore is three-quarters folktales, tells the reader that "it is mainly in their folktales that [black people] have been able to find some relief from their frustrations and give some aggressive expression to their hostilities without endangering their physical well-being" (179). Many of the autobiographical stories the ex-slaves have told are excellent examples of how they adapted the wisdom of Brer Rabbit in their day-to-day encounters with massa. John Mason Brewer, another outstanding black folklorist, feels that Brer Rabbit symbolized the slave himself (1968, 4).

The theme of triumphing over massa is the chief preoccupation of the "John tales," many of which are reported in Zora Neale Hurston's *Mules and Men* (1935). According to David Dalby, the name "John" is Mandingo, and the tales are a recreation of a similar body of slave tales in the Mandingo society (in Kochman 1972, 182). John is the fictive slave who almost always outsmarts massa. And from the numerous imbroglios in which he becomes implicated he is disentangled through a combination of cunning and luck. Like Kwaku Anansi of the Akan (the spider trickster), he is frequently arrogant and boastful. In more recent years the John/massa tales have been largely replaced by tales of individual blacks who outsmart whites. In earlier times "Sis Goose" was characteristic of the tone of the black American folktale. Sis Goose is grabbed by the fox as soon as she comes off the lake, and he accuses her of trespassing. When she replies that the lake is for the benefit of everyone, he insists that they take the matter to court. But the sheriff, judge, attorney, and jurors are foxes. They try Sis Goose, execute her, and eat her (Hughes and Bontemps 1958, 13). The differences reflected in the contemporary tales are to be seen in the following:

These white guys ... got this black guy down in Mississippi somewhere, and they just started shooting around his feet, you know. Say, "Dance, nigger, dance!" And they were just shootin' and he was jumpin' ...

So when they got through he said, "You use all your bullets?"

They say, "Yeah."

He pulled out that blade; he say, "You ever kiss a mule?"
The white guys say, "Naw, but I always had a inklin'" (Dance 1978, 218).

Here one can surely see that the basic formula for the trickster tale is unchanged in the contemporary tales.

The tales in which blacks satirize the traditional concept of heaven, the black and white church, the white justice system, inequality, white womanhood, and the myth of black supersexuality reveal the perspicacity with which Afro–Americans observe American reality and their effective ways of dramatizing the fundamental dishonesty of that society. Frequently such tales are parodies of white myths.

The ghost and conjure tales are excellent preservations of the superstitions of rural blacks. Many of these tales reveal that their creators never took the superstitions as seriously as some scholars have thought they did.

There is a group of tales that have made many blacks very uncomfortable. They are a good index of the self-hatred and self-distrust that centuries of oppression and doctrines of racial inferiority have inculcated in Afro–Americans. It would seem that for the oppressed it is sometimes easier to accept the rationalizations proferred by the oppressor and the concomitant self-denigration than to undertake the often radical action necessary to contest that oppression. John Oliver Killens, in his essays and fiction, has written extensively about self-denigrating black folklore (1954 [1982]; [1965] 1972).

Overall, black folktales abound with insights by blacks into their own life and life in America in general. Most of these tales are humorous, and those that are not are outstanding for their cleverness. Whatever their immediate impact, their principal focus is a greater awareness of the black position in America. We must also add that the verbal "edifice" of the black church, created to transcend stifling racism, is equally manifest in the folktales.

The most obvious connection between the Afro–American folktale and the black novel is the ubiquitous presence of the trickster in both. We shall look at several portraits of the trickster in chapter three.

The folktales surrounding the church in general occasionally set the tone for the fictional characterization of the preacher, as we shall see in chapter two. But it is in the pervasiveness of the tragic and sometimes comic irony in these tales and in Afro–American novels that the resemblance is greatest. The folktale has become a structuring device for many black novelists, including John Killens, John Wideman, Paule Marshall, Toni Morrison, and Ishmael Reed.

Closely allied to Afro–American folktales and straddling them and the fantastic ritual oral arts (my term for the toasts and dozens, to be discussed later) is a category of folklore that Zora Neale Hurston brought to popular attention when her work *Mules and Men* appeared. *Lies*, the term used by those who engage in this type of folklore, conveys its nonmimetic nature. This form has parallels with white folklore. It is probably another area where African and European forms syncretized. The form exists in all Afro–Caribbean communities under different names, such as *garfing, fatiguing*, and *Piquong*. In St. Vincent excellent tellers of such tales are called *garfers* to the extent that the term eventually replaces their actual names.

Lying is an outstanding example of the degree to which "Afro-New Worlders" prize their oral art and their imagination. These lies are challenges in the skill of creating clever exaggerations. The following tale in the Hughes and Bontemps collection of folklore is an example of a "lie." Someone heard a bullet twice—first when it struck him and later when he sped past it (1958, 135). In *Mules and Men* Zora Neale Hurston devotes several pages to showing the keenness with which her informers competed in the telling of lies. According to one of them, it was so hot in Texas once that old stumps and logs crawled off into the shade. To which "Eugene Oliver" responded that it was once so hot that "two cakes of ice left the icehouse and went down the street and fainted." Arthur Hopkins added that once it was so hot, that two men melted out of the serge suits they had been wearing ([1935] 1978, 106–7).

The intention of this type of folklore is principally to entertain and, as Hurston shows in *Their Eyes Were Watching God*, to foster social communion. In *Mules and Men*, it is evident that "lying" is valuable for the distraction it provides those employed at tedious tasks—Hurston's best tales of this nature were collected from workers in the turpentine camps of Polk County ([1935] 1978, 64–190). This folk form functions similarly in St. Vincent, where it is employed, along with others, by arrowroot diggers, who work all day with their backs bent, and cane-cutters, who are constantly being wounded by the sharp edged sugar cane leaves. As such, lying has a function analogous to the worksong. Complementing cards, dominos, and checkers, it is a chief source of entertainment in those rural and urban communities where people for any number of reasons must create their own entertainment.

Cleverness and a carefully worked-out structure, even if the telling is extemporaneous, must be evident in the lies. Obviously the audience enjoys hearing new lies, but the old ones, as seen in *Mules and Men*, are an essential part of the repertoire. We shall look briefly at Forrest's use of lies in chapter three.

It is easy to move from lies to the humor of black people, for the former relies heavily on the latter; both are entertaining and distracting. But here the similarities end. Among Afro–Americans, humor, sometimes self-directed, but mostly directed at the white race, is a vital part of the survival mechanism. In *The Big Sea*, Langston Hughes observed that the black poor of Washington, D.C., often looked at the dome of the Capitol and laughed out loud; this they did, opines Hughes quoting a line from a popular blues tune, "to keep from crying" (1940, 207). Most Afro–Americans will agree with this interpretation of their humor.

Lawrence Levine has written a detailed explanation of the church worship-type atmosphere that exists when a black audience is listening to a black comedian. The comedian reiterates the cruelty of whites, the hardships of black existence, the lapses of blacks, etc., all in a humorous way. In black audiences black humor is organic, with a great deal of evocation. The humorist, however, functions as teacher, castigator, and healer, with the audience always shouting its agreement to what is being said (Levine, 1977, 362–66). Charles Keil has in mind this relationship between the black audience and the performer when he writes that "Certain performances called entertaining by Negroes and whites alike have an added but ritual significance for Negroes. . . . These entertainers are the ablest representatives of a long cultural tradition—what might be called the soul tradition—and they are all identity experts" (1966, 15). One must not ignore the vestigial remains in black American entertainment of the close ties between performer and participating audience in the West African setting.

Humor as part of black audience entertainment reflects the overall tendency of black entertainers to be secular priests to their audiences. In the Afro–American novel humor emerges from the interactions of the characters as they reflect on the absurdities of existence in America. Frequently it is "black humor" on all cognitive levels. This is especially true of the novels of Langston Hughes and John Killens.

Just as black humor, black music, and the black church are essential forms for the exorcism of the pain of injustice, so there are other forms through which intragroup hostility is ritualized and prevented from becoming physical violence. One of these forms is referred to as the dozens.

Verbal warfare with an emphasis on wit, humor, and rhyme, the opponent's mother being the principal target of abuse, best defines the dozens. There is some distinction made between the clean and dirty dozens, the latter being characterized by its obscenities and its fixed expressions, in the same sense as some blues lines are fixed. The same can be played with or without an audience; but an audience is always desirable, for part of this ritual involves showmanship, and the degree of the listeners' shouts of approvals and applause provides a qualitative index of the players' verbal skills.

Most of the interpretations of the function of the dozens have been proferred by white scholars, and as is to be expected some of them are far-fetched. Black civil rights activist H. Rap Brown agrees with those scholars who argue that the dozens represent an initiation into the game of "rapping"—i.e., excelling at verbal skills—and an aggression-releasing mechanism. A dozens player himself, Brown writes that "we exercised our minds by playing the dozens." The following are samples of the repartees cited in his work:

I fucked your mama / Till she went blind.
Her breath smells bad, / But she sure can grind.

I fucked your mama / For a solid hour;
Baby came out / Screaming Black Power.

On the subject of aggression, Brown writes, "What you try to do is totally destroy somebody with words. It's that whole competition thing again, fighting with each other. There'd be sometimes forty or fifty dudes standing around and the winner was determined by the way they responded to what was said" (1969, 26).

Abrahams, offering a critic's interpretation of the dozens, feels that because Afro–American society is matrifocal, the dozens have a liberating effect for the youthful male who feels a compulsion to cast aside the feminine dominance to which he has been subjected. By insulting another boy's mother, the youngster knows that his own in turn will be insulted (*Positively Black* 1970, 41). But recent research into the matrifocal facet of the black family questions the validity of this theory (Willie 1976, 3; Wallace 1979, 114–16; Collier and Williams 1982, 487–89). Abraham's stay in a small section of a Philadelphia black ghetto was too short for him to understand deeply the communal parenting that exists in many black communities. Albert Murray and James Baldwin have written about this aspect of the black community. Murray opines that "further investigation may discover that the actual family of many contemporary Negroes is the neighborhood. Much goes to show that among US negroes parental authority and responsibility have always been shared by neighborhood uncles and aunts of whom sometimes none are blood relatives" (1970, 63). On this subject Baldwin states that when he was growing up in Harlem "every child belonged to every mother and every father" to such an extent that any adult who found children misbehaving could whip them and be assured that when the real parents found out the children would be flogged a second time (Tsuruta 1981, 78–79).

Another element that undermines Abraham's hypothesis is the fact that girls play the dozens. Black Philadelphians with whom I have discussed Abraham's note, appended to the 1970 revised edition of *Deep down in the Jungle*, that girls rarely play the dozens, find his statement laughable. John Dollard's 1939 study acknowledges the active involvement of girls in the game (in Dundes 1973, 285–86). Rap Brown also states that some of the best dozens players are girls (1969, 27).

For a long time it was felt that the game of the dozens was unique to the United States. In a 1951 essay, however, Phillip Mayer reported observations of a similar ritual among Bantu adolescent males. In a later essay, Abrahams states that he was later informed of analogous practices in various African and Afro–Caribbean societies (in Kochman 1972, 217). According to Mayer, for the Bantu lads, to insult one another—the crowning insult

being directed at the other's mother—without eliciting anger or violence is
a profound sign of companionship and solidarity within the group. If such a
friendship should cease these playful insults become unacceptable (31–33).

In St. Vincent preadolescents engage in a limited version of this game,
with frequently resulting tussles. The peer pressure to participate is very
strong, to the point that spectators make a virtual prisoner of unwilling boys
or girls until they participate. Ostracism, sometimes brutally enforced, is
imposed on a defying youngster. The male who fails to undergo this initiation will be referred to, for as long as he remains in the community, as
someone who missed out on some of the activities of his "boy days." It
seems that in later life the relationship between the defiant person and his
peers lacks spontaneity, speech tends to be more formal, and conversation
topics more restricted. It is as if the defiant person never earned the trust of
the group.

In his pioneering study Dollard gives as reason for the existence of the
dozens the need on the part of the black community to deflect aggression
away from the dangerous white community to the black community. It is an
interesting initial remark, but one that Levine dismisses along with Abraham's matrifocal hypothesis as inadequately accounting for the function of
this folk form. I concur (with Levine); though, as I shall show later, I also
feel that the game is bound up with the purging of aggression. Grier and
Cobb see it as ritual preparation of adolescents to ignore the numerous
insults they will hear whites hurl at those they love most (1972, 7).

In St. Vincent, where the black/white dichotomy is less evident and the
matrifocal theory mostly irrelevant, the dozens exist in a highly developed
and elaborate ritual form among adult females. It takes the form of a witty
trading of insults, mostly of an imaginary kind, going back to several generations of the family; when they exhaust the facts, they turn to conjecture.
Nothing is taboo in these exchanges, not even the physical deformities of
relatives, such deformities being attributed to sins the public may or may not
know about. Because of this last, *cussing* or *tracing*, as this ritual is variously
termed in different parts of the English-speaking Caribbean, functions
secondarily to preserve a sort of public morality. Frequently a mother
remarks to a disobedient child, "Do you want to put words in people's
mouths to curse me with?" It is also well known that any heinous crime that
an individual commits leaves a curse legacy for his descendants of several
generations (the family is disgraced).

Because of the large crowd that comes to witness such an event, there is
an entertainment factor. Moreover, as each combatant lists the more
serious lapses of the other (to the shouts of applause and urgings of the
crowd), those present derive a peculiar catharsis—it is as though the parad-
ing of a person's sins in public is a penance for the offender. Adult men
rarely engage in this ritual, active participation therein being considered
effeminate. The antagonists may or may not become enemies temporarily;

but if they do, the enmity lasts only a few days, unless one lied seriously about another, in which case there could enmity for life.

The generalized presence of this ritual among people of African descent in the New World points to its African origin. For what I believe to have been a defensive reaction to the ravages of nature, the West African held life within the clan to be so sacred that if in some societies one murdered a clansman, not only would he be killed or forever banished but a curse devolved upon his descendants (despite the Christian influence and a profound knowledge of the Bible, Vincentian folk believe that a murderer inevitably damns his soul; murder also includes abortion). Such sanctions, over a long period discouraged the use of physical force and resulted in verbal structures for the resolution of hostilities. Language as a weapon, as it is used in black communities everywhere, has its roots, I suspect, in this phenomenon. Of course, on coming to the New World, the rituals, the means to enforce and impress them upon blacks as part of an ethical code, broke down (some were even inverted), but they did not altogether vanish; there were also other needs born of the oppression New World blacks encountered, and so the rituals were accordingly altered.

Afro–American novelists find the dozens a useful rhetorical device to comment on the psychic reality of black Americans. We shall observe this in Wright's and Forrest's use of the dozens in chapter four.

Signifying is sometimes so close to playing the dozens that it is indistinguishable from it. Some folklorists group the dozens under signifying. There are several shadings of this form. Signifying, however, is always marked by innuendo and indirection.

According to Claudia Kernan-Mitchell, a black folklorist, there must exist a shared body of knowledge for signifying to operate properly:

It must be employed, first of all, by the participant in a speech act in the recognition that signifying is occurring and the dictionary-syntactical meaning of the utterance is to be ignored. Secondly, this shared knowledge must be employed in the reinterpretation of the utterance. It is the cleverness used in directing the attention of the hearer and audience to this knowledge upon which a speaker's artistic talent is judged (in Dundes 1971, 325).

An excellent example of what Kernan-Mitchell means is cited in Kochman:

A man coming from the bathroom forgot to zip his pants. An unescorted party of women kept watching him and laughing among themselves. The man's friends hip him to what's going on. He approaches one woman—"Hey, baby, did you see that big, black Cadillac with the full tires ready to roll for you?" She answers, "No, Mother fucker, but I saw a little gray Volkswagen with two flat tires" (Kochman 1972, 244).

Signifying need not be verbal; gestures of the head, shoulders, and hands can be effectively employed (Kernan-Mitchell 1971, 325). According to

Henry-Louis Gates, who is in the process of formulating a new literary critical theory based on signifying, "the black tradition has its own subdivisions of signifying, which we could readily identify with the typology of figures received from classical and Medieval rhetoric...In black discourse 'signifying' means modes of figuration itself...and would include 'marking,' 'loud-talking,' 'specifying,' 'testifying,' 'calling-out' (of one's name), 'sounding,' 'rapping,' and 'playing the dozens'" (1983, 687).

So indigenous is signifying to black American discourse that one finds it everywhere, from the relating of a person's defects in his presence but attributing them to some fictitious being, to speaking in parables. Rap Brown defines it as an exchange of tales and considers it more humane than the dozens. He notes as well that playing the dozens is one's apprenticeship in acquiring the "rapping" skills required for signifying. Brown goes on to say that "signifying allowed you a choice—you could make a cat feel either good or bad. If you had just destroyed someone or if they were just down already, signifying could help them over. Signifying was a way of expressing your own feelings:

"Man, I can't win for losing."

"If it wasn't for bad luck, I wouldn't have no luck at all."

"I been having buzzard luck: can't kill nothing and won't nothing die" (Rap Brown 1969, 27).

In his autobiography, Dick Gregory cites analogous self-directed epithets and ascribes to them some of Rap Brown's functions (1964, 40–42).

One needs to comment on the well-known poetic narrative, "The Signifying Monkey," in which the monkey creates mischief by informing the lion that the elephant has been speaking ill of him. The lion takes the monkey at his word and seeks a fight with the elephant and is badly beaten. The monkey, on the other hand, is entertained by the battle. From this tale it is clear that signifying has another significance from those we have already seen; it involves a clever manipulation of language at another's expense.

As Brown and Gregory explain signifying, it functions to entertain the group and to place the black experience into an aesthetic framework. In this manner it accords with Ralph Ellison's understanding of the blues: the squeezing from pain "a near-comic, near-tragic lyricism" (1964, 78). In the other examples it is a clever and comic rendition of reality that could otherwise be harshly competitive and aggressive. In the case of the monkey it is another use of language as manipulation, an extension of the trickster tradition. Signifying is therefore the grouping of various Afro–American folk tendencies under a single rubric.

The toast is the most recent folk form to be studied by white folklorists. Roger Abrahams credits himself for bringing this form to the attention of the academic community ([1963] 1970, 97). White scholars hotly dispute the meanings as well as the definitions of the toasts (see *Journal of American Folklore* 88: 178–87).

The toast eludes an easy definition and is believed by most scholars to be unrelated to the European practice of eulogizing someone with a drink in hand. David Evans disputes this by saying that "all the toasts [he has] heard ...were recited by informants with drink in hand" (1977, 130). Undoubtedly Evans overstates his case, for toasts are recited at the pool hall, the barbershop, the street corner, wherever large numbers of black males assemble.

Toasts are for the most part unrealistic and obscene narrative, and sometimes lyrical, poems. They include many of the features of exaggeration already seen in lying. Daryl Dance links them to tales of the "Bad Nigger" (1978, 225). The following citation summarizes many of the disparate features of the toast:

The heroes are all "bad": they claim the virtues of courage, physical strength, clarity and coolness of mind, and knowledge of the rules of the game and the ways of the world. They explicitly reject respect for the law; romantic love; pity and gratitude; chivalry or special consideration for women....Shine, Honky Tonk, Bud, and the narrator of "The Fall" are heroes but not gentlemen. Furthermore, the heroes of the toast defy the values of middle-class society in respect to language: in their use of taboo words and their scorn for sentimental and abstract verbiage. They do not, however, reject the aesthetic value of poetry: the intricate system of rhyme, meter, and metaphor shows a great emphasis on the poetic aspect of verbal skills (Labov, Cohen, *et al*, 1968, in Dundes 1973, 335–36).

The function of the toast varies in direct proportion to the number of interpreters. Rap Brown refers to toast-telling as merely "talking shit," the "shit" talkers being prized for their elocution skills (1969, 29–30). For Brown's community, and I suspect for the majority of Afro–Americans who engage in this ritual, the function is entertaining for the audience and status-procuring for the teller. In the socio-psychological area Wepman, Newman, and Binderman, in their collection of toast texts: *The Life: The Lore of Folk Poetry of the Black Hustler*, state that these poems reveal "the special community which creates and transmits the toasts: that black urban community known as sporting life, or, simply the life" (1976, 1). These authors aver that the pimps, supersexual men, and badmen whom these poems glorify were the heroes emulated by black urban ghetto youths before black militancy and organized crime appeared (15).

Roger Abrahams' interpretation is in character with his analysis of the role of the black entertainer. Commenting on "The Great Mac Daddy" toast, he writes:

Life is seen in commodity terms, with about as much worth as the personal limousines or the beautiful "threads" (clothes) which these heroes are described as wearing. These outlaw heroes are regarded as heroic not only because they act aggressively in the face of authority but they also announce that they are pursuers of the American Dream, with its visions of perpetual plenty available to those who are willing to do the pursing. These are the Negro entrepreneurs, those who are going to grab the goods even if society at large seeks to keep the tv sets and the beautiful clothes in the windows of the department stores. These are those willing to be "a flying piece of furniture" to fly around Main Street Heaven for at least an hour (*Positively Black* 1970, 80).

This statement, in its reduction of an important aspect of black American folklore to a quest for crude materialism, is insulting to the black American community. Unfortunately Abrahams sees realism where there exists parody. There is a great deal of signifying in the toasts. To the extent that Abrahams interprets them in a literal way he is signified upon.

Bruce Jackson's introduction to '*Get Your Ass in the Water and Swim Like Me*' (a collection of toast texts) repeatedly links the reality described in the toast world to that of the urban black ghetto; yet at the same time, in what seems to be clever strategy, dissociates the two to such an extent that his statements are sometimes contradictory (this is not to deprecate the value of his work: his perceptions are frequently astute; but in the absence of known explanations he falls into speculations that derive inevitably from white-held stereotypes about black existence).

It is erroneous to suggest that the toast portrays the lifestyle of the black urban ghetto. Of the toast tellers of whom Wepman, Newman, and Binderman write—all prison inmates—none of them meets the criteria for membership in the life. Moreover, to suggest that black youth aspire to the roles depicted in the toasts is defamatory. Do black youths aspire to having their genitalia removed as is Shine's fate in some versions of the Shine toast?

That the toast is psychologically related to the lifestyle of blacks in America is indisputable; its function, however, is vicarious, not actual—no more do blacks aspire to these roles than do boxing fans go out the day after a boxing tournament and slug away at everyone who comes in sight. The toast is as vicarious as the Brer Rabbit tales, as the John tales, as the jokes about "Miz Ann" seducing black men as soon as her husband is out of sight. The same psychological need that caused the creation of these tales also caused the creation of the toasts; it is only the forms that are dissimilar. The toasts are an aggression-releasing mechanism, providing relief from an aggression that is heightened by the stresses of inferior status in a white-dominated society. The targets are the values of that society. The hostility that young dozens players direct at one another becomes directed in later life toward white American society at large. No folklorist is prepared to say that the dozens reflect the aspirations of its players. Why then should folklorists think that toasts do? Black psychologist Kenneth Clark warns those who see the toast as literal reflections of the ambitions of ghetto youths:

Teenage Negroes often cope with ghetto frustrations by retreating into fantasies related chiefly to their role in society.... Some pretend falsely to be pimps, some to have contacts with numbers runners. Their apparent admiration of these models is not total but reflects a curious combination of respect, of contempt, and fundamentally of despair. Social scientists must find a way to unravel this web of pretense if their conclusions are to be relevant (1965, 66).

It is common practice among people of African origin to desecrate what is most valuable in one's enemy. In the Caribbean, because of the great emphasis placed on fertility and sexuality, such curses are most often directed at the relevant parts of an opponent's anatomy. The toast can be shown to be a continuation, as is the above example, of a tradition that still obtains in West Africa. This is R.S. Rattray's account of this tradition among the Ashanti:

There is also a custom known as *bo akutia*—a kind of vituperation by proxy. This consists of an aggrieved person arranging with a friend to accompany him to the house of, e.g., a chief who has offended him, but of whom he is afraid. The man and his companion pretend to have a violent quarrel. In the altercation which ensues, the former will assail the latter with every kind of abuse, all this taking place in the presence of the chief against whom one of the parties has the grievance, and against whom all this raillery is subtly directed. Having thus relieved his pent-up feelings, the offended one professes to feel much better. These interesting customs prove, I think, beyond a doubt that West Africans had discovered for themselves the psychoanalysts' theory of "repressions," and that in these ways they sought an outlet for what might otherwise become a dangerous complex (1923, 155–56).

Elsewhere Rattray describes a ceremony where on certain ritual days the Ashantis have the right to abuse their chiefs and even their gods, using the most derogatory terms: eater of rats, impotent, a pet cat, etc. (1930, xi–xii). Herskovits has observed similar practices among the Dahomeans (1958, 62). It would be foolish for one to think that such abuse was done in earnest, just as it is silly to assume that toasts are overly serious. It is not difficult to see how upon coming to America such customs as reported by Rattray became modified and gave way to the toasts, as well as to signifying. As with its West African progenitor, a great deal of the entertainment found in the toast comes from its iconoclastic nature: its inversions of the mores of puritanical society, its espousal of bestiality, obscenity, extreme cruelty, and ruthlessness. Lawrence Levine alludes to this in his discussion of "Shine" as a brilliant mockery of the postulates of the American dream (1977, 428–29). James Baldwin, commenting on Wright's "Bad Nigger" Bigger Thomas, makes a subtle observation that may be of pertinence here. He says that it is not the monstrous that a white society pushes blacks towards and about which they sometimes fantasize that triumphs in them, but rather their humanity, kept intact by the institutions they have created for their survival

([1951] 1972, 26–29). Perhaps no other aspect of Afro–American folklore dramatizes this duality like the toast.

In a significant number of published toasts there is a moral dimension that seems to have escaped the analysis of those who have interpreted the form. Bruce Jackson implies some awareness of this in his statement that

it is easy to see the street roles portrayed in the toasts as models for black youths, but they are also terribly threatening to them: the badman will beat you up; the pimp will hustle your sister or your mother or your woman; the pusher will sell you a product other people will rob you to buy; the hustler will take your money. I suspect that toasts hold these roles up as models for behavior or success but simultaneously display some of them as figures to be distanced and laughed at (1974, 15).

It seems that many scholars of black folklore blind themselves to those aspects that contradict their hypotheses. How else can one account for the folklorists' emphasis on the criminal activity of the ghetto and their simultaneous ignoring of its fanatical religiousness? I say this to highlight an aspect of the toast that none of its scholars has examined. In several versions of "The Signifying Monkey" it is not so much the violence between the elephant and the lion that is important—though that in itself is highly dramatic—but rather the monkey's delight in creating mischief. The intentions of this toast are, in my view, clearly moral: that one should not permit oneself to become the victim of a puppeteer or a signifier. In some versions of "Shine," after he displays profound wisdom in choosing life over the silly material offerings of people who would in different circumstances despise him, he ends up anticlimactically in a pathetic, drunken stupor in a New York whorehouse or he is in a doctor's office about to have his genitalia removed. Thus, this toast, at least in the version referred to here, has an implicit moral. A youngster hearing this toast is forced to conclude that despite Shine's physical prowess and initial wisdom, he was not so wise after all.

To the discussion of the meaning of the toast Dance adds yet another dimension regarding those toasts that deal with badmen, pimps, and whores. She interprets such toasts in light of the theory expressed by Grier and Cobbs in *Black Rage* and extensively explored in John Killens's novel *Youngblood*—that it is the black mother who must impress upon her son the technique of staying alive in America. And because such a technique involves debasement, the young man often redirects his hostility toward his mother. Dance's own words best express her hypothesis:

The Bad Niggers in folklore are sexual supermen, but their women are enemies to be conquered, humiliated and controlled rather than partners to be loved. The hostility toward the Black woman expressed in the toasts...undoubtedly has its basis in the inhibitions imposed by white American society on Black men.... It has usually been the Black mother who, because of her fear of the slave master, the lynch mob, and the legal system, had to teach her child to mask and repress his normal masculinity and aggressiveness lest these put his life in danger. . . . It is commonly accepted that the Bad Nigger's need to humiliate and subdue the woman (the battlefield is the bed) stems from his antagonism towards her for what appears to him to be her collusion with white American society to emasculate and repress him (1978, 225).

Yet in West Africa the tales that men tell one another are very much full of stories that point to the need to keep women in a subordinate place. Thus, while this tendency reaches a new height in the toast, its origin is not American.

Finally, the toast parallels the dozens, lying, and many of the folktales in that its details are rarely realistic. In some versions, Shine, for example, converses with whales and sharks, does not drown because of "a cork in his ass," and swims the distance from the sinking Titanic to New York in thirty minutes. One must also see the boasts of the badmen in this light. All this reminds us that a principal feature of the toast is to entertain, bearing in mind the psychological needs to which entertainment responds. The toast hero is in the background of the two Bad Niggers we shall examine: Wright's Bigger Thomas and Gaines's Marcus Payne in chapter two.

One cannot ignore the language that transmits the lore. For this reason the phenomenon of jive, by far the most distinguishing trait of Afro–American folk speech, must be addressed. Jive could be defined as a preoccupation on the part of a small group of black Americans, usually urban ghetto dwellers, to invest old words with new meanings and to create new words and expressions. Dan Burley writes that "like copy readers and editorial writers on newspapers jive addicts take infinite care of their latest brain-child. They trim and polish, rearrange, revise, reshuffle and recast certain phrases until they have the best and most concise expression that can be devised" (1944, in Dundes 1973, 22). A glance at *The Dictionary of American Slang* will indicate to the reader the degree to which jive has affected the spoken language of America. That the creators of jive are very active is to be noted by the number of new expressions that keep appearing in the black American vocabulary.

Jive has more than a semantic function. Claude Brown refers to it as "spoken soul" and feels that its essence is more sound than meaning. Soul "possesses a lyrical quality which is frequently incompatible to any music other than that ceaseless and relentlessly driving rhythm that flows from poignantly spent lives. Spoken soul has a way of coming out metered without the intention of the speaker to invoke it" (1968, in Dundes 1973, 234). Jive expressions reflect, therefore, the musical characteristic of Afro–American speech; at the same time it too contributes to the musical vitality of Afro-American folk speech.

Jazz musicians were, as Neil Leonard documents, prolific contributors to jive. Leonard attributes this to jazz musicians' needs to "probe the unknown

or unexpressed with metaphor, oxymoron, and synechdoche in ways puz-
zling to unattuned ears" (1986, 152). Whatever the reason—a feeling of
community as well as acceptable ways of ritualizing stress and competition
are among those reasons that Leonard gives (155)—jazz musicians were
deep reservoirs from which flowed much of the jive that came to enrich the
language of mainstream America.

The mysterious nature of jive is best appreciated when one listens to the
inner circles where it is created. Both Hurston and Burley, themselves
Afro–American, have written at length about the hermetic nature of the
newest jive expressions. Following is an excerpt from a 1942 essay that
Hurston wrote to illustrate the inaccessibility of jive to all but the initiated.

Wait till I light up my coalpot and tell you about this zigaboo called Jelly. Well, all
right now. He was a tall seal skin brown and papa-tree-top-tall. Skinny in the hips
and solid built for speed. He was born with rough-dried hair, but when he laid on
the grease and pressed it down overnight with his stocking cap, it looked just like
righteous moss, and had so many waves you got seasick from looking. Solid man,
solid! (in Dundes 1973, 222).

Here, for the benefit of her white audience, Hurston stylizes the jive
expressions and thins out the hermetic words, leaving only a flavor of the
rhythm and the cryptic vocabulary. Elsewhere Hurston feels that jive springs
from some need within the black man to adorn and "in this respect the
American Negro has done wonders for the English language.... He has
made over a great part of the tongue to his liking and has had his revisions
accepted by the ruling class" ("Characteristics of Negro Expressions," in
Cunard, 24–25).

Wright's interpretation, which leans in the direction of the need for a
secret code, seems more plausible: "We stole words from the grudging lips
of the Lords of the Land... charged" them "with all the emotions and needs
we had" and created a language with voice inflections, "tonal variety, hur-
ried speech," and "honeyed drawls... to be able to speak of revolt in their
actual presence" (1941, 40).

To the foregoing one must add that the myriads of secret societies
devoted to the worship of various West African deities had already pre-
disposed blacks to the need for cryptic languages. Slavery and its concomitant brutality simply reinforced the need for such a language among
the descendants of West Africans.

Jive, then, enriches black American speech, not only in terms of its
imagistic words, metaphors, and rhythm, but also in terms of the new meanings it gives to familiar words. For a while, that is before the expressions
pass into the verbal mainstream, there is little doubt that they confer some
distinction on the users who resist the pressure to conform to the standard
American idiom. Underlying jive is an attitude of revolt.

Allied to the study of jive is Karla Holloway's examination of the language of Zora Neale Hurston's characters and narrators. Holloway notes that it is through language that Hurston's characters reveal the distinctness of their culture. Indeed, so distinct is their speech that on occasion the nuances and denotations are incomprehensible to outsiders. But it is in these characters' use of metaphor, personification, and pathetic fallacy that the Afro–American *lingua franca* predominates (1987, 47–73 passim).

In the black American novel there is only limited room for the novelist to indulge in orthodox jive. To do so would be to alienate most of his readers. What the authors therefore do is apply the jive principle to an interpretation of reality. It is not surprising that the word *jive* in contemporary American usage is synonymous with trickery, for if one were to interpret the words of the jive artist according to their strictest meanings one would be duped. In Barry Beckham's *Runner Mack* (1983), Mack uses jive to effect solidarity with Henry, to form as it were a community with its own codes. In chapter four we shall see the Harlem rioters in Ellison's *Invisible Man* and Forrest's Nathaniel in *The Bloodworth Orphans* indulging the jive faculty.

SUPERSTITIONS AND CONJURE

The superstitions of American blacks are by blacks and whites alike the most vilified aspect of Afro–American folklore. Article after article in nineteenth-century American magazines underscored the "simpleminded-ness" of a people who could harbor such beliefs. As late as 1926, Newbell N. Puckett was still interpreting Afro–American superstitions and conjure in terms of the stereotypes of "laziness," "humor," "sexuality," "love of despotism," "impulsiveness," "short-sightedness"; all but the last he considered to be "traits of the Negro" (8–9). The general belief of whites was that black superstitions were irrefutable evidence that blacks were juvenile in character. Eventually such views became pivotal in the characterization of blacks by white authors, and in the interpretation of black literature by white critics.

What are now loosely termed superstitions, at least those originating in Africa, functioned as a structuring tool in pre-American black society. Many of them are taboos severed from rituals that died on contact with slavery. Devoid of their context, these superstitions frequently appear ridiculous. For example, to die without having had a drink of water from one's loved ones is, in West Africa, the Caribbean, and black America, a fate to be avoided, although in the West Indies and America the reason for this belief is unknown. It is, however, connected to the Ashanti belief that the "death-rattle" sounds are due to the laborious journey the dying person's soul is making to reach the other world. A drink of water given as a thirst-quencher is therefore considered a necessity (Wright 1954, 212–13). When placed in the animist world of West Africa, where functions, duties, and responsibilities are intricately related and must be respected, these superstitions are no more or no less ridiculous than the tenets of most Christian creeds. One needs, of course, to go beyond the actual superstition to the human needs it responds to. Novelists Alice Walker, Toni Morrison, Margaret Walker, Ishmael Reed, and Toni Cade Bambara have all seen in these so-called superstitions metaphors that summarily embody elusive aspects of reality, and have consequently utilized them in their work. Frederick Douglass told of the courage he derived from a piece of John the Conqueror root (1845, 80–82); and Zora Neale Hurston's essay "High John the Conqueror" is an excellent interpretation of the courage the John the Conqueror superstitions provided the slaves in their struggle to make life dignified (1943; in Hughes and Bontemps 1958, 93–102).

An aspect of black superstitions that requires separate treatment is conjuring. Some black critics and writers would argue that it is not a superstition but rather a ritual or series of rituals. Ishamel Reed would not even classify it under folklore; for him it is a religion—but this study considers religions to be folklore. The extent to which conjuring was a way of life among the black folk is to be seen in the references made to it even in the spirituals: "Ole Satan is a liar an' a conjurer too . . . If you don't mind he slip it on you." Here conjure is allied with the devil; but such an alliance equates the conjurer's power with the devil's, which is enormous power indeed. In Dance's opinion, the force of conjuring on the popular black imagination is declining (1978, 37). At one point, however, there was a compulsion by black and white creators of black characters to involve them with conjure, so closely were the two perceived to be allied.

Conjuring must not be confused with Voodhoo or Hoodoo even though the Hoodoo priest could conceivably be and frequently is a conjurer. Conjuring is intended to be a deadly art; Voodhooism, on the other hand, is a religion whose emphasis is on the spiritual wholeness of the community, a wholeness that includes even the dead members, who then become ancestral spirits. Conjuring is related to sorcery, which is in opposition to Voodhooism as the Christian Devil is opposed to the Christian God. In most West African communities individuals who attempted to put sorcery spells on members of their own clan were, if discovered, severely punished. But the clan as a whole sometimes included in its rituals aspects that were designed to conjure its external enemies (personal communication 1983).

It is not difficult to see why blacks as slaves in the New World had a deep need for sorcerers or conjurers. Insofar as the spirits of their ancestors failed to free them from slavery, they turned to conjuring. In her novel *Jubilee* Margaret Walker shows how quickly the white slave driver Grimes loses his confidence in controlling the slaves when he discovers a doll before his door; what frightens him further is that the death of one of his children follows (Walker's novel is based on historical documentation). In addition to the foregoing, there were none of the African controls to prevent the use of conjuring on other blacks: neither the threat of punishment nor the sense of the clan remained. Some of Dunbar's short stories depict the psychological power of conjure on the behavior of slaves. Virginia Frazer Boyle's *Devil Tales* (1900) are an excellent portrayal of conjure used for positive ends.

If the tales of conjure that one reads are true (I suspect they are altered to suit the temperament and memory of the teller and the needs of the audience), then early American blacks accepted as a matter of course an act of conjure and the death for which it was intended, unless they could conjure a reversal. This attitude contrasts with this writer's knowledge of the beliefs surrounding the tradition in St. Vincent, where opinions on the subject are quite diverse. Those, for example, deserving of the spell fall victim to it. There are contradictions to this, however, for one occasionally hears of a spell that was intended for one individual having its effect on another, a situation especially common in the case of the implantation of evil spirits in others. One thing is certain—and even the "unschooled" believe this—that frequently those who believe they have been conjured are victims of the guilt they feel for concealed wrongs. Moreover, the society possesses a mechanism, in the form of a Voodhoo-derived cult, by which persons who believe that they have been conjured may submit to a series of rituals and therefrom obtain release; or, in the case of guilt, exorcism. It is not difficult to see how such rituals are an effective therapy for various forms of mild madness, if only because many of the fears and anxieties from which illusions and delusions are born are effectively purged.

To return to the written accounts of conjuring among black Americans, it seems that conjuring is in some ways related to what in the broader society is termed hypnosis. In conjuring, however, the resignation of the will comes through an object that is believed to be endowed with a force capable of making the victim powerless. One might term it, especially as it is portrayed by Zora Neale Hurston, hypnosis by remote-control ([1935] 1978, 193–251). For this purpose various types of objects are used, some of which reflect European influences on black folk belief—the black cat bone being an example. The use, however, of soil from a grave, popular in both the United States and the Caribbean, suggests that this last is African-derived. There seems as well a greater emphasis in the Caribbean on employing the spirits of the dead as emissaries of evil.

There is an area where African and Caribbean reality are almost identical. Witchcraft, as conjuring is termed loosely in many parts of Africa, and *obeah* or *maljeu*, as it is termed in the Caribbean, is related to communal morality. Basil Davidson writes that among the Nupe in Nigeria witchcraft is identified with those who set aside the social values and thereby show that they reject the communal goals (1969, 133–34). Caribbean village society, like its African counterpart, has a compulsion to know the thoughts and actions of its members. Such societies, moreover, become suspicious of any situation that deviates from the norm. In the case of a poor person becoming wealthy, the society speculates openly as to whether such prosperity may not be derived from a secret trafficking with evil forces. In such gossip it is not hard to identify a deep wish on the community's part for conformity and some sort of uniformity among its members. It moreover shows a strong suspicion of individual initiative from which only the individual benefits. Because of such ingrained tendencies the enterprising individual, so as to be above suspicion, feels the need to make his transactions a public affair. And yet, should that individual become seriously ill, it would not be unusual for a business rival to become suspected of having worked "obeah" on him.

Because of the capitalist nature of American society the relationship between witchcraft and deviation from the social norms is no longer apparent. Individual initiative being a sacred feature of American society, the morality of the group is no longer sufficiently powerful for conjurers to be identified with those who are in conflict with the mores of the group. In most Afro–American novels where the characters resort to conjure, they do so because Christianity or the legal system fails to provide the solutions they seek. In Hurston's *Jonah's Gourd Vine* (1935), acts of conjure are shown to be effective; moreover, the entire community believes that there are solutions that can be provided only by the conjurer. Conjure as psychological trickery indissociable from verbal cunning is an important aspect of Charles Chesnutt's *Conjure Woman* (1899), which we shall examine in chapter three. Of contemporary Afro–American novelists, it is an important facet of Ishmael Reed's literary aesthetics and frequently provides local color in the works of Alice Walker.

We now turn to the utilization of the folklore in the novels.

2

Preachers and Bad Niggers

INTRODUCTION

This chapter deals with some of the popular figures of Afro–American folklore who nonetheless rarely appear as major characters in the Afro–American novel. They include the folkloric black preacher, Black Moses, John Henry, and the Bad Nigger. These figures are popular in folktales, in sermons, in ballads as well as tales, and in the toasts, respectively.

In black fiction the black preacher occurs most frequently as a confidence man. This makes him a trickster and so we shall treat this aspect of the black preacher in the chapter that deals with the trickster. Along with the foregoing, ostentation and lechery are his most visible traits. It is easy to see why such traits—at odds with his vocation—force him to be a trickster. We note, of course, that the Afro–American preacher shares much with medieval church figures in the way they were characterized in folklore and literature. One thinks, for example, of Chaucer's Monk, Abbot, and Pardoner. In St. Vincent and Jamaica, as a subject of folklore the preacher is second only to Anansi (the Akan Spider trickster whose stories were brought to the western world by slaves originating in modern-day Ghana).

The term *Bad Nigger* is quite broad and at times includes all the character types dealt with in this chapter. A Bad Nigger is essentially anyone who in any way menaces the white *status quo*. The term is borrowed from the slave planters, who referred to uncooperative slaves as "bad niggers" who had to be "broken." The clearest example of a Bad Nigger among Afro–Americans was the boxer Jack Johnson, for not only did he "whip the white man" but he lived on his own terms, violating all America's racial and even puritanical taboos (Wiggins 1971, 35–36). Using *The Narrative of Frederick Douglass* as an example, Houston Baker points out that the slave narrative "traces the self's successive movements through the roles of trickster, badman, educated leader, and intelligent rebel" (1974, 10). "Badman" is a synonym for Bad Nigger. It is not unusual to see various combinations of these roles in some of the categories we shall examine here. If we drop the word *educated* from the above quote we shall see that

John Henry is all of these in Killen's portrait of him. None of the Bad Nigger types is devoid of trickster qualities.

THE BLACK PREACHER

With their ancestral roots in Africa, blacks derive from a tradition where priests are wise men totally immersed in the beliefs, traditions, and aspirations of their culture and are mediators between the divine and mortal. In America, the black preacher found that while he was limited to preaching a Christian God and a Christian heaven, the mores of his congregation were a hybridization of those of their white masters and those of their African forefathers (LeRoi Jones 1967, 182–83). Furthermore, himself a product of such an environment, his own lifestyle could not but reflect that fusion. Clearly the degree of Americanization would vary among the members of his congregation, a reality which made the preacher's task extremely difficult.

Stemming from the African tradition was the expectation that the preacher would communicate to his congregations in the forms they understood best—primarily the forms of an oral culture (see Kenyatta, 1965, xvi). Thus beliefs had to be dramatized, abstractions concretized, and contact with the godly spirit manifested. In Africa itself questions were asked of gods and answers expected. Moreover—and some of this was transferred to America—no sharp distinctions existed between the secular and the divine. This feature of black American religion in its earliest phase was its most outstanding point of contrast with its white counterpart. As we have seen in chapter one, Africans even had their ceremonies in which they satirized their gods.

When one takes into account the fact that Christianity was the religion of the slave master, one naturally expects the slaves to be loathe to embrace it. With good reason they wondered whether this god would assist them against the master. They therefore had to make him into their god. In his novel *Clotel or the President's Daughter* (1853), ex-slave William Wells Brown captures the flavor of the Christianity that the masters taught their slaves and the contempt slaves held for that version of Christianity. The white Methodist minister teaches them that revolt against their master or dissatisfaction with their lot will impair their chances of going to heaven; moreover their condition as slaves, since it liberates them from the cares of their own well-being, gives them an advantage over white people in that it avails them more leisure to prepare their souls for heaven (97–99).

But back at the "quarters" the slaves are shown reflecting on the sermon. They are certain that their master gave the sermon to the minister, that the people who made the Bible were foolish—"such a great big book and put nuttin' in it but servants obey your masters"; they laugh heartily at the concept that black folks were created to work for white folks; and one of them affirms that there is much more in the Bible that white folks did not want black folks to hear (103–4). The supreme irony of all this is that not long after this sermon, a mulatto slave, disguised as a white woman, escapes from the plantation with a black slave who poses as her "nigger."

In an environment like the one that Brown described, the slaves were forced to alter Christianity to make it serve their needs. A curious tension developed, for while they supplemented it with their own forms and beliefs, they also felt a need to satirize it. Very soon, therefore, a huge corpus of deprecatory lore developed around their religion, the black preacher who interpreted it, and even the heaven that was supposed to be its end.

In his essay, "The Black Preacher Tale," which analyzes the preacher tales of Brewer's *The Word on the Brazos*, Hubbard writes that the tales "are a means for the people to work out cultural tensions through the use of humor directed at their preachers." The humor, according to Hubbard, takes some of the edge from a racially-oppressed congregation's anger (1987, 341). As mentioned already, the preacher of folklore is lecherous, greedy, alcohol-loving, power-hungry, boastful, ostentatious, cunning, lazy, unprincipled, and occasionally militant. Of course, all these qualities do not appear in every portrait. Clearly, aspects of various Afro–American mythic heroes have spilled into the tales of the preacher. When black Americans talk about the black church it is evident that their opinion is colored by many of the folktales they have heard about the preacher.

The preachers I shall examine here are those who are in some way related to their prototype in folklore. We begin with an examination of one of Dunbar's preachers.

Dunbar's portrayal of the black preacher is multifaceted, and for this reason is best understood after one has examined all of Dunbar's stories in which the black preacher is a central or peripheral character (an undertaking which will not be done here). For the most part, it is the black preacher maligned by the lore who holds sway in Dunbar's stories. Foremost among the reasons for this is that Dunbar's stories in general are profoundly influenced by plantation lore in texture and in form. One such story, "Supper by Proxy," is an adornment of a well-known plantation tale. The numerous anecdotes about the black plantation preacher in Rawick's *The American Slave: A Composite Biography* show that the drama, humor, irony, and wit germane to black plantation tales are equally abundant in such tales about the preacher. Another reason is that Dunbar was deeply interested in delineating the personal gain that motivates much of human endeavor. Since black preacher lore focuses on the preacher's egocentrism, greed, cunning, and clumsiness in masking his motives, it fits readily into Dunbar's overall philosophical preoccupations. Another reason, one related to the self-interest drive, is Dunbar's wish to show black religion on the plantation as an important part of the strategy planters employed to control their slaves. In fact, most of Dunbar's preacher stories, whether set on or off the plantation, suggest that traditional black American religion is a game of trickery in which the congregation and occasionally the preacher are duped. But Dunbar had very clear views about the role that black preachers should play in the lives of black Americans. These will be discussed later.

By virtue of the space he occupies in Dunbar's short stories—appearing in five of them—Brother Parker is Dunbar's most visible black preacher. Each time we encounter him it is from a different perspective, and each time it is another quality of the preacher from the lore that is amplified.

When we encounter him in "The Walls of Jericho," he is confronted, like many of his counterparts in the lore, with the loss of his congregation. It is as a strategist that Dunbar portrays him here. He is prepared to attend the revival meetings where many of his congregation are falling to the charming ploys of the Reverend Johnson. Dunbar's intentions in the story are sinister. They are an attack on black folk religion, and both Johnson and Parker are employed to that end.

The story, a very humorous one, evokes the spiritual "Joshua Fit the Battle of Jericho"; and it is by enacting the "Jericho March," interspersed with copious eating, that the Reverend Johnson is able to win over, at least for the moment, Parker's congregation. Drama, then, not substance, it is suggested, is what much of plantation religion was about. And as for the slaves' beliefs in Old Testament phenomena, seeing in them a reflection of their own struggle, Dunbar implies that this is false. The test comes when the mischievous white Mordaunts cause trees to crash, and blow a horn upon the sixth and seventh rounds. Ostensibly, if the slaves accepted this theology, they should have interpreted the noise and the horn as a fulfillment of their wish. Instead they and their preacher run for dear life. Parker is the only one present who does not quit the scene, partly because it will prove that he is not a coward, a fact that will give him renewed value among his congregation and thereby help him win it back, but mostly (one suspects) because he did not believe the stories he told his congregation.

One does not have to look far for models for this story; the story of John, who prays daily for death, but who runs when massa, disguised as death, knocks at his door, is, no doubt, one of them: the irony of both stories is in fact their kernel.

"The Walls of Jericho" dramatizes the extent to which the black preacher sets the pace of the religious "game" and plays on the sentiments of his congregation. Here the preacher is unmasked so that the reader can discover what is behind his verbal facade. In fact, all Dunbar's folk preachers undergo some form of unmasking.

In "How Brother Parker Fell from Grace," we are presented with another story that relies for its success on the irony that suffuses the plantation lore. Brother Parker sets out to reprove the gamblers on the Lord's Day, but ends up being enticed into playing cards with them.

The story dramatizes, through its trickster figure and antagonist Jim, that there have been those who could pierce the preacher's mask, and in the case of the trickster, recognize him as one of them. It is by appealing to what Jim knows is Parker's vanity that he is able to trick him into playing cards and consequently humiliate him before his congregation.

The battle for ascendancy between Jim and Parker is continued in the story "Jim's Probation." This story, more than any other of Dunbar's preacher stories, underscores the profit motive satirized by black preacher lore. Both Parker and his master Stuart Mordaunt are shown exploiting sickness to bring about conversion; in Parker's case, it is for power and profit, in Mordaunt's case, for profit.

Both Mordaunt and Parker are apprised of Jim's rheumatism, and Mordaunt prevails upon Parker to use this fact to effect Jim's conversion, the reward for Parker being a huge supply of his favorite tobacco. The argument Parker uses with Jim is standard among confidence preachers; i.e., that the redeemed do not suffer from bodily afflictions. Jim, whose desire is to find relief from pain, agrees to accept religion. Mordaunt is delighted: it means fewer stolen "shoats" and pullets, less worry for the overseers, and fewer injured "negroes." It is a patent revelation of Parker's function on the plantation.

But the superstition that Mordaunt believes black religion to be does not fully conquer Jim, for on the evening of the Sunday that he is given "the right hand of fellowship" he goes possum hunting. It is in this act that Dunbar clinches the story and further reveals Parker's hypocrisy. Parker discovers Jim with the possum and is quite prepared to overlook this violation of the Lord's Day in anticipation of sharing the possum with Jim. Next day, however, when he shows up uninvited, citing the rule of his church that entitles him to dine at Jim's house, Jim simply withdraws his church membership. Parker is shown in this story to be Mordaunt's tool; in turn Parker turns his congregation into self-serving implements. Again, one trickster recognizes another and will not play by the other's game.

The Brer Rabbit tales seem to be operating somewhere in this story, particularly "Tar Baby." In essence, Parker is Mordaunt's snare or Tar Baby. Jim's fate, like the Rabbit's, seems sealed until, of course, he realizes that religion is a trap and would not allow it to ensnare him permanently. This story exploits the folkloric elements of the preacher as tool, confidence man, and glutton.

Dunbar held very unequivocal views about the role of the black preacher in the black community. Two of Dunbar's stories, along with his poem "Religion" and various comments in his essays present that position. The preacher should be a literate man dedicated to providing leadership; i.e., showing the community alternatives to crime, poverty, and despair.

These sentiments are dramatized in the concerns that the Reverend Dokesbury has for the Mount Hope community, where crime, alcoholism, gambling, violence, and despair claim the lives of the young without opportunity. The reader is shown the self-pride that success brings as well as the example one successful individual provides for the shiftless.

In the story "Old Abe's Conversion," Dunbar relegates to meaningless-ness the shouting, hollering, and moaning of the black folk church. To do so he sets up an opposition between the traditional black preacher Abram Dixon and his son, a modern, educated preacher, uninterested in the theat-ricality of the black folk church (for which reason his father's congregation finds him useless). Robert invites his father to the church he pastors in the city and shows him the role of the church in rescuing young people who fall into crime simply because they have no other option. Abram eventually agrees with his son that the church's function should be to help others in a concrete way. When he preached in his son's church, "it was a gentler gospel than he had ever preached before" (*Heart of Happy Hollow* [1904] 1969, 121).

Praiseworthy in Dunbar's depiction of his folk preachers is his refusal to let the lore eclipse the characters' individuality. It is the essence of the lore and lore-derived inspiration that are foremost in his preacher stories.

Hurston wanted to show the collision between the animist and puritan tendencies in black American Christianity, and chose her protagonist as a focus for such a collision. A folklorist herself, Hurston had already reflected deeply on the issue before she sat down to sketch the character. She tells us that her father and his colleagues "told the best stories on the church ...funny stories at the expense of preachers and their congregations..." (1942, 77). Richard Dorson has observed the facility with which these ten-dencies exist in black preachers: "Despite his long educational background, Reverend Altheimer had absorbed completely the traditions of Southern Negro Culture and related comic fictions, grim accounts of slave life and supernatural legends. Surprisingly he believed in hants and hoodoos..." (1967, 40). These observations show to what extent black preachers used humor to mitigate the seriousness of their calling and how easily Christian and African strains coexist without contradictions in the same being.

Regarding the creation of John Pearson, Hurston told James Weldon Johnson that her character was to be "a Negro preacher who is neither funny nor an imitation puritan ramrod in pants. Just the human being and the poet that he must be to succeed in the Negro pulpit"; and outside of the pulpit the preacher should not be constrained by his occupation (cited in Neal's introduction to *Jonah's Gourd Vine*, 1971, 5). In Pearson, Hurston explores two of the elements that characterize the preacher of folklore: his lechery and the manner in which he is called to preach. There are others too, such as the preoccupation with power and vanity. Greed in him is absent, however, as is trickery.

Even as a young man John Pearson must struggle not to fall into the arms of every young woman on the Pearson plantation. This is Hurston's method of setting him up as someone whose urge to conquer women is inordinate and hence as someone who, when he becomes a preacher, would have great difficulty living within the laws of sexual continence prescribed by his church. He can control this sexuality when he must do so for some gain. For example, he restrains himself, prior to his marriage with Lucy Potts. But the marriage ceremony ended, he gives way almost immediatly to slaking his sexual thirst.

Hurston combines disasters attendant on these sexual escapades with Pearson's call to preach. Prior to Pearson's visit to Mehaly, Deacon Moss notes his "fire" and "good straining voice," and is sure that he is called to preach. To ensure that the readers do not miss "the African connection" the narrator informs them that Pearson "rolled his African drum up to the altar and called his Congo Gods by Christian names. One night at altar call he cried out his barbaric poetry to his wonder workin' God that three convicts came thru religion under the sound of his voice" (*Jonah's Gourd Vine*, cited hereafter *JGV*, 146). We note that the narrator excludes any reference to the Holy Spirit, which is considered the prime mover in such matters.

But John's sexuality is more important to him than the contemplation of what he feels may be a call to preach, and so he sets off to see Mehaly. On his return he almost drowns. This brings about the first adversity that the person called to preach must undergo. Following his recovery he remembers the vow, but a new woman in town distracts him. This sets him up for his second adversity—it ends with his having to run from home at night. Hurston wishes to show that the passion that others identify in Pearson's religious utterances also manifests itself in his need to be polygamous.

When Pearson moves to the all-black community of Eatonville and experiences a great deal of happiness (On Lucy's initiative he succeeds at carpentering and acquires a five-acre plot), partly because he feels esteemed as a result of Lucy's love and partly because he has a wife whom other men envy, he accepts the call to preach. This is how he articulates that decision: "He called me long uhgo, but Ah wouldn't heed tuh de voice, but, brothers and sisters, God done whipped me tuh it, and like Peter and Paul Ah means tuh preach Christ and Him crucified" (*JGV*, 180). These words are part of the ritual declaration of one's intention to preach and would have been uttered by anyone else who had felt a similar urge to preach. They should therefore not be used in assessing Pearson's personal behavior. They are an artifact of the black folk community.

This call to preach, Hurston states elsewhere, "comes three times. It is never answered until the third time. The man flees from the call, but is finally brought to accept it. God punishes him by every kind of misfortune until he finally accepts that he is beaten and makes known the call" ("Conversions and Visions" 1933, 32). Hurston's observation is borne out by the "Tales of Religious Conversion" included in John Mason Brewer's *American Negro Folklore* (1968, 254–59).

Hurston, we have seen, places the emphasis on Pearson's dramatic skills. His knowledge of theology is unimportant, for she shows him to be barely literate. However, earlier on, we are told that in Pearson's telling of folktales, Brer Fox, Brer Rabbit, and various characters walked the earth. Consequently Pearson acquires his preaching skills while performing secular lore. This corresponds to Hurston's view, expressed in her autobiography, *Dust Tracks on a Road,* that the principal function of the black church is a drama of catharsis (1942, 280–82).

Hurston concocts a situation with a great deal of potential for drama: Pearson's lecherous disposition versus the nonadulterous injunctions his ministry forces on him, and this *vis-à-vis* a congregation that is affected in varying degrees by the animist and puritan characteristics of the black church. Naturally the pulpit does not dampen Pearson's sexual fire. It seems to provide him with more opportunities. Some members of his congregation attempt to rationalize his conduct, but it is clear that his behavior is an embarrassment to the church. But given the choice between a lecherous minister and one unable to take them to the peaks of ecstasy in their Sunday services, they choose the lecherous minister. They continue, however, to persecute him because of his lechery.

Pearson tries to circumvent the accusations with humor—a habit that characterizes the preacher of folklore everytime he is caught literally with his pants off. Some of Pearson's responses are excellent examples of black folk humor and were probably culled from the tales Hurston's father and his preacher friends told:

Yall been looking at me fuh eight years now, but look lak some uh yall been lookin' on me wid unseein' eye. When Ah speak tuh yuh from dis pulpit dat ain't me talkin', dat's the Voice of God talkin' thru' me. When de voice is thew, Ah jus' unnother man—one uh God's crumblin' clods. Dere's seben younguns at mah house an' Ah could line 'em all up in de courthouse and swear tuh eve'y one of 'em. Ahm uh natchel man but look like some uh yall is dumb to de fack (*JGV*, 197).

Don't it look funny dat mah ole pleasures done got to be new sins. Maybe iss 'cause Ahm gittin' ole. Havin' women didn't useter be no sin. Just got sinful since Ah got ole (*JGV*, 262–63).

You see, dey is ready for uh preacher to be uh man uhmongst men but dey ain't ready fuh 'im to be uh man uhmongst women (*JGV*, 282).

Pearson's responses derive from the tradition of the black preacher tales. One such example is a tale of a preacher who, while pointing his finger in a member's face, tells him that he smells whiskey on his breath, to which the member replies that he smells "pussy" on the preacher's finger. In another tale, a deacon suspects the preacher of sleeping with his wife, and wishing to confirm his suspicion invites the preacher to his house in his absence. When the deacon returns and finds his wife in bed with the preacher, he shouts, "Gotcha!" but the preacher replies, "If you set a trap for me and bait it with pussy, you bound to catch me" (Dance 1978, 56). Such examples, along with Pearson's responses, are variations on the theme of being "uh natchel man" and "uh man uhmongst women."

According to Pearson, one of the women most vociferous in laying charges against him had unsuccessfully sought his sexual services. Hambro, his friend, says of Deacon Harris, one of Pearson's antagonists, that women avoid him because he is impotent. These remarks and reactions are rooted in black American folk culture. One is reminded of Deacon Brown's death, which leaves all the women, including the preacher's wife, inconsolable, for their giver of sexual joy is gone and they know of no replacements among the congregation (Dance 1978, 62). According to the terms of black American folk culture, Pearson had failed his congregation, for a standard joke in that community—West Indian and American—is that a preacher has to serve the sisters. Even Deacon Harris is riveted in the lore when he tells Pearson's second wife that most of the congregation accept that every man gets as many women as he can; and since Pearson is the best-looking among them (and mulatto too), he gets the most.

Pearson manages his congregation effectively while his wife is alive. After her death he becomes involved in one scandal after another until he eventually gives up pastoring at Zion Hope Baptist Church and thereby becomes the target of the community's scorn. This inability to get around his congregation is a weakness. Hurston eliminated the preacher's usual cunning, through which he manages to hold on to his church without having to abandon his vices, from Pearson's character to provide a basis for continuing the story. But she is sure to include exactly what happens to preachers who succumb to church criticism. In giving up his pastorate, Pearson evinces weakness and elicits the scorn of the community. Weakness is not favorably looked upon in the black community. If one lacks the physical prowess to defend one's self, one must compensate with cunning. It is a theme that runs through all Afro-American folklore.

Pearson is thus not the clever politician he should have been to survive in the black pulpit, a quality we have already seen in Dunbar's folk preacher. We see him killing an actual snake, but the snake of duplicity he never cultivates. Though an expert teller of folktales he neither internalizes nor applies their wisdom. Of course, this may be due to his physical prowess, his principal means of defense all his life. But beyond this he is a very shallow character. Hurston wished to show him as a weak character incapable of functioning without the "arbor" of a strong woman to keep him upright. Being a Jonah's gourd vine, without such an arbor he must literally crawl along the ground.

Much has been said about the inadequacy of John Pearson's character, stemming from the fact that as a man he could not distance himself from his urges and thus gain insight into himself (see Hemenway 1977, 200), and

of his inability to integrate himself effectively into the community he pastored. Hurston virtually drowns Pearson in folklore to the point where he
becomes the embodiment and victim of the community's folk outlook and
beliefs. He therefore never emerges as a man, for the sort of caricature that
one identifies in folktales—quick and unsubtle sketching—clings to him.
Nevertheless, through John Pearson and his congregation's response to
him we are provided with some remarkable scenes of black folk life in the
early twentieth century American South.

James Baldwin's Gabriel Grimes in *Go Tell It on the Mountain* (1952) does
not fall strictly into the category of the preacher of the popular imagination.
In fact, he is the complete opposite of Hurston's preacher, for he is a
guilt-ridden man who has learned nothing about the survival skills—those
that the lore satirizes—of the black preacher. He despises such preachers.
Gabriel accepts puritanical Christianity to the letter. Slowly it robs him of his
humanity, for despite his efforts he can never get beyond the mask of purity.
In all other respects, his manner of conversion, his manner of being called
to preach, his search for revelations through visions, his blaming of the
woman with whom he commits adultery, etc., he is a folk preacher.

In a sense Baldwin approves of the preachers whom Gabriel condemns,
for they, with their outlets of humor and their ability to put the black
religious experience into a wider human perspective, escape the cumulative
guilt that is destroying Gabriel. We see Gabriel's refusal to acknowledge his
son born out of wedlock result in the death of both mother and son. To
relieve the guilt he feels for this action he punishes his second wife and her
son, also born out of wedlock.

In Gabriel's church in Harlem all the cathartic rituals are intact; everyone
but Gabriel benefits from them. Catharsis is not his lot, for as he looks at his
son Roy, the offspring of a lawful union, being lost to the sinfulness of the
city, and sees the uprightness of the "bastard" John, he is rendered doubly
jealous. Gabriel's understanding of God is in Old Testament biblical
terms—a God of vengeance. To see "Ishmael" inherit the kingdom that is
"Isaac's" is for Gabriel a sign that God has chosen to afflict him personally.
And so instead of finding comfort in the rituals of the church, he finds a
scourge; for he can find no ritual to appease the guilt he suffers for not
having given to Royal the parenting that was his due.

In a roundabout way, then, Baldwin shows through Gabriel how vital are
the qualities of black religion that are joked about in the folklore—that in
complementing their religion with a folklore that ridicules it, blacks infuse
existence with paradox, a paradox that Baldwin elsewhere tells us white
America is eager to stamp out (1949, 16). This lore is a reminder of the
preacher's flesh-and-blood status, a status that puritan dogma negates. Since
Gabriel rejects the lore but remains man, he is fated to experience conflict
and guilt. In Baldwin's last novel, *Just Above My Head* (1978), Julia the
child-preacher observes that a religion that tries to imprison man's sexual

instincts is not worth adhering to. In all Baldwin's novels there are negative portrayals of puritanical religion. In Gabriel's case puritanical dogma destroys his humanity.

In Hal Bennett's *Lord of Dark Places* (1971) we encounter two preachers straight out of the folklore. Sex, greed, and curious forms of sacrificing characterize Titus Market, and sex and sacrifice of others characterize Reverend Cobb. To such an extent is the novel's emphasis on sex that for the protagonist his virility and oversized penis become both a scepter and the means of defending that scepter. Sex is also the medium through which the characters relate to one another. It is quite clear too that communication between the black and white race is limited to the sex act. Those willing to go beyond sex are crippled by social conventions; the farthest they can get is to wound each other physically, while claiming that they do so out of love. For to show love is to show weakness, and to set one's self up to be abused. Since the novel implies that the only difference that exists between black and white Americans is the degree of power each group possesses, and that everyone sets out to humiliate the other, Bennett must rationalize the preacher to this world view. He uses him to underscore the dominant themes of sex, money, power, and death which dominate the novel.

Titus Market, the first of these preachers, is the son of a black cultist and her nephew-husband. His church is based on the worship of the human penis. Already sexually developed at twelve, Titus's son Joe is made to strip each night just before the collection is taken. This act moves the sisters to ecstasy. The narrator tells us that all church sisters wear clean underwear, for their conscious wish is to be ravished when they "pass out." When Joe is sixteen Titus changes the name of the sect to "The Church of the Naked Disciple," and consolidates the practice that he had already begun of having Joe provide sexual service, for a fee, to those brothers and sisters who come looking for it. Joe comes to believe that his penis represents the redemption of the world and that everyone of every sex should crave it. And they do—some overtly, others covertly. Clearly what Bennett is doing is recasting black preacher lore into his own personal form of romance, for in keeping with the redeemer idea, the time comes when Titus attempts to sacrifice Joe. But Bennett twists the conventional myth, and it is Titus who is sacrificed. He is buggered to death by Southern white policemen. After Titus's death Joe escapes North to New Jersey, where he continues to believe that he is a sex god, willing some to suffer and others to die.

The second preacher, Reverend Cobb, is Joe's preacher in Virginia who later moves to Cousinville, New Jersey, where he cuts his wife into fine pieces and throws them into the Passaic River. We learn of him principally from what Joe tells us. At his electrocution Joe is delighted to "watch a preacher fry." At the time of Cobb's electrocution Joe tells the reader:

You'd have thought they were going to electrocute God.... For the office of preacher among black people is their most sacred totem; and while Mr. Cobb was a self-confessed and convicted murderer, he was still a minister of the Gospel and therefore a messenger of God to the minds of most people of Decatur.... Black preachers are forever doing wrong, and are forever being pardoned by their people, since it is thought that preachers have some sort of special mandate from God to be less restrained than even Roman Catholic priests, and everybody knows how they are, wearing dresses and everything. This mandate for libertinism is thought to express itself in his enthusiasm for fried chicken, free pussy and chocolate cake, in that order of edibility. In the neighborhood of free pussy, the black preacher is especially fortunate, since devoted sisters of the church have long ago convinced themselves that to fuck their preacher is one and the same with fucking their God, which they consider the insanest and sweetest kind of love. They are the ones who make totems out of preachers... (*Lord of Dark Places*, 182).

If elsewhere we are uncertain about Bennett's purpose in this novel, here we have no doubts: it is strictly to entertain. In the blues the preacher has long been established as a subject of ridicule. The following are samples of his treatment in the blues:

> Preacher in the pulpit, Bible in hand,
> Sister in the corner, cryin', "There's my man."

> One night pa got to preachin',
> And forgot and left the sermon out.
> Sister Fullbosom over there in the Amen Corner,
> Mad anyhow, she let all the secrets out.
> She hollered, "Sisters and brothers, thoroughly understand,
> The Elder he's my man.
> Now I don't mind you goin' to talk to Elder occasionally,
> But nix on standin' out there holdin' his hand.
> I washes hard both day and night,
> Catch you with that Elder we gonna have a miserable fight,
> Do you hear me?..." (Jones 1929, in Oliver [1968] 1970, 51).

The setting in which the message is delivered and the fact that it is addressed to men and women make the whole quite dramatic and comical. In another blues song we are told:

> Well the preacher used to preach to save our souls,
> But now he preaches just to buy jelly roll.
>   Well he calls that religion...

> Went from the church last night fast as I could be,
> That ole preacher was tryin' to take my wife from me,
>   Well he calls that religion...

Old Deacon Johnson was a preachin' king,
They caught him round the house tryin' to shake that thing.
   Well he calls that religion ...
(Carter and Vincson 1932, in Oliver [1968] 1970, 51–52).

The next selection pretends to come to the preacher's defense:

The preacher must get some sometime,
Where and whenever he can;
The preacher must get some sometime,
Just like any other man
(Robinson and Lewis 1932, in Oliver [1968] 1970, 52).

Another trait of the preacher in the blues, that of his being a thief, is explored in the citation below. But rather than stealing corn, sheep, watermelons, etc., as in other blues songs, the composer blends his thievery with lechery and portrays the preacher as stealing other men's women.

Some folks say a preacher won't steal,
I caught three in my cornfield.
One had a yeller, one had a brown;
Looked over in the middle, one was gettin' down.
   Now some folks say, that a preacher won't steal,
   But he'll do more stealin' than I get my reg'lar meals
(Joe and Minnie 1931, in Oliver [1968] 1970, 60).

As a target for tale tellers and as a subject of jokes and blues musicians' lyrics, the preacher as metaphor for hypocrisy is well established. He is every black entertainer's target. Why not the novelist's? Bennett simply extends the tradition of the preacher jokes to the novel. He knows, like all the other entertainers, that the preacher is venerated by his black audience and so any ridicule of his person is replete with drama.

Before concluding this section on the preacher, it needs to be said that blacks in the New World expect political and spiritual guidance from their preachers. In most novels, when there is trouble in the black community, everyone heads to the church and seeks the preacher's opinion. Insofar as these practices are deeply ingrained in black folk tradition they need to be mentioned. We see them in Martin Delaney's *Blake or the Huts of America* (1859), Walter White's *Fire in the Flint* (1924), Richard Wright's "Fire and Cloud" (1940), Lorenz Graham's *South Town* (1958), Margaret Walker's *Jubilee* (1966), Sarah Wright's *This Child's Gonna Live* (1969), Mildred Taylor's trilogy: *Song of the Trees* (1975), *Roll of Thunder, Hear My Cry* (1977), and *Let the Circle Be Unbroken* (1981), and Ernest Gaines's *In My Father's House* (1978), among others.

With the exception of the trickster-preacher, Hurston's Pearson and Gaines's Martin, the black preacher rarely occurs as a protagonist in a novel. He may be given significant roles, as in the case of *Jubilee*, but even such a function is not the rule. One can only be tentative about the reasons for this. In the first place the overwhelming majority of black American writers are concerned with black survival; and to create intriguing fictional portraits, it would seem that the preacher, like other professionals, is not sufficiently interesting to continue to explore him in fiction. What needed to be shown has been undertaken by the earlier writers—James Weldon Johnson, Zora Neale Hurston; in the case of satirizing the preacher and by extension those he dupes, there is very little left to be said. Consequently, it is in the realm of political action that the more recent portraits of the preacher—Gaines's Phillip Martin, for example—focus. Ultimately, unless the preacher's role is only incidental or tragic, he risks becoming a stereotype.

BAD NIGGERS

In discussing the Bad Nigger, Black Moses, John Henry, and the slave insurrectionists, one is dealing with types that blend into one another. Dance notes that the "Bad Nigger is and always has been bad to whites because he violates their laws and he violates their moral codes" (1978, 224). She adds that he is "ba-ad," underscoring the contemporary meaning and pronunciation of the word among Afro–Americans, "to black people who relish his exploits for exactly the same reason" (1978, 224). The word *ba-ad*, as it is used among black Americans and in black American literature since the 1960s, describes situations or individuals diametrically opposed to white control of black existence. John Henry, Black Moseses, the slave insurrectionists, Malcolm X, Adam Clayton Powell, even Martin Luther King and Jesse Jackson are all "ba-ad niggers." The toast protagonists are "bad" niggers.

Yet each of the categories listed at the beginning of the last paragraph is unique. Dance, although she includes John Henry under the rubric of the Bad Nigger, defines the latter in terms of the most extreme properties: "The Bad Nigger of folklore is tough and violent. He kills without blinking an eye. He courts death constantly and doesn't fear dying . . . He values fine clothes and flashy cars. He asserts his manhood through physical destruction of men and through his sexual victimization of women" (1978, 224–25). This description accords well with legendary toast heroes like Stagolee.

JOHN HENRY

Interpretations of John Henry have been diverse and often erroneous: Bad Nigger, Uncle Tom, vagrant, etc. But it is hardly for any of these that he is a black folk hero. Alan Dundes observes with acuity that American blacks had their trickster on the one hand and their Bad Nigger on the other;

they needed a middle figure, which John Henry became (Dundes 1973, 568–69). Richard Dorson's essay, "The Career of John Henry" (Dundes, 1973, 569–77) is an excellent review of many of the portraits of John Henry in straight folklore, in music, and in literature. Guy B. Johnson, *John Henry: Tracking down a Negro Legend* (1929) is among the first attempts to interpret as well as to compile several versions of the John Henry myth. John Henry is especially popular among black rail liners, who sing his praises in their worksongs and for whom he is the equivalent of a patron saint. He is equally a hero among black people, who recite his feats in ballads and folktales. He has been interpreted by many outstanding black poets, including Margaret Walker and Melvin B. Tolson; he is also the subject of a young adult novel by John O. Killens.

Is John Henry a historical reality? Johnson says that no one knows. The other character, John Hardy, who is sometimes associated with John Henry, is known to have been a superior steel driver and to have been hanged for murder in 1894. He too worked on the Big Bend Tunnel in Virginia, where John Henry is alleged to have defeated the steel driving machine, though the effort kills him (G. B. Johnson, 1929, 44).

Regardless of what is said or written about John Henry, his psychic value for black America lies chiefly in his assertion, "A man ain't nothin' but a man"; his physical stature—he was well over six feet tall and a giant of a man—permitted him to assert his manhood and to defeat the steam engine, a feat that made him superhuman. In the American South and even in the North where black people were (and still perhaps are) considered three-fifths human and treated accordingly, they needed mythic figures to accomplish for them what they in actuality were not permitted to do— defend themselves and their loved ones against indignity. Thus John Henry's conquest of the white machine could be interpreted as his triumphing over white intelligence and capitalist indifference, a feat all oppressed blacks would want to perform. In the fact that whites sought John Henry to undertake the most difficult tasks—a savior-figure of sorts—he achieves mythically the kind of valuation that most blacks desired but had little opportunity to obtain. Blacks invest themselves with value vicariously through John Henry; there is a survival function at the core of the John Henry myth.

It is Killens's portrayal of John Henry that we shall focus on. In this portrait John Henry is presented not only as a character to emulate, but, as suggested by the book's title: *A Man Ain't Nothin' but a Man* (hereafter cited *A Man*), as a primer of Afro–American manhood. Here Killens portrays what Sterling Stuckey expresses in essay form: "Blacks later found their greatest symbol of manhood in John Henry, descendant of Trickster John of slave folk tales" (1968 [1972], 447). This type of portrayal, too, conforms to Killens' view that Afro–American literature should inspire blacks to free themselves from the negative white icons about blackness that blacks have with grave consequences adopted (1965, pp. 364–66). But Killens also knows the conventions surrounding the epic character, and he inserts those that the John Henry myth does not already possess. Simultaneously he updates the myth to make it relevant to a technological society. The novel traces John Henry from his birth to his death. Killens's challenge is to make John Henry very human, very anthropomorphic, a demand imposed by fiction.

In John Henry and the characters surrounding him, Killens constructs an entire ethical system that operates before us as John Henry affirms himself and negotiates the world around him. This ethical system includes self-affirmation, self-realization, fidelity to one's promises, devotion to one's people, pride in one's identity, humility, cunning, leadership, and fighting for one's rights. This approach to John Henry is part of Killens's overall aesthetic vision: "I am a writer, first of all, and precisely because the world stinks and I want to change it. Yes, I mean it, and any writer worth his salt is up to the same subversive business" (1965 [1972], 361).

John Henry's antagonist from beginning to end is the machine: American capitalism that reduces human beings to profitable tools. The machine is as much Southern peonage and those who enforce it, as it is the railroads and their agents. In all cases, therefore, Killens depicts the men and the machinery itself with similar qualities.

John Henry's first assertion of his manhood and his equality—his single most dominant characteristic (which he encapsulates in the refrain "a man ain't nothin' but a man")—comes when he refuses to continue picking the white man's cotton. This refusal, the narrator shows, could have been costly: the plantation overseer points his rifle at the departing John Henry in order to dissuade him from leaving the plantation, for John Henry's departure does not fit into Cap'n Jack's practice of having his "niggers" well-rested on weekends so they would be energetic at picking cotton on Monday morning (*A Man*, 20–21). The point made in this episode is that blacks must not allow white intimidation to prevent them from asserting themselves, even when they know there is the risk that they might be killed. Thereafter John Henry insists that no white man call him "nigger" or "boy," thus refusing to comply with the practices white society had instituted to inculcate feelings of inferiority in blacks and reinforce feelings of superiority in whites. When the railroad Captain, with a gleaming gun on each hip and two armed state troopers flanking him, addresses John Henry as "boy" to humiliate him before his peers, John Henry asks him:

"How big do men grow where you come from Cap'n?"
"What you say, boy?"
"You ain't talkin' to no boy when you talkin' to John Henry, Cap'n. You talkin' to a natcherl man" (*A Man*, 159).

But John Henry's understanding of manhood goes considerably further than challenging derogatory appellations. It extends to not depriving a man of his livelihood, a decision he makes despite his penniless state, and one which makes his would-be victim a lifelong friend. Moreover it is John Henry's understanding and his demonstration of that understanding—that one should not use one's advantages for personal aggrandizement at the expense of others—that most underscore his moral principles. When he refuses to cooperate with the railroad captain, the latter resorts to spreading lies about him, so that he would lose his friends and so that they would consider him "snivelling" and ostracize him. But part of his conception of being a man is honest confrontation, which reveals to the other workers who the real enemy is.

Furthermore, John Henry knows that he must use his skills for the advancement of his race, essentially because he understands that it is more important for his white colleagues to be white than to be good men (A Man, 153). Consequently, "John Henry was fiercely proud of the fact that he John Henry, Black man, was the undisputed greatest steel driver in the land or in any other land.... That was something to be proud of. And he was proud of being black" (111). Through John Henry's statement Killens implies that talent in black people, regardless of its form, should be used to glorify the race—a somewhat difficult practice in a society that emphasizes individualism.

Foresight too is one of his character traits. He looks both to the future and the present and at the resources lacking in the black community of the 1890s. Of his unborn child he says to his wife:

I was worried that beingst as how you make such admiration over me you'd be putting in that boy's head to be a steel-driving man just like his no-count daddy.... 'Cause I wants him to be a doctor or a school teacher, a leader of the people, something like that.... Besides the way I'm hearing tell of them machines that drive steel by they self, they ain't gon be needing no hard-working fool like me (A Man, 127).

Thus a hero of the people would be concerned about the people's leadership.

He should also know his limitations and attempt to deal with them. We see this in John Henry's decision to have Polly Ann, his wife, teach him how to read, as well as his trusting her superior judgment (male supremacy is alien to his way of thinking) except in the vital domain of his vocation as a steel-driving man, the only source of conflict between them. This excludes John Henry from the category of the Bad Nigger who humiliates the weak, especially women, who must perpetually prove that he possesses complete mastery over others, must make them cringe, plead for mercy, and reaffirm their enslavement to him. Since this is a young adults' novel and since Killens is deeply concerned about the psychological health of black children, he makes John Henry reflect those attitudes that lead to stable, healthy families (1965 [1972], 364–65).

Finally John Henry knows that the weaker masses come to expect leadership from those who possess outstanding talents. And although it is unpopular to oppose the machine, for the general thinking is that it is retrogressive to do so, John Henry knows his peers are looking to him to be their savior: to save their jobs that "the machine" would soon be gobbling up. Thus John Henry asserts that "It ain't right to shove men aside like beasts of burden" (*A Man*, 160). Moreover "the first to be laid off gon be our people, black people!" (166). John Henry provides leadership in the only way he knows, he challenges the machine—"Before I'd let that steam drill beat me down, I'll die with my hammer in my hand" (*A Man*, 162). He proceeds with his challenge, outperforms the machine, and because of the exertion, dies from a heart attack. He manages, however, to save the jobs of those who would have otherwise been terminated. In a sense, John Henry, like Bontemps' Gabriel, is a martyr.

It is not the "folly of John Henry's decision" that should interest the reader but the nobility of his motives in challenging the capitalist machinery in all its forms, in all its disregard for humanity. Usually the John Henry story ends with his collapse, but Killens appends a new element. He lets John Henry live long enough to advise his co-workers of the foolhardiness of trying to outdo the machine; rather they should find ways of accommodating it.

In choosing to make of the John Henry character a blueprint for the way black people ought to be, Killens puts into fiction what he writes in his essays: "A people needs legends, heroes, myths. Deny them these and you have won half the battle against them" (1965 [1972], 367). Besides, in excluding certain versions of the John Henry narrative—the compliant tool of the white man, in Leon Harris's version, for example (1925, in Dundes 1973, 157)—and by adding to the character the behavior traits that could unite and further add to the dignity of black people, Killens leaves none of the ambivalence that is usually evident in the folk narratives. One needs to note as well that John Henry's wit and cunning, his survival techniques, and his language and styles of communication are purely Afro-American. This is Killens's way of saying that black Americans possess their own system of perceiving reality, and it must be their frame of reference. One can hardly dispute his membership among those writers termed Cultural Nationalists—with an avowed intention to make literature reflect and become a part of the survival of black people (see Karenga [1968] 1972, 478–79; LeRoi Jones 1966, 247).

BLACK MOSES

In the case of Black Moses the emphasis is on courage and leadership, and defiance is never an end in itself, nor is violence. It is rare in the black American novel to encounter fully developed Black Moses. Rarely do they exist beyond metaphor. Because they represent longings in black folk they are usually projected onto whichever leader comes along. In black folklore Moses is a trickster and a hoodoo connoisseur, as in Ishmael Reed's *Mumbo Jumbo* (1972). As the procurer, through Jethro, of the knowledge that is at the root of the "Jes Grew" phenomenon that threatens to supplant puritan capitalistic staidness in America, he is also functioning through the inheritors of the hoodoo tradition as deliverer. Zora Neale Hurston's *Moses Man of the Mountain* (1939) relies heavily on the black concept of Moses learning from his Ethiopian father-in-law the hoodoo skills that give him access to the godhead. Any character who in a sense leads the people out of oppression can be given the appellation of Moses (the South from the very first time the slaves heard the story of the Israelites in Egypt became Egyptland; the North after freedom could be had there became the Promised Land—in later years, as is evidenced by the title of Claude Brown's autobiography *Manchild in the Promised Land*, with profound irony). Harriet Tubman, very deservedly, was nicknamed Moses. A character like Tucker Caliban in Kelley's *A Different Drummer* (1962) is a Moses figure.

The pervasive presence of spirituals like "Go Down Moses" and "Joshua Fit the Battle of Jericho" keeps the memories of the Moses figure alive in black American consciousness. We note characters in fiction referring to him: Mary Rambo in *Invisible Man*; Aunt Sally in Walker's *Jubilee* prays, "Lord, when you gwine send us a Moses" (1966, 70); Jane Pittman and the other folks in the "quarters" identify one: "Jimmy...by the time he was twelve he was definitely the One" (Gaines 1972, 208). Gideon, in Dunbar's "The Strength of Gideon," is an abortive Black Moses (1900, 1–23). The Founder in Ellison's *Invisible Man*, with his close resemblance to Booker T. Washington, is certainly described in terms of an ironic Moses; and the protagonist, as Wilson Moses sees him, conceives of himself as a messiah (1982, 196–206); in Cullen's *One Way to Heaven* and Childress's *Short Walk*, Garvey is shown as a Moses figure, in both cases ironically. Paule Marshall's *Brown Girl, Brownstones* and Louise Meriwether's *Daddy Was a Number Runner* gives Moses-like attributes to Father Divine (Father Divine certainly perceived himself in that light) (Hughes and Bontemps, 1958, 273–74). Alice Walker's *Meridian* could certainly be seen as a Moses figure and, in some respects, a Christ figure.

It is, however, in the leaders of the slave insurrections that the Moses characteristics come most alive. This is especially true of Arna Bontemps' Gabriel in *Black Thunder* (hereafter cited *Thunder*), whom we shall examine here. For a somewhat contrasting picture, we shall also look at Toni Morrison's Shadrack in *Sula*.

If Bontemps had wished to create a Moses figure strictly according to black folklore, Nat Turner, who felt that God had put him aside for some great purpose, would have been a better choice of historical figure. However, the character Bontemps was most interested in was one for whom the revolt for freedom "was a less-complicated," straightforward affair, free from the mystic elements in which Denmark Vesey's and Nat Turner's revolts were couched (Bontemps, preface to *Black Thunder*, 1968). Bontemps modifies the historical facts to suit his aesthetic purpose. He portrays Gabriel as a general and leader who understands troop psychology, who fires his men with righteous indignation so that they believe theirs is a holy war, who provides them with the appropriate slogans to reassure them in times of doubt. What in folklore would be termed *hoodoo* becomes in Bontemps' Gabriel knowledge derived from observation and motivated by the need for dignity and freedom for himself and his people. Gabriel also understands that most slaves cannot remember abstractions, and that it is therefore necessary to codify reality in metaphor and allegory. Thus his brethren dwell in Egyptland and they need their Moses and Joshua to lead them to the Promised Land, which in history and in the novel was the elimination of slavery from the state of Virginia.

When we first hear of Gabriel it is in connection with his being a Black Mason. Ostensibly the purpose of this order is to plan strategies to put an end to slavery. Bontemps wanted the reader to perceive Gabriel as a thinker and strategist, traits that consistently characterize him throughout the novel. It is also important, since the reader is told in parentheses that it is an African vision of reality that obtains among the slaves on the plantation, that Gabriel convince his fellow slaves of his leadership ability—both in terms of his physical prowess (which he demonstrates by defeating Ditcher, who had the reputation of being the strongest black on the neighboring plantations) and his cunning.

However much Bontemps wished to distance Gabriel from the religious personage that he was historically, he realized that to make Gabriel the inspiring leader that emerges in the novel the slaves had to believe deeply in the rightness of their cause. Furthermore there was the propaganda of the planters—who cite the Bible in support of slavery—to counter. To do so, Bontemps created Mingo, a free literate black, to read to the slaves those parts of the Bible that oppose slavery. Thus, using the same Holy Scriptures that the slavemaster employs to justify his holding others slaves, Mingo discredits the slave owners and inflames the slaves with a deep sense of outrage, which would soon impel them to revolt. This other knowledge is part of what black historian Sterling Stuckey describes as the ethos the slaves developed to avoid being imprisoned within those definitions the larger society sought to impose on them (1972, 440). Even more important is the confidence Mingo imbues in the slaves that God will fight on their side. One message, which Gabriel encourages the men to listen to, is important for its linking of freedom with warfare, death, and destruction:

"There, there," Gabriel said abruptly. "Mingo. Read that once mo'."

"He that stealeth a man and selleth him, or if he be found in his hand, he shall surely be put to death..."

"That's the scripture," Gabriel said. "That's the *good* Book what Mingo's reading out of" (*Thunder*, p. 45).

Several additional passages of Scripture are read, for the purpose of showing that the slavemaster, in upholding slavery, violates his own creed and that God will cause him to be punished for it. From Gabriel's strategic interruptions it is evident that he and Mingo had carefully devised this ritual ahead of time. Consequently we must see it as part of Gabriel's strategy for reassuring the revolting slaves that even the god of the slavemaster was on the side of the slaves. Bontemps wished the reader to see Gabriel's interest in the Bible not as a religious man but as a general who must provide moral support for his troops.

This trait of strategist is seen in several other places. At Bundy's deathbed when the slaves engage in their rituals of prayer, reminding God of their condition in "Egyptland," Gabriel stands by but refuses to participate in the ritual and thus prevents his anger from being tempered. Because Bundy's death is the result of a whipping from Master Prosser, ostensibly because Bundy is too old to be profitable, the slaves are indignant. In this, Gabriel finds an opportune moment to announce his plans for the capture of Richmond. To do so he interrupts the following prayer before it succeeds in dissipating the slaves' grief: "Oh, battle-fighting God, listen to yo' little Chilluns; listen to yo' lambs. Remember how you brung deliverance to the Israelites in Egyptland; remember how you fit for Joshua. Remember Jericho. Remember Goliath, Lord. Listen to yo' lambs. Oh battle-fighting God..." (*Thunder*, 55). It is on "battle-fighting God" that he halts the prayer; ostensibly it is they, the slaves, who are to become God's warriors. His exact words are "That's enough.... Hush moaning and listen to me now. God don't like ugly. Some of y'-all heard Mingo read it," and they imply that he expects action from them. The narrator tells us that "he gave a quick summary of the Scripture Mingo had read. Then he paused a long time. His eyes flashed in the growing dusk. He looked at those near him in the circle, one by one, and one by one they broke their gaze and dropped their heads" (55). This is excellent nonverbal assertion of leadership. Before the final details of the plan for capturing Richmond are communicated, Marse Prosser appears on the scene, and Gabriel commands those present to strike up a song, showing that even the finest details of camouflage had already been worked out. This strategy includes a knowledge of the enemy's firing power, the exact locations of the munitions, who guards them, etc. Gabriel's work is rendered somewhat easier than one would have expected in these circumstances because of the slaves' belief that somewhere someone was going to be called to deliver them from bondage.

Thus Bontemps relies heavily on the atrocities of slavery to provide the motivation necessary for the slaves to revolt. Gabriel's task is to harangue them, to underscore these atrocities, and to remind them of the indignity of their present plight. When Ben hesitates to lend his support to the plan, Gabriel merely has to ask him if he does not wish to be free. Whenever doubt comes to any of the participants, even the feebleminded Criddle, it is Gabriel's slogans he remembers: "Anything what's equal to a groundhog wants to be free" (93). This slogan appeals not to some faraway authority but to the slaves' pride as human beings.

The manner in which Ben is co-opted into the plan continues to depict Gabriel as a strategist. Ben had been urged several times to join the Black Masons but had refused. With Bundy's death the slaves around Ben suggest to him that he owes Bundy this, for such had been the dead man's last wish. This is how they orchestrate it: Martin,

the smaller of Gabriel's two brothers, stood up to speak,
  "Is there anybody what ain't swore?"
  Ben wrinkled his forehead, scratched his salt-and-pepper whiskers.
  "Swore about what?" he murmured.
  "I reckon you don't know," Martin said. "Here's the Book, and here's the pot of blood, and here's the black cat bone. Swear."
  "Swear what?"
  "You won't tell none of what you's apt to hear in this meeting. You'll take a curse and die slow death if you tells. On'erstand?"
  Ben felt terrified. All eyes were on him. All the others seemed to know. Something like a swarm of butterflies was let loose in his mind. After a dreadful pause his thought became clear again. Well, he wouldn't mind swearing to keep his mouth closed. It was no more than he'd have done had he not come to the burying....
  "I won't tell nobody, Martin," he said. "I swears" (*Thunder*, 54).

Both Ben and General John are old and trusted slaves, but while General John shares Gabriel's ideals, Ben is the sort of house slave that all slaves distrusted for his having grown too fond of his master (see Genovese 1974, 133). Gabriel and the other slaves know that Ben could best be controlled by psychological fear, and it is for this reason that he is made to swear the oath before he understands its implications. Ben's participation is indispensable to the success of the strategy. Gabriel says, "We want Ben to go to Caroline County. Him and Gen'l John can get off and travel 'thout nobody thinking nothing. They's old and trusted like. Nothing much they going to have to do; just be there to tell folks what's what when the time comes..." (59). The sign that the revolt has started, Juba's wearing of Marse Prosser's riding boots while riding the colt Araby, is intended to be fear-allaying. This clearly is a sign that the slave has taken over from the master. If Gabriel could outfit his girlfriend in Marse Prosser's riding boots, then, he must be a brave man, one could imagine the slaves opining.

In both the novel and history the revolt fails because of the torrential downpour on the evening that it should have come off. In both as well Gabriel is betrayed by Ben and Pharaoh. In the novel, however, Ben undertakes his task with Pharaoh accompanying him, and only gives up when the torrents of water overturn the gig. What makes him join the plot, apart from his earlier oath, is the bitterness he feels over his children, who had been sold to distant plantations. Moreover Ben disagrees with Pharaoh's betrayal but realizes that if he is going to save his neck he too will have to pretend to have betrayed the cause. It is not the rain as such that prevented the revolt, but the impassable waters cutting off the slaves from some of the adjoining plantations and preventing access to Richmond. Despite the fact that their numbers diminish as the downpour continues, it is only when they face the impassable waters that the plan is halted. However, they do not abandon the plan; they merely defer it, but are betrayed on the day they should have effected it.

Bontemps ends the novel on a note that shows Gabriel as someone from whom blacks desirous of leading their people could derive important lessons. To the white court Gabriel says, "I tell you. I been studying about freedom a heap, me.... And everything I heard make me feel like I wanted to be free.... Something keeps telling me that anything what's equal to a gray squirrel wants to be free. That's how it all come about" (210). When in an effort to trick him into revealing the names of the participants in the plot, someone hints that he may yet live, Gabriel's reply is that "a lion what's tasted man's blood is a caution to keep after that.... On'erstand? I been ready since the first time I hooked on a sword. The others too—they been ready.... The stars was against us, though; that's all" (211). When asked if he thought that "well-fed, well-kept slaves" would have joined him, his answer is laconic and to the point: "Wouldn't you jine us, was you a slave, suh" (213)?

The foregoing speeches are historical approximations. Elsewhere, however, Bontemps alters the facts. In actuality the informers were made free blacks (Aptheker [1943] 1969, 221). But Bontemps keeps them within the slave community as a way of showing how the community dealt with them. Both Ben and Pharaoh fear for their lives; both have been victims of stab wounds; and in the end Pharaoh is so harassed with conjured articles that he goes mad, convinced that he has been conjured. In choosing to characterize the slave community's reactions in this way, Bontemps stays close to history. Eugene Genevose cites several authorities to document his assertion "that no greater crime existed for the slaves than that of betraying one another to the whites" (1974, 622).

On returning to the Black Moses framework, we could ask whether or not Gabriel felt a commission from God to liberate Virginia. In Gabriel's case it is not relevant. What is important is that the people feel so. Gabriel's own dialectic is freedom or death. Clearly the mission fails and the people should wonder about the truth of all those scriptural passages Mingo read.

For them, however, the response is that Gabriel erred only in one small detail—he had not consulted those who are in touch with the African gods: he should have had a "hand." And, according to Ditcher, he should have awaited a sign. One could say Bontemps wished to underscore those leadership qualities he perceived to be valuable to the community by characterizing a legendary hero. Bontemps himself felt that there existed an analogy between Gabriel's revolt and Dr. Martin Luther King's. As late as 1968 Bontemps saw the black liberation struggle as an ongoing reality; he felt that the inspiration for its continuation could be derived from contemplating the black heroes of history and folklore (1968, viii).

Morrison's figure provides no such inspiration—only pathos. Shadrack is the product of a community that started as a "nigger joke" (i.e., a joke played on "niggers") and the trauma he experiences in World War I, on the battlefield and in a military hospital. He returns to Medallion, Ohio, where he finds an identity as a madman prophet and establishes the National Suicide Day ritual.

The neighborhood that produces Shadrack originated in a joke; it is the "Bottoms" located on the hill overlooking the white town. Its rituals—dancing the cake walk to a harmonica, camouflaging pain behind laughter, etc.—are the residents' way of preserving their sanity and hiding their sorrow from outsiders. Morrison's depiction of the community makes us wonder about the relevance of such a community in a highly individualized, technological society. Such behavior would be more pertinent in a society organized along communal lines, for the rituals are directed against no one, do not reflect the competition that is largely the *raison d'être* of America; instead they center on the containment of pain.

Morrison's narrator goes on to tell us a great deal more about this community, which occupies a central role in the novel:

They did not believe doctors could heal—for them, none had done so. They did not believe death was accidental—life might be, but death was deliberate. They did not believe Nature was ever askew—only inconvenient.... The purpose of evil was to survive it and they determined... to survive floods, white people, tuberculosis, famine and ignorance. They knew anger but not despair, and they did not stone sinners for the same reason they didn't commit suicide—it was beneath them (*Sula* 77–78).

Therefore, while at first we might think that these people had found the sort of quiet contentment that white people think blacks are prone to—that is, that they become easily resigned to suffering—we are later forced to question their relationships to the future. The survival techniques enumerated here respond to the immediate present. But even beyond all this, suffering had served to make them strong, stoically strong, and for this reason they could not compartmentalize joy and pain.

Turning to Shadrack's war experience in December 1917, we are told that he "saw the face of a soldier near him fly off...But stubbornly, taking no directly from the brain the body of the headless soldier ran on, with energy and grace, ignoring altogether the drip and slide of brain tissue down its back" (*Sula*, 7). Shadrack later comes to consciousness in a military hospital in the United States. His first perceptions are the food on the tray, his hands which grew as he attempted to use them, his resulting shrieks that bring the male nurse who commands him to eat, the upsetting of the tray, and finally the straitjacket. The narrator tells us that Shadrack occupied needed space and either that or his violence resulted in his release, at which time he was given "$217, a full suit of clothes and copies of very official-looking papers" (9).

Upon his release from hospital, Shadrack's contact with the world is hardly different from that of an infant uncertain of his movements, and he is as equally disoriented. And so he begins an aimless wandering. One passage in this regard is especially poignant:

Twenty-two years old, weak, hot, frightened, not daring to acknowledge the fact that he didn't even know who or what he was...with no past, no language, no tribe, no source, no address book,...he was sure of one thing only, the unchecked monstrosity of his hands. He cried soundlessly at the curbside of a small midwestern town wondering where the window was, and the river, and soft voices outside the door (*Sula*, 10–11).

Not long after he is picked up by the police, taken to jail, and eventually back to Medallion, which is twenty-two very long miles away. "In the back of the" sheriff's "wagon" amidst sacks of squash and "hills of pumpkins," he "began a struggle that was to last for twelve days." Finally "he hit upon the idea that one day a year" devoted to death would exorcise all thoughts of it for "the rest of the year...In this manner he instituted National Suicide Day" (12).

If we focus on the joke that caused blacks to be living where they are, the institutionalized prejudice that keeps them impoverished and on the border of despair, the imperialist venture that had brought their ancestors as slaves to America, and link these with the imperialist crisis that culminated in World War I as well as the purely materialist reason that caused Shadrack to be discharged from hospital as soon as he appeared to have regained consciousness, then we begin to see the interrelationships of racism, greed, brutality, and power—those forces the Medallionites devised their rituals to combat, albeit passively.

National Suicide Day is Shadrack's ritual of catharsis—a vicarious suicide for the real suicide he does not himself commit. By talking about suicide he found sufficient relief from the pain that otherwise might have impelled him to kill himself. "On the third day of the new year, he walked through the Bottom down Carpenter Road with a cowbell and a hangman's rope calling the people together. Telling them that this was their only chance to kill themselves or each other" (12).

National Suicide Day, therefore, is another ritual introduced into the community. It should have been ignored but is instead added to the other rituals. One can safely say that a second joke is played on the Bottoms. "Shadrack was crazy but that did not mean that he didn't have any sense or...power. His eyes were so wild, his hair so long and matted, his voice so full of authority and thunder that he caused panic on the first, or Charter, National Suicide Day in 1920" (12).

These John-the-Baptist traits invest him with a prophetic aura. It is merely a question of time before the power that Medallionites see in him becomes mesmeric. We are told that "once the people understood the boundaries and nature of madness, they could fit him, so to speak, into the scheme of things" (13)—that is to say, they found a place for his ritual among them. And so Suicide Day becomes a vital part of the Bottom's calendar: before Suicide Day, after Suicide Day became ways of reckoning time. Eventually "Reverend Deal took it up, saying the same folks who had sense enough to avoid Shadrack's call were the ones who insisted on drinking themselves to death or womanizing themselves to death. 'May's well go on with Shad and save the Lamb the trouble of redemption'" (Sula, 13–14).

Before Morrison could move on to show the desperate side of the Black Moses longing, she provides the reader with more specific details about the residents of the community. The episodes are highly gothic—Eva cuts off her leg to get the insurance money to feed her children; she burns her son Plum to death after he returns home crazed from his war experience; Sula drowns Chicken Little, and Nell, who witnesses it, never reveals the secret; Sula watches her mother burn and simply admires the spectacle. These are only a sampling of the bizarre episodes that occur in the community. Clearly the adjustments the community made to the problems prejudice created brought other forms of psychopathology. Although the incidents appear too many to be credible, especially the disasters with which Sula is identified, the overall impact of these details is to evoke a sense of desperate survival in dire circumstances and with minimal energy. Jones and Vinson argue that this quality is present in all of Morrison's novels (Jones and Vinson 1985, 7–21).

From the following passage one gets the sense from the narrator that perhaps the people had overaccommodated the adversity in their lives:

They would no more run Sula out of town than they would kill the robins that brought her back, for in their secret awareness of Him, He was not the God of three faces they sang about. They knew quite well that he had four, and the fourth explained Sula. They had lived with various forms of evil all their days....The presence of evil was something to be first recognized, then dealt with, survived, outwitted, triumphed over (102).

This description of the community is both damning and complimentary. It is damning principally because the community fails to draw a line between what it considers acceptable and unacceptable behavior. Paradoxically this failure to delimit the unacceptable results in a tolerance for all aberrations and hence an absence of real bigotry. Insofar as the Medallionites accepted the diversity of human behaviors they felt no need to stone sinners or to burn effigies, and it is in this regard that the description is complimentary. But in their perception of God as containing an evil dimension they program themselves for the visitation of evil, and yet we are told that they struggled to overcome such evil. Unable to rely on their God for defense, the Bottom dwellers believe passionately in nothing and accommodate everything. One cannot but wonder about the psychological devastation such accommodation has on their lives and about the adequacy of their rituals to effect the manifold reconciliations required for such a general acceptance of things.

Just before the catastrophe occurs, the residents of the Bottom had hope; they had abandoned their refuge of cynicism, and consequently had put themselves in a somewhat vulnerable position. Two incidents, which could be interpreted as the evil side of Providence sporting with them, had come to break down some of the cynicism: Sula's death meant that the evil with which they associated her would disappear and there was news that the tunnel project which had been started and abandoned was definitely going to be realized and that blacks would find work on it. Once more they are disappointed, and the bitterest winter ever known with a vast array of suffering intensifies their frustration. For this latest bout of suffering they have no resources, except Suicide Day.

Ironically the cold disappeared on January 1, when the temperature shot up to 61 degrees. Blades of grass were visible on January 2, and on January 3, the sun and Shadrack came out—the latter with "his rope ... his bell," and "his childish dirge." The narrator provides both a description and an analysis of what happened.

As the initial group of about twenty people passed more houses they called the people standing in doors and leaning out of windows to join them; to help them open further the slit in the veil, this respite from anxiety, from indignity, from gravity, from the weight of that very adult pain that had undergirded them all those years before, called to them to come out and play in the sunshine....

When they got to the tunnel excavation ... their hooded eyes swept over the place where their hope had lain since 1927. *There was the promise: leaf-dead. The teeth unrepaired, the coal credit cut off, the chest pains unattended, the school shoes unbought, the rush stuffed mattresses, the broken toilets, the leaning porches, the slurred remarks and the staggering childish malevolence of their employers.* All there in the blazing sunlit ice rapidly becoming water....

Old and young, women and children, lame and hearty, *they killed as best they could, the tunnel they were forbidden to build.*

They didn't mean to go in, to actually go down into the lip of the tunnel, but in their need to kill it all, all of it, to wipe it from the face of the earth... *they went too deep, too far....*

A lot of them died there....

And all the while Shadrack stood there. Having forgotten his song and his rope, he just stood there high up on the bank ringing, ringing his bell (137–39; emphasis added).

This portrayal of the tragic culmination of the National Suicide Day ritual captures decades of frustrated hope and the Promised Land to which the people escape via death—the Promised Land of the spirituals that the victims, a very religious people, must have sung quite often. To what extent we hold Shadrack responsible is difficult to say. It is clear from the manner in which he describes the value of his ritual that he senses a submerged despair in his people. His role as Moses, however, leading them out of their Egypt, is inverted for he does not precede the throng, he merely supplies the mesmerizing sounds of the bell that urge the people on. This inversion is constant throughout the novel. He blasphemes, comes to his project through madness rather than study, and claims no high goals for the solution he offers, nor does he lead. Self-sacrifice is not his goal. Unable to wreak vengeance on the world that sent him to war and that refused to heal the wounds from that war, he turned to fashioning a ritual sacrifice where he was willing to be sacrificer.

Several of the passages cited here are quite light-hearted in tone. Inasmuch as a people in the dire circumstances of the Bottom's residents must clearly be awaiting deliverance, Morrison's jocular tone and inverted Moses figure bring considerable irony to her subject. The ironic tone is derived from the superstitions of the people, their seeming folly in following Shadrack, but most of all from the narrator who refuses to see how close to despair these characters are. This ironic element creates the impression of a strong aesthetic detachment between Morrison and her subject matter. Morrison identifies this dissonance between events and language as part of her writing technique (Ruas 1985, 222).

Essentially, then, Bontemps and Morrison approach their Black Moses figure quite differently. In a sense Shadrack is one who preys upon his people's beliefs for self-gain; he is therefore like many of the trickster characters we shall encounter in the chapter on the trickster. Gabriel, on the other hand, corresponds to the "myth, the hope... that some day a Black Messiah will arise from among the people and lead the black race out of bondage and slavery" (Williams 1972, 120). Morrison focuses on the pathology, derived principally from racism, that drives the black community in desperate moments to follow madmen whom they mistake for Moses.

THE BAD BAD NIGGER

We shall now look at the sociopathic Bad Nigger, for whom violence is a virtue. He has always been an ambivalent figure for black Americans. Lawrence Levine tells us that "black singers, story tellers, and audiences might temporarily and vicariously live through the exploits of bandit heroes but they were not beguiled into looking at these asocial, self-centered and futile figures for any permanent remedies" (1977, 419). As I have stated elsewhere, the protagonists of the toasts are the quintessential Bad Niggers. Both of the characters we shall examine here reflect many aspects of the Bad Nigger—Wright's Bigger Thomas in *Native Son* deifies violence, and Marcus in Gaines's *Of Love and Dust* is a focus for Gaines to examine the dual role of the Bad Nigger that Levine alludes to.

Richard Wright, for whom the Bad Nigger provided much inspiration for *Native Son* and (though he does not mention it) *Uncle Tom's Children*, lists several versions of the Bad Niggers he had encountered, including the bully type that Dance refers to. "The Bigger Thomases were the only Negroes" he knew of "who consistently violated the Jim Crow laws of the South and got away with it, at least for a brief spell. Eventually...they were...hounded until they were either dead or their spirits broken" (1941, ix). This perspective provides a vital key to understanding the two Bad Niggers we shall examine here.

By referring to Bigger Thomas as the "nigger" of American creation, James Baldwin acknowledges his origins in folklore ([1951] 1972, 29). Ralph Ellison commends Wright for his folklore in those works where it appears but regrets what he perceives to be an absence of folklore in *Native Son* (1977, 421). Black literary theorist Charles Davis shares Ellison's opinion; commenting on the youths in "Big Boy Leaves Home," he writes, "We sense in their gamboling haunted by fear of reprisal a living contact with the land, in their songs a musical heritage extending back to slavery and in their banter the authentic voice of a submerged black culture." But this quality, Davis feels, is lacking in Wright's later work (Davis 1982, 276). But in choosing to create Bigger as a Bad Nigger with whom blacks could find little vicarious empathy, Wright was writing the sort of book that *Uncle Tom's Children* is not, for *Native Son* was to be a book "bankers' daughters" could not "weep over" (1941, xxxvii). Bigger Thomas was therefore intended to shock America as he did and does.

There is a close relationship between Bigger and the toast heroes, who are criminals and profaners of American values. Moreover, Bigger and the creators of the toast heroes share the same environment—the black ghetto—and are streetmen.

After one makes allowances for the greater complexity that fiction demands over folklore, one is still amazed at the close resemblances between Bigger and the toast characters. It is true that Bigger sometimes breaks under the strain of action, and that toast characters, being essentially romantic heroes, never really do. But in the traits of brutality and ruthlessness as well as the propensity for power—all of which causes them to be contemptuous of human life and societal values—Bigger and the toast heroes are identical. Of course, the creators of the toast intend them to burlesque the American dream, which they feel excluded from. Wright's character is also deformed by his exclusion from pursuit of the American dream. Wright, however, takes his character one step further: instead of Bigger's creating toasts and engaging in an imaginary destruction of America, he eventually becomes his own toast hero, made complex by the dramatic qualities of a hostile environment.

At the beginning of the novel Bigger is simultaneously confronted with the poverty of his family's life and the hypocrisy of American morality. The election poster he notices reads "If you break the law you can't win," but Bigger knows that whoever possesses the "graft" to pay off politicians wins. Wright follows this up with the movie Bigger needs to see so that he can fantasize about a life he knows nothing about, and with Bigger and his friends' plan to rob Blum's delicatessen. In fewer than two pages Wright brings these three elements together in Bigger and in them dramatizes that he is a creation of his environment.

When Gus comes along conversation turns automatically to the exploitation they suffer from their landlords. Their remarks about the sun imply a longing for better times; and a plane in the sky reminds Bigger that white folks "get a chance to do everything," and that he could "fly one of them things if" he "had a chance." But Gus remarks that that would be possible if Bigger "wasn't black," if he had money, and if he was allowed to attend aviation school (Native Son, 19–20). Bigger's subsequent contemplation of the ifs Gus had mentioned is Wright's way of stripping the petals one by one from the flower of the American dream as it applies to the residents of the black urban ghetto. To relieve the horror of their realizations the boys decide to play "white." Whiteness for them means power to declare war and to sell stockmarket shares (21–22).

They must soon give up this play and find another escape: the inevitable pool hall. There they are joined by their "sidekicks," GH and Jack. From there it is to the movie house, where their unreality is reinforced by false pictures of American life—of wealthy women with millionaire husbands—and the boys articulate their fantasies freely: "Them rich white women'll go to bed with anybody, from a poodle on up" (33).

This completes the environment that shapes Bigger. Wright's focus thereafter is on how Bigger survives in this environment. His mother sings the spirituals—especially those that advocate stoicism: "Life is like a mountain railroad / With an engineer that's brave / We must make the run successful / From the cradle to the grave..." (14). Bigger, however, terrorizes those who are weaker than himself. He carries around a gun and a knife, never really to attack the white race, for he is afraid of its power. And though he suggested the robbing of Blum's delicatessen, when the time comes for the robbery he must find an excuse. He must accuse Gus of being late, and, to belie his cowardice as well as to frighten the other boys into never mentioning it, he resorts to terror. First he kicks Gus. Next he continues by drawing his knife and putting the blade to Gus's throat. Next he commands him to lick the blade. Bigger then makes him stand with his hands above his head, while he pushes the blade against his stomach, threatening to push it in. This is the type of humiliation the toast characters subject their victims to, except that the toast hero is never afraid of the powerful. In the toast "The History of the Dog," for example, the behavior code is "Never teach a lame the game unless you make him pay," and when "the hustlers" begin "stalking their prey...the weakest are doomed to pay..." (Dance 1978, 232). Bigger has a similar ethic. He makes Bessie pay for being a woman; i..e., for being physically weaker than he is. He commands and she obeys, knowing that noncompliance evokes his swift violence, whether the demand is sex or theft of her mistress's property (which on one occasion he is even prepared to use as "blackmail" to force her into further theft). One finds an analogue for Bigger's behavior in "Pimpin' Sam":

> He say, "Shet up, bitch! Don't say another mother fuckin' word!
> If you do I'll put my foot in your ass...
> I'll pull a bitch outta bed at half past fo'
> And make you jump in Lake Michigan if it's ninety feet below.
> If you shiver when you come to sho',
> Well, I'll kick your asshole and make you swim some cock suckin' mo'..."
> (Dance 1978, 235).

When we first encounter Bigger his fear of the powerful is the only difference between him and the sociopathic toast hero. But Bigger too will get to the stage where he is unafraid of the powerful.

When Bigger gets the job at the Daltons' (the millionaire real estate owners who exploit ghetto residents and soothe their conscience by giving back a million of these dollars to black charities), the world that Bigger knows disappears, and uncertainty, fear, and distrust come to characterize his life. The knowledge he has of the way whites live comes from the movies. Kindness and equality as Mr. Dalton's daughter and her boyfriend Jan think they offer are outside of Bigger's conception of white people. He lacks the psychic apparatus to deal with such acts from them. Separated from each other by geography and knowing each other only through stereotypes, neither group can truly grasp the other's reality. For Bigger the violence that served him in street life cannot serve him in his relationships with white people. In such a situation, as notes Kathleen Gallagher, what happens to him is "a question of luck, context, and semantics" (1984, 293).

Therefore, Bigger can only think, as Mrs. Dalton comes to the room where he has just taken the drunken Mary, that if Mrs. Dalton discovers him she will feel that he is there for one reason only, to rape Mary. The white shadow of a blind Mrs. Dalton is powerful enough to provoke panic in him; and the consequence is that he suffocates Mary in his attempt to keep her quiet. But those brutal instincts he had perfected for his survival return to him and help him hack the body to bits and put them in the furnace. This act, despite its accidental nature, frees him from his fears of the white race, and gives him a new sense of power.

Now, like a toast hero, he exploits his advantage: he could extort money from the Daltons before escaping; Bessie, his girlfriend, would become his tool, after which he would dispose of her. Consistent with Wright's view of the failure of the Bigger Thomases, Bigger's plans are foiled. Wright goes on to characterize him with a depravity and egocentrism so great— equivalent only in the toast hero Dolemite—that shortly after escaping from the Dalton household after the discovery of Mary's bones in the furnace, he lures Bessie into an abandoned building, where he rapes her and kills her with a brick. The similarities between Bigger's conduct and that of Dolemite are too close to be accidental. Dolemite "screws" his "bitch to death" to get her out of the way so he could continue "kicking asses and fucking up in the hall" (Dance 1978, 231). Bigger's total dehumanization is later conveyed graphically as the reader witnesses him leaping from building to building like a chased cat.

There is one other element of the toast hero that characterizes Bigger: the absence of remorse for his crimes. The toast hero—and this is especially evident in the characterization of Stagolee—sees life as a power game and is quite content to accept, when someone stronger comes along, that his game is over. Death is as natural to him as life. Since the exercise of violence and brutality gives meaning to his life, at death he regrets nothing. Bigger, of course, finds existential meaningfulness in his killing of Mary Dalton and the media coverage and speculations about him; the attention accords him a self-importance he had never before imagined. He regrets nothing. The closest he can come to remorse is to say that had he not been excluded from the things he wanted he never would have resorted to murder. His final vision of what he has done is thus expressed: "What I killed for must have been good...When a man kills, it's for something...I did not know I was really alive in this world until I felt things hard enough to kill for 'em..." (392).

The literary critics failed to see this particular aspect of Bigger, partly because outside the black ghetto community little knowledge of the toast form existed until the appearance of Roger Abraham's *Deep down in the Jungle* (1956), and partly because the black–white dialectic of Wright's work was too overwhelming for the critics to pay attention to much else. Dan McCall briefly alludes to Bigger's "Bad Nigger" status and abandonment of reason by pointing out that in every case when Bigger attacks he goes for the victim's head. In noting Bigger's recurring dream, that he carried a package with his own decapitated head, McCall underscores Bigger's subconscious awareness of his having sacrificed his reason (1969, 74–75).

Allusions to the toast form do not appear in the novel; there are none of the rhythmic bantering or verbal insult that one associates with the toast form. A writer like Cecil Brown tells the Efan tale to let the reader know that his protagonist is a modern-day relative of the plantation trickster. Wright had several justifiable reasons for excluding such references: he wanted a fast-paced narrative in which Bigger's actions would speak for themselves. Another was that for Wright to characterize Bigger as sympathetic to any art forms, even a criminal's art, would have risked diminishing the total monster that Wright wished him to become by the time of his capture. Wright would not let Bigger create a personage to perform the feats Bigger was unable to, rather he let Bigger be that personage himself. McCall feels that for Wright to have invested Bigger with "a folk tradition in the slum—that is, to create whole human beings in a brutally fragmented world—would not be to take that world seriously" (1969, 85). McCall overstates his case: the existence of a rich, black urban folklore contradicts him. In Wright's novel, however, such folklore would have been defeating. The conversion of folklore to realism, by extracting its principles and discarding its rituals, evident in Wright, will become more and more noticeable in later Afro–American writers.

From the point of view of self-awareness, Ernest Gaines' Marcus Payne in *Of Love and Dust* (1967) is a more complex character than Bigger Thomas. The behavior of both characters, however, is deeply influenced by their environments. Each rejects the ritual controls that mark their parents' lives. But the reactions of Marcus and Bigger to their environment are different, for whereas Bigger is a stumbler, Marcus is a schemer. Moreover, Marcus can identify how certain personal experiences altered his perceptions of reality and caused him to modify his personality to deal with that reality. Marcus's sphere is considerably more vast: he is not Bigger Thomas, afraid of white people; instead he set out to defy them.

Like the Bad Nigger of folklore, Marcus determines for himself what is moral. He is contemptuous of the subservience he observes in his grandmother, in Jim Kelly, in Aunt Margaret, Bishop, and all others who live exclusively within the confines of a white-demarcated reality. But Marcus is also the Bad Nigger as brute, the murderer of another man simply because he wants that man's woman, an act for which he feels no remorse. This absence of remorse coexists at the beginning of the novel with a lack of gratitude and filial affection, indifference to the kindness of others, and a renunciation of friendship for pure egocentrism. He attributes his attitudes to the crass violence and exploitation he was subjected to by black people at his work place and later in prison.

Marcus shines best in his attempt to fight Southern white supremacy. Having committed murder, he is now in the throes of the powerful plantation owner, Herbert Marshal, whose power over blacks and cajuns is almost infinite. Marshal has arranged Marcus' release so that he could use this Bad Nigger to kill his cajun overseer Bonbon, who having committed murder for Marshal, now uses its potential as "blackmail" to enrich himself from Marshal's plantation. Egotist that he is, Marcus is concerned with freeing himself from the murder charges; he is too disdainful of blacks who accept the humiliation of plantation life to ever submit to the backbreaking job of corn-harvesting with Bonbon on his horse always six inches behind him. It is implied in the text that Marshal arranges this scenario so that the contest of will between both men would lead to violence and eventual murder, a sure way of ridding himself of Bonbon. Gaines thus brings complexity to his plot by introducing an element never associated with the Bad Nigger, his being a tool of whites.

The most popular trait of the Bad Nigger is his violation of sex taboos. While blacks, who are victims of such taboos, derive vicarious satisfaction from the Bad Nigger's open defiance, they nevertheless fear the consequences; they know that the vengeance whites inflict for such violations always engulfs the black community. Furthermore, each time the Bad Nigger upsets the status quo, the defenseless position *vis-à-vis* white violence in which blacks find themselves is always accompanied by guilt and questions of self-worth; in peaceful times such feelings become submerged in rituals. Therefore when the Bad Nigger comes into town the black community's fears surface. His presence among them is a reminder of their victim status, and they seek to restrain him. What Gaines' community fears happens: Marcus openly courts Bonbon's wife.

The strategies the community devises to prevent Marcus from being with Louise and the counter-strategies of Louise and Marcus account for some of the most exciting parts of the novel. Gaines' rhetorical purpose, however, is to reveal to what extent the Bad Nigger is a reaction to the preabolition codes that govern Southern black–white relationships. Bishop, the butler at the plantation house, takes it as an affront that Marcus does not say *Mr.* Marshal and an even greater affront that Marcus, the descendant of a slave, had dared to hold open with his foot the door of a house that slavery had built. Bishop's own protestation to Marshal that he had been promised a lifetime on the plantation provided he remain a "good boy" is indicative of the servile nature of the community and the antebellum codes by which it operates. In Marshal's scorn for Bishop, Gaines dramatizes the contempt Southern whites feel for their "good black boys" who never make an effort to become men. That Bishop is an ardent church goer implies that religion is part of his "good boy" armor. Little wonder then that Marcus is a nonbeliever in everything but his self-affirming actions, for religion is as much a part of the preabolition contract as is the tacit understanding that black women become the mistresses of white men by command, not consent—Pauline and Bonbon being the examples given in the novel. Marcus' trait of believing in his own actions is, of course, a fundamental characteristic of the Bad Nigger; but Gaines does not take this for granted. He ensures that his plot provides some justification for Marcus' conduct.

Gaines wishes to have the reader see Marcus as more than just another Bad Nigger; thus we see that although Marcus becomes interested in Louise for purely selfish reasons—for vengeance against Bonbon—her loneliness and her expectation that he will free her from Bonbon's slavery affect him to the point where he discovers that he is in love with her. Sherley Anne Williams notes that "Marcus falls from the only promontory which a streetman considers worthy of climbing, that of controlling any game which he tries to run on others. In loving Louise he loses sight of his reason for having her" (1972, 196). But this way of regaining his humanity is at odds with the customs of the South, and here his defiance reaches its acme. While Marshal is prepared to provide Marcus with a car and the money he needs to take Louise away, Marshal cannot accept the miscegenation that Marcus insists on. Marcus's act threatens to crack the very foundation of southern society, whose rationale is white hegemony—the disbarring of black-initiated, black–white copulation being a tenet of that hegemony. This is Gaines' way of revealing the principal threat that the Bad Nigger represents for the white status quo. Had Gaines not shown Marcus as a remorseless murderer and a beater of those women who refuse his sexual advances, Marcus would have been a hero (but a less intriguing character). The expensive, flashy clothes he wears to work in the fields—his way of expressing contempt for the work—, his refusal to ever accommodate to the pace of field work, i.e., to be "broken," as well as his aforementioned brutality are all traits of the Bad Nigger. The end result is that Bonbon shoots Marcus, not because he wants to or because of outrage over his wife's consorting with him, but on account of Marcus' need to fight Bonbon as a way of asserting his manhood, of living up to the Bad Nigger code.

In the fact that Bonbon does not wish to kill Marcus, that night riders do not come to terrorize the community, and that Bonbon profits from the occasion to escape North with his mulatto mistress and their two children (who cannot openly call him father), Gaines shows that it takes the defiance of the Bad Nigger to reveal the weaknesses of southern taboos. Gaines's own Bad Nigger proves that the fear of the taboos is greater than the reality they seek to enforce. Moreover it takes the affront of the Bad Nigger to inspire Bonbon with the courage he needs to be a man and marry the mulatto woman he desires rather than being forced to have a white wife whom he disdains. In fact, Bonbon would have been happy to see Marcus leave with his wife. In his treatment of Marcus in the field and of his children and Pauline, Bonbon wears the mask that an oppressive society forces him to don. The Bad Nigger redeems him, provides a way for him to break the social stranglehold.

Like Wright, Gaines is interested in the black community's response to the Bad Nigger. We have already seen the community's fear of him because of his callousness and his daring. But the element of admiration that the Bad Nigger inspires is there too. After the culmination of the events, Jim Kelly notes that he "didn't blame Marcus anymore. I admired Marcus ... And that's why I wanted to hurry up and get to the front. I wanted to tell them that they were starting something that others would hear about, and understand, and would follow" (*Love and Dust*, 270). This is the same Jim Kelly who marshalled whatever forces were at his disposal to keep Marcus away from Louise, the same Kelly who despised Marcus in the beginning. Jim's statement expresses the need that created the Bad Nigger of folklore; but blacks have shown in all their Bad Nigger tales that however much they might admire the violence directed at the white man, they know that such violence is itself dehumanizing and will invariably be turned on them at some point. For Jim, what is important in Marcus is that aspect that Grier and Cobbs feel is positive in the Bad Nigger: his defiance, which is "a reminder of what manhood could be" (Grier and Cobbs 1968, 55). It is for this reason that blacks cannot dispense with him and eagerly seek his many incarnations.

Wright's and Gaines' portraits of the Bad Nigger are intriguing because of the angle from which each writer chose to create his character. Wright's hero is the victim of confused notions of the American Dream, of the lack of opportunity to give himself an identity outside of violence, and of his sequestration from the various institutions that inculcate and reinforce humane values. Gaines' Marcus knows why he rejects humanity, despises blacks and whites, acts according to his needs, and refuses to be the puppet of white society. These differences in the portrayals of Wright and Gaines have to do with the environment of the characters as well as the intentions of the authors. But they are all facets of the Bad Nigger.

These then are a look at portrayals of the black preacher, John Henry, Black Moses, and the Bad Nigger in the Afro–American novel. Considering their importance in Afro–American oral culture, these heroes are under-represented in the written literature.

Other folk heroes that are still awaiting their due in the Afro–American novel are slave insurrectionists and blues/jazz protagonists. Bontemps' Gabriel, created more than half a century ago, shows us the fictive richness inherent in the former. In the case of blues/jazz heroes, some of these characters appear alongside other characters—Leroy in Ntozake Shange's *Sassafras, Cypress and Indigo* (1982), Rufus in Baldwin's *Another Country* (1962), Scooter and Luzanna Cholly in Albert Murray's *The Train Whistle Guitar* (1974), Ursa Corregidora in Gayle Jones's *Corregidora* (1975). Scooter and Luzanna Cholly are caught up in the rituals of the blues rather than in its performance and lifestyle. Ursa is a restrained blues singer protagonist and therefore fails to do justice to the ebullient blues singer. This is not to say that the foregoing writers and others not mentioned have not contributed in transposing the blues from music to literature—there is a definite literary blues tradition, especially in poetry and drama, but a dearth of authentic blues/jazz protagonists. Looking however at what Ishmael Reed has done for Afro-American aesthetics in the manner in which he uses hoodoo, what Toni Morrison has done with Pilate and Therese as culture bearers in the African *griot* sense, Toni Cade Bambara for the black folk healer, and Alice Walker for the black revolutionary, and most of these in the 1970s, one expects most of these gaps to be soon filled.

3

Tricksters

INFLUENCES ON THE AFRO–AMERICAN TRICKSTER TRADITION

> White folks do as they please
> and black folks do as they can.
> (Haskins 1972, 67)

> Our Fader which art in heben,
> White man owe me leben and pay me seben;
> Dy kingdom come, Dy will be done;
> Ef I hadn't tuck dat I wouldn't git none.

These statements have survived to become a part of the folk repertoire because they contain the kernel of an entire philosophy of black survival. In both examples the white man is unethical; in both examples the black man is victim; and in both examples the black man must deal with such unethical behavior as he is able to. According to Ostendorf, the final line of the second folk rhyme "captures well that curious dialectic between cognitive and cathartic functions: it expresses the collective determination to survive and the knowledge that this survival has to be paid for with a temporary acquiescence" (1982, 37).

Thus to be black in America and survive necessitates being a trickster. The folktales surrounding Brer Rabbit and John teach this chiefly. In the accounts the slaves gave of their conduct *vis-à-vis* massa, one sees how astutely they put to use the wisdom they ascribed to Brer Rabbit in his dealings with animals several times more powerful than himself and to John in his dealings with massa. In masking their exploits behind these figures and in telling these stories in the presence of whites, subtle bragging and ironic laughter directed at the "all-powerful" whites is apparent. These stories were, moreover, told night after night at the slaves quarters, and the young never had to ask what they meant. Consequently the Afro–American trickster tradition, in which the forces of cunning are marshalled against white society and with its sanctioning art couched in entertaining allegory, was firmly established long before the abolition of slavery and continued to thrive in the almost equally oppressive system of peonage, white-capping (the prevention of blacks from engaging in any profitable form of business activity), and Jim Crow of the American South.

Turning to the folklore surrounding the Euro–American trickster (confidence man), the African trickster, and the Amer–Indian trickster, in relationship to the complex character of the Afro–American trickster, one begins to see a merging of all these influences on him, especially in fiction. Yet each of the aforementioned figures has distinct differences. The West African trickster, knowledge of whom the slaves brought with them, is a figure that embodies and reconciles through cunning all the disparate elements of human existence—from the divine to the despicable (Pelton 1980, 223–24). His linguistic dexterity is preserved in the Afro–American trickster—it is quite evident in John. Some of his excesses are there too. But the redeemer element is lost. Of course, the communal, societal structure that in West Africa made the redeemer quality imperative was considerably altered in America: a hostile nature no longer had to be appeased; taboos against offending beneficent ancestral spirits and gods no longer had to be observed; and there was no self-defined political structure to reinforce and account for by way of a unifying mythology. The immediate problem for the slaves was finding ways to affirm their humanity—the rationalization for slavery being that slaves were not human. Hereafter in this study John, together with Brer Rabbit and Brer Terrapin, will be combined under the rubric of the plantation trickster. His name will represent individual success, and his cunning is always directed at the white race.

The influences deriving from the Amer–Indian trickster are somewhat harder to identify. They are important in the sense that, because of the similarities that exist between the Amer–Indian trickster and the West African trickster, the one kept alive memories of the other. Paul Radin remarks that the North American Indian Trickster "remained everything to every man—god, animal, human being, hero, buffoon, he who was before good and evil, denier, affirmer, destroyer, and creator..." (1956, 169).

The Euro–American trickster tradition is different from either of the above—its rationale is deception for its inherent power and control. According to Warwick Wadlington, the Euro–American trickster tradition is not sanctioned by myth but by fiction, whose purpose is to find things out (1975, 4). He further states that the confidence game is deeply ingrained in American tradition, for, given what appears to be the inchoateness of "a dark, silent disorder," the trickster's deceptions become "convenient counters to express a powerful psychic energy and at the same time to elicit repeatedly the confidence that he needs to exist" (1975, 6). In his role as linguistic manipulator, the confidence man merges with the aboriginal trickster. But the peddling of assurance, faith in self, and the sanctity of

capitalism—all germane to the American ethos—bring interesting ramifica-
tions to the Afro–American trickster tradition; for while the white race still
remains an unconquerable fate, the black trickster turns to preying on
members of his race, in closer conformity with American individualism.
Thus the John versus massa framework of the plantation trickster becomes
considerably modified. It then becomes simply "putting folks into tricks,
running games on them, or merely hustling, and black people will applaud,
admire and envy these heroes even as the heroes run games on them"
(Williams, 1972, 58). This type of character, whose essential quality is that he
preys on all folk, black and white alike, shall be referred to simply as the
confidence man.

The black preacher too has been given many of the attributes of the
trickster. This is no accident; in the earliest times of slavery his office was a
form of subterfuge; in the later period he was often clandestinely literate
and frequently worked surreptitiously with the abolitionists to disseminate
information regarding the work being done to liberate the slaves as well as
to set up and coordinate stations of the Underground Railroad. On a
somewhat sinister level, following emancipation, most educated blacks
could find work only in teaching or preaching; this fact encouraged blacks
to question the degree of commitment their preachers brought to their
work. Besides, blacks were also well aware of the legends about preachers,
especially itinerant ones, who employed the gospel to become wealthy.
Langston Hughes's Laura in *Tambourines to Glory* and Alice Childress's
Mountain Seely in *A Short Walk* are both trickster figures. These I shall
examine under the subcategory of the trickster–preacher.

CHESNUTT TO ELLISON

While elements of the trickster appeared in many of the fictive characters
of early Afro–American writers, it was not until Chesnutt's *The Conjure
Woman* (1899) (hereafter cited *Conjure*) was published that one began to see a
serious attempt to portray the trickster in fiction. Chesnutt's Julius McAdoo
is an ex-slave whose function is to tell antebellum tales, and each story is
organized around a tale. The tales show for the most part how the slaves,
often through conjure, frequently outsmarted massa and occasionally
themselves. Moving away from the tales and focusing on their teller, we find
that McAdoo has a specific motive for telling each one. In the case of "The
Goophered Grape Vine" it is to dissuade the would-be proprietor from
purchasing the property, for to do so, though Julius never reveals it to the
purchaser, would deprive him of his livelihood. In telling "Po Sandy," Julius
wishes to prevent the dismantling of an old unused schoolhouse, which the
seceding members of the Baptist Church—Julius is among them—would
like to use as a meeting place. "Mars Jeem's Nightmare" is to persuade his
employer to rehire Julius' lazy grandson; "The Conjurer's Revenge" con-

vinces his employer to buy a blind and lame horse, which purchase earns
Julius an excellent commission; "Sis Becky's Picaninny" convinces his
employer's wife of the need to carry a rabbit's foot and vindicates Julius'
carrying one; "The Gray Wolf's Hant" is to discourage his employer from
destroying the forest that harbors the bees that supply Julius with honey;
and "Hot Foot Hannibal" helps effect a reconciliation between his employer's niece and her fiancé, from whom it is suspected Julius hopes to procure
additional employment.

How does Julius proceed? First it seems as if he is full of stories and only
awaits his chance to tell one, having decided in advance what benefit he
hopes to derive from its telling. Secondly, he is aware that his employer's
wife, Annie, is interested in stories about slavery and is deeply affected by
them. And as Robert Bone notes, Julius knows that a good story teller is like
a conjurer (1975, 83).

Let us examine some of Julius' techniques for controlling others through
language. He approaches his subject by indirection, in a matter-of-fact way.
Here is how he begins "The Goophered Grape Vine":

Well, suh, you is a stranger ter me, en I is a stranger ter you, en we is bofe strangers
to one annuder, but ef I'uz in yo' place I wouldn' buy dis vimya'd....

Well, I dunno whe'er you believes in conj'n'er not,—some er de w'ite folks don't, er
says dey don't,—but de truf er de matter is dat dis yer old vimya'd is goophered (11).

The first three clauses are quite metrical so as to enchant the unsuspecting
listener. Moreover, like every good trickster, Julius knows that he should
convince the would-be victim that he has his welfare at heart. John, the
white proprietor, whom Chesnutt uses as the author's narrator, tells the
reader that Uncle Julius "imparted this information with such a solemn
earnestness, and with such an air of confidential mystery, that I felt interested, while Annie was evidently impressed and drew closer to me..." He
entered so well into the world of his tales that he seemed to be back in that
world, completely removed from the present (*Conjure* 11–12). Thus Uncle
Julius possesses the best trait of the trickster: the ability to immerse his
entire identity in his art.

Part of Julius' cunning is to wear the Sambo mask. Hugh Gloster notes
that Julius is not, however, the compliant Sambo that one sees in the fiction
of Thomas Nelson Page (1948, 35), nor, it might be added, in many of
Chesnutt's other characters: Mammy Jame and Sandy, for example, in *The
Marrow of Tradition*. Julius' use of the Sambo mask is comparable to the
juggler's distractions for the purpose of deceiving his audience.

The following passage, which introduces the first story not long after he
meets John and Annie, is all calculation: "Now if dey's an'thing a nigger lub,
nex' ter possum, en chick'n, en watermillyums, it's scuppernons. Dey ain't
nuffin' dat kin stan' side'n de scuppernon' fer sweetness; sugar ain't a

sukumstance ter scuppenons..." (13). Just before this statement he had referred to himself as "just a ole nigger" (12). With this introduction, Uncle Julius, who does not yet know his listeners, deceives them into thinking that he is the type of "nigger" that accepts white folks' stereotypes of "niggers." This effective donning of the Sambo mask and Julius' triumphs over his "massa" are no doubt the basis of Arlene Elder's remark that "in *The Conjure Woman* the conflict between the white and black forces is fierce, despite a deceptive overlay of Southern romance" (1978, 153).

This battle extends even to Julius' world view. When John becomes amused over Julius' carrying a rabbit foot and remarks that such practices retard the progress of the black race, Julius does not get angry. He simply resorts to art and tells the story of Sis' Becky's troubles. John notes at the end of the story that Julius had not proven anything about carrying a rabbit's foot; but Annie surmises that Becky's troubles came from her not carrying a rabbit's foot (It should be noted that here the rabbit's foot takes on the power of an encapsulating metaphor, encompassing the slaves' vision of reality, their ruses, and survival techniques, which, quite clearly, Sis' Becky did not fully embrace). When, days later, John discovers Annie with a rabbit's foot, we smile at Julius' triumph over the whites' so-called "unsuperstitious" mind.

Julius' successes are abetted by his profound understanding of the white mindset. He can remark that from fear of being conjured, white slave-masters refrained from punishing conjurers—though, of course, they never admitted these fears. But Julius' conjure remains essentially a verbal one, capable of conjuring the white man with his own reality. Motivated by the commission Julius hopes to collect for persuading John to buy a lame, one-eyed horse, Julius first distracts him with a tale; next he deplores the younger generation for telling lies, particularly the lie that the earth moves; finally he juxtaposes his going to prayer-meeting and calling upon the owner of the horse to tell him of John's interest in it. The passage is a masterpiece of deception:

"Ef you makes up yo' min' not ter buy dat mule, suh," he added, as he rose to go, "I knows a man w'at's got a good hoss he wants ter sell,—leas'ways dat's w'at I heared. I'm gwine ter pr'armeetin' ternight, en I'm gwine right by de man's house, en ef you'd lack ter look at de hoss, I'll ax 'im ter fetch 'im roun'" (*Conjure* 127–29).

Rooted as John is in a western Christian context he probably could not associate going to prayer-meeting with duplicity, and so he is a victim of Julius' trick. For Julius too his tale-telling functions in ways similar to the manner in which the slaves, the central characters in Julius' tales, employed conjure to get more from the white race than it was prepared to give—to trick a planter into returning a slave to his former plantation or to reunite a young child with his mother or to get a master to treat his slaves more humanely. Here, however, Julius' interests are strictly material and perhaps self-congratulatory in the sense that he, the "ignoramus," can outsmart a literate white man.

Since Julius' employer describes himself as being benevolent, one could ask if Julius' tricks might not be self-defeating over the long run. But one could say as well that Julius is enough of a cynic not to trust declarations of noble intentions from white people. We see that despite John's perception of himself as a nonracist, he is nevertheless very bigoted: "He was not entirely black and this fact, together with the quality of his hair, which was about six inches long and bushy... suggested a slight strain of other than negro blood. There was a *shrewdness in his eyes, too, which was not altogether African...*" (9–10; italics mine). Evidently shrewdness of character, in other words, intelligence, could not be associated with the African. This observation on Chesnutt's narrator's part makes him another conventional white man of his day; and, as Sylvia Lyons Render observes, a racist (1980, 64). In "Dave's Neckliss," one of six stories intended for *The Conjure Woman* but excluded from it, John states:

The generous meal he had made put the old man in a very good humor. He was not always so, for *his curiously undeveloped nature was subject to moods which were almost childish in their variableness. While he mentioned with a warm appreciation the acts of kindness which those in authority had shown to him and his people, he would speak of a cruel deed, not with the indignation of one accustomed to quick feeling and spontaneous expression, but with a furtive disapproval which suggested to us a doubt in his own mind as to whether he had a right to think or feel...* (1889, in Render 1974, 133; emphasis added).

This passage, which we can hardly take as a valid characterization of Uncle Julius, instead reflects the speaker's ignorance and is intended to disclose to the reader how effectively Julius wears his mask of trickster. What John fails to recognize is that these reactions are the careful calculations of Julius, reflecting the slaves' expression, now immortalized among their descendants: "Got one mind for what I know is me, and another for white folks to see." Julius could not reveal the truth of what he felt to the white man; had he done so he would never have survived slavery.

The tales Julius tells obviously belie John's interpretation of him. Let us take for example the story of Tenie and Sandy. Both of them love each other dearly and cannot tolerate being separated. But Marse Marrabo decides that Sandy should be hired out to various distant plantations. Tenie, who is a conjure woman, turns Sandy into a tree during the day and turns him back to a man at night. With his branches sometimes lopped off, Sandy meets with more than enough worries. Eventually, one day just before Sandy and Tenie effect their plan to run away, Tenie is forced to go to a plantation twenty miles away, and in her absence Sandy is converted to lumber. The school house that contains the lumber is said to moan perpetually. In this story conjure is trickery; the lopped off branches represent the wounds of slavery; the lumber into which Sandy is transformed conveys effectively the utilitarian aspect of slavery; its being used to build a school house reflects the taints of slavery even in society's noblest institutions; and Sandy's moaning ghost attests to the continuation of sufferings originating in slavery.

As a white man John is no more perceptive than Joel Chandler Harris, who admired and recorded the cleverness of the tales of the plantation "darky" but felt that they were created and perpetuated by buffoons. Thus we see that in his art Julius reveals his true feelings about slavery; but in their mythic, allegorical context, the reality the tales embody is not evident to someone enslaved to conventional views of who "negroes" are.

Still, apart from Julius' wiliness, his having endured slavery, his belonging to a Baptist Church, and having a grandson, we know little of him. Noel Heermance feels that it is Julius' intervention on his grandson's behalf that rescues him from being an all-out allegorical figure (1974, 183) instead of the realistic characters we expect in fiction. We have already seen John's perception of Julius. That the overwhelming majority of readers in Chesnutt's day would have seen nothing ironic in John's perception of Julius is astonishing to readers in 1987; but more than this it reveals how severely limited white America was at the dawn of the twentieth century in its perception of black humanity. It was this pervasive limitation in his white audience that forced Chesnutt to couch Julius' humanity in folklore and discouraged Chesnutt from revealing a maskless Julius within the black community.

Chesnutt's other trickster, Grandison, is less complex than Julius—he uses slavish compliance and the Sambo identity to its fullest, even to the point of returning from Canada where his master's son had taken and abandoned him. But while massa is boasting about Grandison's fidelity and using it to support his view that slavery is a benevolent institution, Grandison quietly escapes with his wife, his mother, father, four brothers, and a sister (*Wife of His Youth*, [1899] 1978, 201). This story is thematically similar to Dunbar's "The Ingrate" but less successful.

Because of the paucity of lifelike details about Chesnutt's tricksters—outside their acting role—one may speculate that Chesnutt felt that since these characters were tricksters it was not necessary for the audience to see the character outside his role of performing tricks. It must also be noted that since Chesnutt was among the first Afro–American novelists to explore folklore in a significant way, he had no predecessors from whose mistakes or successes he might have benefited; thus he relied on his intuition. Together, these factors caused him to create trickster figures that the critics label as stereotypes or modified stereotypes (see Payne 1981, 25).

Various parallels are evident in the plantation tricksters and in Julius. When Julius earns his commission on the horse he tricks John into buying, we see an analogue to the various benefits the slaves derived from massa through lying (see Courlander 1976, 430–31). In the instance where Annie resorts to carrying a rabbit's foot for protection we hear echoes of the plantation trickster's triumphant laughter—we are reminded of massa's impatience with John for not killing the bear, of John's subsequent invitation to massa to take his place, and of John's laughter as massa dodges the bear to avoid its hugs (Courlander 1976, 425). The metamorphoses we witness in John the slave trickster's form as he pits his conjure against massa's are paralleled in the metamorphoses that the conjure woman in Julius' tales effects; but they are, even if less prominent, present too in Julius' flexible mask. At the center of Julius' creation, then, is the plantation trickster.

Chesnutt and Dunbar started the tradition of using figures from folklore as major characters in fiction. In Chesnutt's trickster figures, we see him portraying for the most part the plantation trickster—Grandison is wholly that, Julius mostly so—and moving in the direction of the confidence man, many of whose traits Julius already displays.

Dunbar, who was Chesnutt's contemporary, made trickery the theme of some of his short stories. We have already seen the extent to which he invested his black folk preachers with plantation cunning. But, apart from Josh Leckler, a slave, who, like Chesnutt's Grandison, completely wins his master's trust as part of his plan to escape to freedom, Dunbar's tricksters are all literate blacks who operate along the lines of Melville's Confidence Man—to prey on the gullible, the ignorant, and the greedy.

Dunbar's confidence men—Ruggles, Scatters, and Buford—are the standard confidence men of American literature and folklore. Dunbar alters the characterization slightly from story to story, but it is essentially the same schema that he employs to create each character.

Mr. Ruggles, in "Aunt Mandy's Investment," is simply the confidence man who shows up in the community, promises the people great returns on their money, and disappears without being heard of. This confidence man, however, leaves some doubt about his intentions, for he returns Mandy Smith's five dollars along with ten dollars interest. By keeping the investors' hopes alive, he discourages the robbed from seeking his whereabouts.

In the case of Scatters ("The Mission of Mr. Scatters"), his game is very original: he is purportedly bringing back the wealth of the deceased John Jackson to his brother Isaac Jackson. Such an act provides him with the mask of the scrupulously honest man, behind which he is able to "borrow" sums of money from the town's dwellers. It is the people's communal solidarity, seen here in an exchange of information about Scatters' behavior, that leads to suspicion about his intentions, and eventually to the discovery that the papers that were supposed to represent $5,000 in notes and bonds were worthless.

At the trial of Scatters, however, he plays his final confidence card—he flatters the white judge, the white prosecuting attorney, and the jury, which is also all-white. They are a people of honor and mercy, befitting their status as aristocrats; he even praises the Confederacy. On that basis he is acquitted and manages to escape the angry residents of Miltonville precisely because the judge allows his carriage to be used to transport him to the train station.

While the confidence man is interesting because of Dunbar's precise delineation of his physical and even mental traits, Dunbar's preoccupation is with revealing the plight of ignorant blacks who could be easily preyed upon by unscrupulous individuals. Provided the exploiter was on good terms with the white establishment, he could continue his criminal activity with impunity. Here, then the confidence man is part of Dunbar's rhetoric for social commentary.

Buford, in "The Promoter," is shown to "feed" on the desire of blacks to own their own homes; he entices them into doing so by offering them unrealistic terms so that eventually they lose their money, which goes to Buford, and their property, which Buford resells. Part of his game, the narrator tells us, is to exploit the "exodus longing" in blacks.

Dunbar complicates the plot by introducing Sister Dicey Fairfax, who proves to be quite full of plantation cunning. Buford persuades Sister Dicey to change her name to Jane Callender so that she can collect the pension of the deceased Jane Callender. Soon after, Sister Dicey is arrested. In court Dicey is truly "the innocent." She stages her conduct to give the impression that she is a maladroit plantation woman incapable of defrauding anybody. Because she had been the "mammy" of the prosecuting attorney, she spends most of the trial treating him like a naughty, ill-raised boy to be asking her such questions. Her clumsiness has its desired effect, and she is able to tell the court at its request who the real criminal is.

In helping the law trap Buford, Dicey is the opposite of the awkward plantation woman, alerting the reader to the fact that such behavior was mere theater. Indeed she turns a deaf ear to Buford's pleas that she refuse to cooperate with the white authorities. She gives him every impression that she will, in the meantime setting the trap for his arrest, which leads to his being stripped of his ill-gotten wealth.

Both Sister Dicey's cleverness and Buford's appeal to her in the name of racial solidarity are the pivot of the story. Anyone with Sister Dicey's intelligence, but for greed or an overzealousness to "better his/her lot," would not fall prey to confidence men like Buford. In Buford's appeal to Sister Dicey, there is considerable irony; racial solidarity presupposes not robbing the members of one's race.

The presentation of the stories is such that our sympathies are not with these confidence men. Dunbar is very careful to reveal kind, charitable, upright people as their victims. The black middle class, especially in its burial societies and insurance companies, perpetrated a great deal of fraud during the period in which Dunbar wrote. Moreover, these stories appear to agree with many of the ideas Dunbar expressed in his essays, especially his

comments about community-building, which could not occur in an atmosphere of distrust. He wrote, "if the better class negro would come to his
own he must lift not only himself but the lower men whose blood brother
he is, for the fate of all blacks is his fate" ("Negroes of the Tenderloin," *Paul
Laurence Dunbar Reader*, 42). These stories would have been read by the
black middle class; Dunbar expected them to have a didactic effect. We feel
revulsion towards his confidence men; they are quite different from Chesnutt's Julius, with whom we feel a certain vicarious empathy.

Our next trickster figure comes some twenty-five years later, at the time of
the Harlem Renaissance, when black writers were exploring the distinctive-
ness of black culture (see Hughes 1926, in Gayle 1971, 172). Countee Cullen's
Sam, in *One Way to Heaven* (1932) (hereafter cited *Heaven*), is a delightful
inversion of the stereotype trickster-preacher; he is the trickster-convert. He
is portrayed along the lines of the black confidence man. His motives are
similar to those of the preacher: money, sex, adoration. Of course, as with
the preying preacher, it is the black congregation who are the victims of his
tricks. Sam is essentially a wanderer and is certainly averse to hard work.
One-armed as he is, he not only knows that his appearance at the "mourners'
bench" would evoke pity in the congregation but that a staged relinquish-
ment of his cards and razor would heighten that pity. The congregation, he
knows, would perceive him as surrendering the vices that maimed and maintained him and would feel obliged to offer him money so that financial need
will not force him to "backslide" (As we shall see in chapter four, blacks
attach a profoundly mystic importance to the conversion experience).

Sam's act achieves its end, and Mattie, who had been indifferent to the
altar call, changes her mind after seeing Sam's performance. Sam, however,
is caught in the briar patch, when the evangelist recognizes him as the
person who had performed a similar feat in a southern state several years
before, not to mention the numerous other evangelists he had heard talk of
Sam's behavior at their revivals. Cullen rescues Sam in true trickster style: in
folklore the trickster is indestructible. The evangelist does not expose Sam.
His argument for not doing so is that Sam's staged conversion had created
the desired emotional impact on the congregation, stirring nine people to
heed the altar call on a night when the sermon and other theatrics had
failed. Thus Reverend Johnson acknowledges Sam to be the superior artist.
Of course, Cullen's interest here is highly rhetorical; since sinners were
supposed to be moved by the Holy Ghost, Cullen uses Sam's act to ridicule
some of the black church's staid beliefs. The preacher too could find
rationalization for his not exposing Sam. He could argue that God moves in
mysterious ways to perform His wonders—Sam's giving up his cards and
razor being one of them. At the end of the service the preacher tells Sam, "I
am not sure that you are not the most despicable man I have ever come
across; I'm not sure that you aren't a genius in your own way, and I am far

from being certain that you aren't an unwitting instrument in the hands of heaven" (*Heaven*, 33).

In witnessing this, the reader is aware of the extent to which a trickster can manipulate the entire religious process. An act done to procure money, without any additional motives, is shown to have far-reaching, controlling significance. Religion, then, is another confidence game. As Reverend Johnson relates to Sam all the various stories surrounding his performance, of the congregations who fondly remember him and still lead clean, holy lives, and of the dramatic impact of Sam's story on others, Sam merely thinks of whether he is going to succeed in the sexual advances he will make to Mattie. Cullen's narrator tells us that "next to getting religion and making it pay, Sam hankered after women.... He had never joined church yet but it had led to an affair. As lightly as he had taken his religion he had taken his women, and as often" (28). This brings Sam very close to the hustler, who reduces everyone to utility.

While walking Mattie home after his conference with Reverend Johnson, Sam discovers that Mattie had asked Johnson for the razor and the cards; these she vows she will keep in memory of her conversion. Already Sam can see that Mattie's weakness is one of excessive gratitude, and he begins to lay down his plans to exploit it.

He manages to get her to convert her gratitude to love, and very soon they are married. Marriage for him, however, means a wife who is working, thereby assuring him food, shelter, and sex for that winter. Once spring comes and, contrary to his plans, he finds work, Mattie loses her importance. There follows a conjure seance proposed by Aunt Mandy as a way of regaining Sam. There is also Sam's final trick before he dies of pneumonia: he hears the women despairing over the salvation of his soul and Aunt Mandy talking about signs that occur before death. He therefore fabricates a vision of heaven, which he recounts to the women's delight; and because of this vision Mattie convinces Reverend Drummond to preach Sam's funeral sermon, for he had died a saint. In a sense, Sam manipulates his own funeral and the memories that will outlive him. This he does clearly for the sheer delight he gets from manipulating others.

Throughout, Cullen shows him as a character devoid of emotion. His acts towards others are uniquely related to his need to exploit them. His preoccupations never exceed the current day's needs, a trait that keeps him close to his folkloric counterpart, who never shows foresight.

Sam, then, is simply an American trickster, another confidence man, who devises his confidence games according to the material at hand. Unlike Chesnutt and Dunbar, Cullen characterizes his trickster with various biographical traits: we know his birthplace, how he lost his arm, about his voyages in the freight trains, etc. But Uncle Julius is a more engaging character who acquires the reader's respect and whose acts find some justification within their context. He is not the parasite that Sam is, nor is he the cynic. As a character, Sam is a failure; he is too shallow to gain the reader's sympathy.

When Ralph Ellison's *Invisible Man* was published in 1952, considerable debate had already taken place about black literary aesthetics, and several types of novels had already been written, including Zora Neale Hurston's predominantly folkloric works and Richard Wright's landmark *Native Son*, "the bible of protest novels." Today these two writers are deemed to have established the aesthetic poles of Afro–American literature (Jordan 1974, 5). Sutton Grigg's novels, Arna Bontemps' masterpiece, *Black Thunder* (1936), and William Attaway's minor masterpiece, *Blood on the Forge* (1941) had been written. No longer were Afro–American writers without models, and lively debates over Afro–American aesthetics were taking place. The result of much of this is to be seen in the publication of *The Negro Caravan* in 1941—an anthology that has become the most important book on Afro–American culture up to that date and that pioneered the attempt to establish a historical and cultural framework for the study of Afro–American culture. Thus black writers of the 1950s had a very diverse selection of works for models and at least a tentative attempt to articulate the Afro–American cultural tradition. In the 1920s and 1930s the number of collections of black American folklore had multiplied considerably. The mass migration of blacks to the cities had resulted in a huge urban population with somewhat altered rituals; and blues and jazz had become institutionalized largely because of such urbanization. It is therefore not surprising that two of Afro–American's best novels, Ellison's *Invisible Man* and Baldwin's *Go Tell It on the Mountain*, were published in that decade. A close look at both of these novels reveals that they incorporate a wide perspective, achieved through history, folklore, and culture that had taken several generations of creative trial and error and scholarship to fashion, and from which these authors benefited.

Ellison's novel, like Wright's *Outsider*—another 1950s novel—is preoccupied with identity. In Ellison's case such a preoccupation is with what it means to be American and Afro–American. Ellison's protagonist finds out that Afro–American means nonexistence as far as the majority culture is concerned. As we follow the protagonist through the novel we learn, as he does, that those blacks who circumvent the "blueprints" of white intentions and who learn the art of subterfuge survive best in the invisible sphere to which they are relegated. In short, they survive by being tricksters. All except the protagonist learn quickly to distrust whatever is said. We are shown somewhat allegorically, through the experiences of the protagonist, what happens to those who take expressed American values at face value. The protagonist goes to a white audience to vaunt his knowledge of American ideals and finds out that white America has a twofold plan for him: one, to castrate him—effectively shown, George Kent notes, in the naked white female on whom he is supposed and not supposed to look (1972, 158) and two, to make him their blindfolded plaything.

Ellison's literary strategy is to lead the protagonist through every possible institution—except that of black folklore—that proclaims itself to be the black man's savior: white liberalism, black leadership, the Communist Party, Black Nationalism, and even the urban factory that lures residents from the South to the Promised Land, only to show these institutions as masks that hide an essentially destructive or enslaving nature; those who escape from these institutions are left more desperate than they had been. These institutions become, as Per Winther observes, prisons (1983, 115). Addison Gayle sees the protagonist as a symbolic figure commenting on post-slavery Afro–American reality (1975, 204). The protagonist finally realizes that all those who survive in the world of the novel have one thing in common: they are all tricksters. Essentially, then, the advice the protagonist's grandfather gives on his deathbed is valid:

Our life is a war and I have been a traitor all my born days, a spy in the enemy's country ever since I give up my gun back in the Reconstruction. Live with your head in the lion's mouth. I want you to overcome 'em with yeses, undermine 'em with grins, agree 'em to death and destruction, let 'em swoller you till they vomit or bust wide open (*Invisible Man*, 16).

In other words, his advice is to wear the mask of deception always—a practice that greatly benefited the slave. The protagonist soon realizes that Afro–American reality as the white world perceives it can be summed up in the formula that produces "optic white" paint: blackness must be negated to obtain a whiter whiteness. If one follows that formula blindly one becomes, like Lucius Brockway, relegated to the basement, completely hidden from sight—stoking the fires of a capitalist hell.

The protagonist's solution, then, is to find an identity in his invisibility. It is not a solution that he accepts readily or for that matter totally. Susan Blake feels that "what functions as black folklore in the novel is everything that the protagonist rejects as representing a Sambo mentality and finally learns to accept as basic to his identity" (1979, 126). It is not really Sambo that he accepts, for Sambo is compliance; rather it is John. Through Clifton's dolls Ellison implies a few comments on Samboism. One either becomes Sambo (which Clifton and the protagonist refuse to do by refusing to be confined to the dictates of the Communist Party) or one acts out the role, i.e., transforms it into art. Clifton makes Sambo dolls, which he uses to act out white fantasies about blacks; the protagonist changes it to an art of invisible sabotage. The protagonist survives, Clifton does not, for Clifton offers white America the icon of Sambo; America dictates that Clifton be Sambo.

Finally, the protagonist, who still yearns for a visible American identity, finds out, like all other Afro–Americans, that jazz and the blues, the black church and the black folk sermon contain secret survival codes, and are part of the folklore apparatus that redeems invisibility; in short, that black folklore is a necessary shield if the black man is to survive the trauma resulting from his existence in the cellars of white America. This ability to manipulate and to resurge is a central part of Ellison's vision. His protagonist makes art of his nightmare experiences, as does the blues musician; he is reminiscent of the plantation trickster, who as a way of defying massa employs the conjurer's art to metamorphose into various shapes (see Courlander 1976, 433).

What Ellison's protagonist finally knows is that his identity resides within the icons and forms of his culture. What he has seen is that those who survive—Trueblood, the Vet, Bledsoe, the Blues Singer, Rhinehart—do not follow the white world's "blueprint," for that blueprint negates their humanity. Through the trickster's cunning they circumvent the "blueprint," even though Ellison does not like the term trickster to be used in describing his characters (see *Shadow and Act*, 52, 57). Yet what is evident here is a reality that the black characters can negotiate only through cunning. When we finally see the protagonist, he is like the mythic figure John, Sambo's opposite, for what John learned by eavesdropping, the protagonist learns from experience: how to deal with white reality and how to survive, using one's "mother wit" against the heinous aspects of that reality.

One could discuss Rhinehart as a separate character from the protagonist or as a projection of the latter's ego. The reader never sees Rhinehart but feels his force by listening to what other characters say of him, and by watching them react to the protagonist whom they mistake for him. This mistaken identity supports the argument that the various facets of Rhinehart are the psychic projections of the protagonist. On yet another level it suggests that self-realization, an identity, could be found in assuming a gallery of "Rhinehartian" roles. Here is what Ellison says of Rhinehart:

Certainly B. P. Rhinehart (the P. is for Proteus, the B. is for Bliss) would seem the perfect example of a trickster figure. He is a cunning man who wins the admiration of those who admire skulduggery and know-how; an American virtuoso of identity who thrives on chaos and swift change; he is greedy, in that his masquerade is motivated by money as well as by the sheer bliss of impersonation; he is god-like, in that he brings new techniques—electric guitars, etc.—to the service of God, and in that there are many men in his image while he is himself unseen; he is phallic in his role as "lover"; as a numbers runner he is a bringer of manna and a worker of miracles, in that he transforms (for the winners, of course) pennies into dollars, and thus he feeds (and feeds on) the poor...but Rhinehart's role in the formal structure of the narrative is to suggest to the hero a mode of escape from Ras, and a means of applying, in yet another form, his grandfather's advice to his own situation ...(*Shadow and Act*, 56).

Although Ellison favors, if any criticism at all, formal criticism, one does not have to follow his objection and refuse to see Rhinehart as a trickster.

Ellison agrees that Rhinehart possesses many of the traits of the trickster; and elsewhere, years later, in an interview he said: "Rhinehart is my name for the personification of chaos. He is also intended to represent America and change. He has lived so long with chaos that he knows how to manipulate it. It is the old theme of *The Confidence Man*" (*Shadow and Act*, 181). Rhinehart can equally be conceived as Bledsoe's urban counterpart— Bledsoe's techniques adapted to the ghetto. Instead of getting what he wants by flattering white people, he gets it from exploiting the needs of desperate black people. He is the best articulator of his intentions, in the handbill the children distribute in front of his church:

> Behold the Invisible! ...
> I See all, Know all, Tell all, Cure all. . . .
> I DO WHAT YOU WANT DONE (*Invisible Man*, 484).

These words encapsulate the various roles Rhinehart plays: they echo the fact that the protagonist never encounters him in person, only his influence; they penetrate to the core of Afro–American longings as they are expressed in the spirituals and prayers, and even extend to conjure, healing seances, etc., that are part of the Afro–American world picture; they project Rhinehart as a Black Moses (we remember the character Mary longing for one); they echo Jesus' words: "Come unto me all ye that labor and are heavy-laden and I will give you rest" (Mt. 11:28). They imply his willingness to transform into reality all the wish fulfillments couched in the Afro–American stories of the preacher as stud, orator capable of turning hell into heaven, bringer of heaven, etc.; the word "invisible" connotes as well his membership in the "life."

Inside the church, Rhinehart's coded meanings become somewhat clearer, and some of the reasons for his success are evident. There are, for example, the old-fashioned prayers where the "voice rose and fell in a rhythmical, dream-like recital—part enumeration of earthly trials undergone by the congregation, part rapt display of vocal virtuosity, part appeal to God" (485); the guitar and piano boogie-woogie music; the assistant dressed in rich red and functioning as a singer, i.e., as entertainer; and the pulpit decorated in rich white and gold with "LET THERE BE LIGHT" written above it in gold letters. These words, given Rhinehart's claim to invisibility, are highly evocative. They remind one of Milton's depiction of God in *Paradise Lost* and of T. S. Eliot's reference to God as being "light invisible" ("Choruses from the Rock," in *Collected Poems*, 59).

The protagonist's contact with the congregation makes him realize the congregation's complicity in Rhinehart's game. One sister sells records of Rhinehart's sermons and collects the money from those raising it for the building fund. She also distracts Sister Harris, who is new to the church and naive in that she thinks the Rhinehart she had heard preaching when he was twelve years old in the South is still the same Rhinehart "doing the Lord's work" (485). When we come to Langston Hughes's Laura we shall see a similar though less effective character portrait.

Using the technique of indirection, Ellison shows the effectiveness of Rhinehart's confidence game—constructed from his knowledge of black needs, black rituals, as well as western rituals and beliefs. This combination results in a powerful character whom the reader never sees. Whether Ellison intended it or not, the trickster too is invisible, living as he does in the minds of those who created him. It is in this sense, then, that Rhinehart could be interpreted as the projection of the protagonist's psyche.

The question then arises as to whether the protagonist can emulate Rhinehart. The protagonist does not think that he can. We must bear in mind that Rhinehart pays bribes to the police. He is part of the "sporting life." Nor can we see in the protagonist the ruthlessness it requires to become a pimp, even though it is hinted that he has all the outward appearances. Finally we see the protagonist stumbling into his version of "invisible" survival. That he benefits from his experience with Rhinehart as far as the parasitic meanings of invisibility are concerned is evident with one difference: he does not prey on black people. Laurence Holland points out that he uses the creativity that Rhinehart fashions into masks in another way: to tell his story (1980, 71). Actually the creativity derives from every character who mediates life through art: from grandfather, Trueblood, the Vet, Bledsoe, The Blues Singer, Todd Clifton, Rhinehart, and Dupree. The telling of the story, however, does not relieve him of his invisibility. It only puts it into context.

Bledsoe too is a trickster. Addison Gayle regards him as the "living exemplar of the image of the wily slave, a dissimulator *par excellence*, 'a spy in the enemy's camp'" (1975, 207). There is little doubt that Bledsoe wishes to be seen as someone who outsmarts white people at their game. But he is no John, whose cunning results in massa's radical reform to the point where he serves his slaves roast pig; rather he is an American confidence man, interested in personal power and wealth, but also possessing a vast array of the trickster techniques of the plantation slave. An exceptional cleverness characterizes Bledsoe's game and the ruthlessness with which he implements and defends it. Homer Barbee, blind preacher and quintessential orator, is brought to the chapel to declare to the white trustees and students of the institution Bledsoe's worthiness to rule. Ellison, who read Lord Raglan's study of the hero while writing *Invisible Man* (*Shadow and Act*, 18), put aspects of that theory to maximum ironic use in his creation of Bledsoe. Homer Barbee, whom we are to see as being no more than Bledsoe's ventriloquist's dummy (so that Bledsoe can preserve the mask of humility intact), describes Bledsoe in terms that sometimes suggest Moses and sometimes Jesus Christ. Since the Founder, to whom ignorant blacks had flocked for saving knowledge, had passed his mantle on to

Bledsoe, Bledsoe then becomes either Joshua or Peter; and the connotations are interesting, for in the improvements that Barbee claims Bledsoe made to the campus, Bledsoe is projected as having taken blacks to the Promised Land, or like Peter, as having built the "black church of knowledge," the instrument of black salvation.

It is with this general omnipotence derived, contrary to Barbee's suggestion, from guileful cunning that Bledsoe describes himself when speaking in confidence to the protagonist. But that cunning involves telling white people what they want to hear and showing them only what, from long study of them, he knows they are willing to see; and these never include the truth about black reality. In addition, Bledsoe communicates to the protagonist that if one knows how to protect white people from ever having to confront their guilt (which the protagonist, in taking the white Mr. Norton into the black slum, had not done), he could rise to prominence in America. Furthermore, "the dumbest black bastard in a cotton patch knows the only way to please a white man is to tell him a lie" (137). He even goes on to suggest that the real education of blacks is learning the art of dissembling to whites. All in all, Bledsoe believes, and the experience of the protagonist bears him out, that if blacks presented whites with truth, black institutions that took one hundred years to build would be torn down in a day; that's the "difference between the way things are and the way they're supposed to be" (139).

We see subsequently that Bledsoe is no bumbling trickster but one who has studied black–white relations and manipulated them to carve a niche for himself:

Negroes don't control this school or much of anything else—haven't you learned even that? No sir, they don't control this school, nor white folk either. True they support it, but *I* control it. I's big and black and I say 'Yes, suh' as loudly as any burrhead when it's convenient, but I'm still king down here....

These white folks have newspapers, magazines, radios, spokesmen to get their ideas across. If they want to tell the world a lie, they can tell it so well that it becomes the truth; and if I tell them you're lying, they'll tell the world even if you prove you're telling the truth. Because it is the kind of lie they want to hear....

It's a nasty deal and I don't always like it myself. But you listen to me; I didn't make it, and I know that I can't change it. But I've made my place in it and I'll have every Negro in the country hanging on tree limbs by morning if it means staying where I am....

I mean it, son.... I had to be strong and purposeful to get where I am. I had to wait and plan and lick around.... Yes, I had to act the nigger!... Yes! (*Invisible Man*, 140–41).

One notes that the statements are replete with apologies, but the process has made him a monster:

"Hee, hee!" Bledsoe laughed. "Your arms too short to box with me, son. And I haven't had to really clip a young Negro in years. No," he said getting up, "they haven't been so cocky as they used to...

"Ole Doc's been 'buked and scorned and all of that. I don't just sing about it in chapel, I *Know* about it. But you'll get over it; it's foolish and expensive and a lot of dead weight. You let white folk worry about pride and dignity—you learn where you are and get yourself power, influence, contacts with powerful and influential people—then stay in the dark and use it" (142).

Bledsoe has therefore been metamorphosed into the capitalists who have made him; but unlike them, he does not believe the hypocritical statements he is sometimes forced to make in order to preserve his position. With the protagonist the unmasked Simon Peter, the unmasked Joshua, is a monster and is unapologetic about it. Had Homer Barbee possessed any *vision*, one wonders whether he could have portrayed Bledsoe as reaching the Promised Land, unless, of course, he were an advertiser, paid strictly to sell a product.

In Bledsoe, therefore, the trickster tradition is taken too far. Here folklore does not nourish, it dehumanizes. Ellison wished his reader to be repelled by Bledsoe whom he intended as a symbol of black leadership, of which he says, "beyond their special interests they represented white philanthropy, white politicians, business interests and so on...they acknowledged no final responsibility to the Negro community for their acts and implicit in their roles were acts of betrayal" (*Shadow and Act*, 18–19). It is evident, then, that rather than emulate Bledsoe as a model of black survival, one should run from him. His suggestion of using power in the dark is, however, utilized somewhat comically by the protagonist in terms of the number of light bulbs he uses to illuminate his cellar. Addison Gayle faults the protagonist for not using Bledsoe's techniques (1974, 208); but clearly Ellison does not want him to.

What we see in *Invisible Man* is a delicate working into fiction of the folklore surrounding the trickster. Here Ellison does not sacrifice fictional demands to folklore or let folklore attempt to do what fiction should. He does not let the folklore stand in place of authentic characterization or situations that motivate the characters. But Ellison's characters reflect on the folklore resources available in the community and use them for survival purposes.

By way of his trickster figures, Ellison makes several comments on the nature of Afro–American survival. The Bledsoes—self-seekers masquerading as leaders—further chain blacks to white oppression. The black confidence man in his protean guises is a dazzling parasite who feeds off the white folk while reinforcing their illusions. In the Vet one sees marginal benefits from the plantation trickster's clever oratory, but still he remains the inmate of a psychiatric institution. The protagonist affirms that because staying alive and staying sane are paramount, trickery is valid until such time as white America permits black America to share in the fullness of America. He categorically rejects blacks who survive by preying on their people, either as confidence men or as enforcers of white restrictions. He employs instead the plantation trickster's cunning to siphon off "power" from the power-holders, and to create an art of self-understanding. It is an art that is created, like the blues musician's art, from the very ropes intended to strangle him, and thereby he paradoxically avoids strangulation. Yet the final "note" is that the invisibility imposed on him makes useless his undertaking of what is necessary to be fully American—his playing a constructive role in American society. Having converted his odyssey into art he is no longer certain of its value. After all he is well aware that language is a vital part of the confidence game, and he must wonder whether his own art does not trick him further into invisibility. In short, the wearers of masks possess no certitude about their identity and are not fully sure of the efficacy of their acts.

THE LATE FIFTIES AND BEYOND

Richard Wright's Tyree in *The Long Dream* (1958) bears many of the marks of the trickster. To the white chief of police, Cantley, Tyree behaves like a Sambo. Yet he is clever in that he saves evidence of all the bribes he pays to Cantley for his permission to operate houses of prostitution and gambling dens in places that are evidently fire hazards.

Wright uses the burning of the Grove, the name of one of Tyree's whorehouses, and its resulting forty-two dead bodies to focus on the limitations of trickery. For despite Tyree's precautions, his grinning, etc., it is not these that would save him, but rather his ability to point to the chief's culpability, to be tried by a jury of his peers—in short, his fundamental rights as an American citizen. When Wright shows that Cantley can order the interception of Tyree's incriminating evidence, can shoot Tyree down as soon as he perceives him to be a threat, Tyree's boasts about his cunning evaporate. Thus, implicit in the novel is the question of the value of this type of folk behavior. It is as if Wright, responding to Baldwin's criticism of *Native Son* for its absence of the institutions of black survival, sets out to question the relevance of such folklore. Part of his strategy in doing this is to show the limits of folklore in the figure of the trickster.

Wright's return to an overt fictive use of black folklore after a lapse of twenty years can be accounted for in several ways. Baldwin's criticism of Wright for failing to deal with black institutions in his fiction had again become the subject of much debate, rekindled by the publication of *Invisible Man* (1952) and *Go Tell It on the Mountain* (1953). In addition, Wright's trip to the Gold Coast in 1953, from which resulted *Black Power* (1954), caused him to reflect deeply on the function of folklore. Wright was savage in his attack on African folklore, and black and white critics were equally savage in their attacks on *Black Power*. In 1957 the essays comprising *White Man, Listen* appeared; in them Wright comments on the negative functions of religion and black folklore in general, on folklore's retarding role in the development of the identities of nations emerging from colonial domination, etc. The topic of folklore was therefore foremost in his thoughts and certainly in the thoughts of the critics of Afro–American literature. Wright prolonged the debate in fiction. He invites his readers to look closely at the so-called "black institutions" (underscored in Baldwin's essays) by which blacks survive. He characterizes the trickster as a pimp (a portrayal reinforced by other writers: Hughes and Ellison, for example). He makes Tyree an undertaker in a triple sense: he buries the actual dead; he buries the ghetto's "living dead" in prostitution; and through his false assurance in the value of his own cunning promotes his own death. There are several references describing the blacks of Clintonville as dead; one of them is particularly vivid: noticing how cleverly his father defends himself against a charge by another black, Fishbelly observes his father's effectiveness when dealing with "dead folks" and his ineptitude when dealing with "white folks."

In Tyree, Wright no doubt hoped to silence Baldwin's criticism. *Bona fide* social institutions in America, he implies, confer trial by a jury of one's peers, a right to prove one's innocence, and a right to pursue legitimate forms of commerce. Since trickery in the South can procure none of these, since it is a tool for the further prostituting of the black race, and since it undermines the morals of the black community, what then is its value? Let the trickster seek his basic American rights and he is gunned down. The argument is unquestionably a powerful one but it lacks nuancing (In the next chapter we shall see that in this work he demolishes all the arguments in favor of the black church). In Fishbelly's escape to France, Wright suggests that one flees such a reality; one does not accommodate it. Undoubtedly Wright puts forth the other side of the trickster's dialectic, but in promoting it as the whole reality, he trivializes the trickster's complexity.

In Cecil Brown's *The Life and Loves of Mr. Jiveass Nigger* (1969) (cited hereafter *Life and Loves*), in which the protagonist George Washington is given many of the attributes of the trickster. Two salient points emerge from Brown's depiction of his trickster. The first is that cunning can give one a sense of superiority if one is able to turn notions designed to humiliate into profit. George Washington is aware of this since his adolescence. The second point is that unless carefully employed, trickery can transform an individual into a parasite, at which point it ceases to contribute to his self-esteem, and can bring about his degradation, making him therefore a victim of his own games. George realizes this in Copenhagen when he becomes aware that what he deemed survival through cunning was essentially the life of a gigolo, a life that robs him of authenticity.

As a young man George derives a certain pleasure from tricking white people. In so doing he shows that it is essentially by manipulating his knowledge of white racism, the guilt from that racism, and white stereotypes about blacks that he is able to succeed. He is able to get two dollars from a "cracker" by telling him that he and his friend are visiting from Harlem where "you kin go for weeks without a mouthful to eat" (*Life and Loves*, 28). Moreover, in Harlem, one of his brothers had died from starvation; and it was for this reason that he had returned to the South to find something to eat. The "cracker" then talks of his grandmother who travels halfway across town to feed a poor "colored" family. The "cracker" is later moved to demonstrate his own generosity, as it were, to live up to the tradition of "Southern hospitality"; he therefore asks the question for which George had set the stage: "Have you boys had any breakfast?" George replies that they have had none in a long time. When the "cracker" suggests that they stop to get some, George, who wants the money to buy wine, states that they did not want to eat with white people, thus letting the "cracker" think that George knows "his place." Quite pleased with such exemplary conduct, the "cracker" gives them some money "so you kin buy a decent meal." Before they part George tells the "cracker" that someday he is going to be a writer and he will publicize the South as the place where all the starving colored people of the North should go to get something to eat. George gets the two dollars and celebrates his victory with his friend Reb, who remains astonished by George's facile lying. It should be noted that George had never left the South and that he and Reb were merely skipping school that day.

Behind George's game is the careful observation of white southerners' opinions of themselves as saviors. In this incident, which occurs early in the book, Brown outlines the trickster's psychological terrain. George goes on to state his philosophy: "I jive people if I don't trust them, see. I jive that motherfucker because I don't feel right with him . . . That white cracker ain't no friend of mine so I jive him" (*Life and Loves*, 31).

Brown lets Doc tell the old plantation story about Efan, who gets in trouble for his boasts, and who, when confronted with someone several times his strength, slaps his master's wife, and thereby frightens his opponent into running away. This story is told ostensibly to point out the long tradition of trickery in the slave psyche and probably to show that an element of desperation, maybe even childishness, is to be found in the trickster.

In Denmark, George uses his knowledge of the white psyche to get money from Miss Smith, the American consul. But when she finally decides to give it, she demands that George become her stud; not to comply with her wish means deportation. George also has ample opportunity to observe other black males in the process of "tricking" white women. Finally he comes to realize that he is no more than a gigolo who must comply with the stereotypes of those he thinks he is duping. After much analysis of his lifestyle, George understands his trickster role as "not living from your insides" (121). In the "epilogue" the author as narrator suggests strongly that what passes for trickery may be merely an illusion, for whites "need to understand you. Need to. If they fail to understand how you live they'll kill your ass..." (213).

It is quite possible that Brown wished George-as-gigolo as a metaphor of the real life of a trickster, for when one focuses on both lifestyles one begins to find parallels. Addison Gayle probably had such an idea in mind when he wrote that Ellison's Rhinehart is invalid as a metaphor of Afro–America (1972, 208). George-as-gigolo is Miss Smith's toy as much as Tyree is Cantley's tool. George's realization that unless whites control the game they kill you is, as we have seen, exactly what happens to Tyree. On still another level, Brown shows that his trickster perpetuates the minstrel tradition, for he must pare his image to fit the white lens; the reality is pare or perish, much as early black minstrels acted out the white man's fantasies of blacks as lechers, half-wits, cannibals, etc.—for a little pay. We do not see here the plantation trickster who gets to know massa's plans ahead of time and sets out to frustrate him; for example, agreeing with massa to provide him with the tops and then planting turnips (Courlander, 1976, 438–40).

Published at the height of the Cultural Nationalism debate, Brown's novel reflects the dominant thesis at the time: that black culture should reject the defensive postures blacks had adopted to conform to white demands of them. Brown's epilogue, in which the author literally tells the moral of the story, is characteristically didactic; one cannot but note the parallels with Addison Gayle's feeling that the function of black literature is to liberate blacks to be themselves (1972, 205). According to Carolyn F. Gerald, one of the articulators of Cultural Nationalism, the new black writer is expected to be an iconoclast ([1969] 1972, 349). Hoyt Fuller, equally a promoter of the New Aesthetic, writes that "the new literature is characterized by a...rejection of values that have proved useless or destructive or debasing" ([1970] 1972, 338). It is exactly this posture that George Washington assumes.

Brown makes it obvious to the reader that he is writing a contemporary fable. And as with all fables we seek to know its meaning and we find it in what he says about the trickster. In the story of Efan, trickery is shown to have been valid during slavery, even if it was born out of desperation; today the chief value of such stories, Brown implies, is the feeling of community that such tale-telling gives the group—in the case of the novel, the community of blacks in Copenhagen. In George's and Reb's game on the "cracker," trickery is appropriate for adolescents. As an attribute of manhood, however, it is self-prostituting. A forward-looking, self-liberating people cannot tote along defenses that were appropriate when they were a subject people. To do so would negate their freedom. It would be analogous to adults perpetuating the games of adolescence. It is on this basis that Brown relegates the trickster to the past. In the definition that Brown provides for blackness—"strong will," "true identity," "return to origin,"—it is authenticity of self that he affirms. Except as an icon in the evolution of the Afro–American people such a definition excludes the trickster.

If there exists a way of labeling Leon Forrest's *The Bloodworth Orphans* (1977) (cited hereafter *Orphans*), it would have to be as elemental art, art whose preoccupation is with origins. Forrest focuses on the people's rituals although he lets the masks slip often enough to reveal the insecurity they hide. Folklore is his road into his characters, and the forceful impact of the lore on the reader is clearly what Forrest intends, the lore fused in metaphor and effervescing ritual. The title of the novel is its unifying metaphor, which echoes in the line from the spiritual "Sometimes I feel like a motherless child" all the way through the work. What Ellison does in very lucid prose Forrest does somewhat cryptically—that is, he explores the Afro–American soul via its sojourn in America. That Forrest chooses, however, to integrate several strands of international folklore makes enormous demands on the reader. Slavery, disguised in varying forms, is omnipresent, like a heart throb not always immediately felt; it represents the absence of a foundation, it creates a need to camouflage such an absence, and it produces an ongoing scarring: the result of monstrous seeds having been sown. Looming at the center of this fictive universe is the orphan status of the characters, orphans who do not know their parents and who discover sometimes with tragic results that a spouse is indeed a brother or a sister. The penitentiary from which Noah and Nathaniel eventually escape is the novel's symbol for the existence whites permit blacks in America.

It is difficult to weave a literary garment for Forrest's trickster figure, Ford. This is due undoubtedly to Forrest's idea that all art must be innovative (1977, 631). It is an innovation which, while the reviewers praised his work for it, has resulted in the critics ignoring it. It is impossible to give a plot summary of *The Bloodworth Orphans*. How can one linearize the earlier novel, *There's a Tree More Ancient than Eden* (1973) before beginning to analyze it? Evoking an ethos is Forrest's principal preoccupation, and thus the traditional function of narrative becomes radically modified.

In attempting to fictionalize all the facets of the trickster in Ford, Forrest certainly gave himself an enormous task. He seeks to present him as a mythic force embodied in character. We get three versions of him: one from La Donna Scales, whose Roman Catholic convent upbringing ill equips her to deal with him and leaves her his victim; another from La Donna's recently discovered brother Thig-pen; and the third and least reliable but most creative from Noah Grandberry, who is a long associate and sometimes partner, and who so much resembles him and is so closely associated with him that he is glad to be in hiding.

After listening to Noah's account of Ford's exploits, many of which Nathaniel knows are the products of Noah's fertile mind and masterful techniques of oral artistry, he wonders, "how many persons were collected in the body of this Ford? how many tumblers of tall tales made up the circular tower of this evil one?" (*Orphans*, 339). We know that the building in which Noah and Nathaniel are imprisoned is emblematic of white control over black life. This point is reinforced when we see how Noah and Nathaniel outwit the authorities by making a creative life of their imprisonment. They begin by creating new games out of the games they find hidden in the cupboards of the room. They are also able to devise contraptions that assure them enough power to keep the television and lights operating.

Although imprisoned on the sixtieth floor, Noah and Nathaniel are able to devise strategies whereby Nathaniel can leave the prison and seek outside what is needed to complement the resources on the inside. They tie together bed sheets and strait jackets to form a rope and paint the prison uniform so that it resembles a dashiki. "With a tarred-up and rough-looking pistol, Nathaniel robbed two meat stores at gun point and stole back into the hospital." On the way up he steals medicine from the intensive care ward for Noah's cold. Inside the prison, they are also able to get more than the system wishes them to have. Noah acquires a store of bourbon; Nathaniel knocks down a guard and steals his reefers (285–86).

This type of portrayal is allegorical, conveying not only the survival techniques of Afro–Americans but also their morality fashioned in reaction to the dominant one. Here, one sees in Nathaniel and Noah the survival cunning that is personified in Ford and that Ralph Ellison describes as establishing a culture "on the horns of the white man's dilemma" (*Shadow and Act*, 301). Nathaniel's painting of his prison tunic—his seal of imprisonment—to make it into a bright dashiki conveys Afro–American cleverness in manipulating and transforming into survival art those forces intended to dehumanize them. The bedsheets, blankets, noose-like strait jackets that comprise the rope by which Nathaniel is lowered into the streets show the patchwork of the trickster's tools and his facility at improvising whatever is at hand into creative survival. The reefer that Nathaniel robs from an orderly, along with Noah's stock of bourbon, by which they stay "high," reflects the wisdom of turning away from situations one cannot momentarily modify. There is a new element in Nathaniel's and Noah's cooperative trickery; together they are able to accomplish what singly they could not do. Such cooperative trickery already existed in the folklore. A folktale affirms that it was through cooperative trickery that blacks gained their freedom from slavery. It is through such combined efforts that Noah and Nathaniel are finally able to escape from the Refuge Hospital. In short, then, it is Forrest's vision of the way Afro–Americans will defeat racism.

From none of the three portraits given of Ford can we quantify him. It is amusing that Nathaniel is imprisoned for the purpose of giving information that the authorities hope will lead to Ford's arrest. The joke that Nathaniel and Noah share is, which Ford do the authorities wish to arrest? For when all the strands of Ford are united, he becomes unquestionably the embodiment of Afro–American cunning and confidence men in general. Nathaniel, in the acts we have already witnessed, incorporates Ford; even more so does Noah whose Ford is mostly his own confabulation. And Amos Thig-pen prides himself on his "Fordian" qualities: his early use "of duplicity and manipulation as a way of getting back at life...and as a way of embracing the highest form of survival and manipulation of life" (*Orphans*, 245). Yet Ford represents ruthlessness, a total embrace of human beings as tools, of human dreams as raw materials to exploit; for him the world must always be victim, himself victor. But as a weapon against oppression, as we see in Nathaniel, he represents salvation from total oppression; and as art, for Noah, he represents therapy. In the extreme, though, he is destruction. He represents God in terms of the total power he is sometimes invested with as well as in his indestructibility and the promise he holds out to those duped by his games. Thig-pen speculates on this aspect of Ford, particularly his invisibility, noting that it was to Ford's force that people responded; he was present only in times of crises. All in all, Ford, as we shall see in terms of the expectations of others, is the secular equivalent of that force that gives magic flesh to the "dry bones" in the desert of America—when blacks are not listening to their preachers effect the reincarnation.

Let us look at the three portraits of Ford. La Donna's diary informs us that he wears a green cape, and "a broad white hat" sporting red and blue feathers. His greenish-blue eyes change colors and hold a penetrating gaze. His face is ageless and "he moves with the grace of an eighteen-year-old youth." Depending on whether he is standing or sitting one is very uncertain of his height. He exudes a very strong, goat-like odor.

Habitually he carries around miniature globes, which he gives to acquaintances as a symbol of trust. He believes in astrology and makes whatever positive connections he is able to between his own and his listener's astrological sign. He is proud of the fact that Dr. Martin Luther King and Jesus Christ were, like him, Capricorns. He dazzles with conversation in such a way that the listener forgets the subject matter. Building bridges between people by giving people bridges to build is his method of operation (242–43).

In this impression of Ford Forrest infuses the trickster with the metamorphosing qualities with which he is described in his aboriginal habitat. Here one sees too the symbols—the globe, for example—with which he confuses in order to manipulate, as well as the associations that function, like a juggler's distractions, to further deceive.

Thig-pen, as we have already seen, admires and emulates Ford's duplicity and is even prepared to attribute a deistic quality to him. In addition, and in keeping with Thig-pen's own psychological state, he describes Ford as asexual, a further suggestion that Ford is for him too a projection of his own ego.

Grandberry's portrait of Ford is enriched with borrowings from jive and "lies." As in the blues narratives and the John Henry narratives, the teller becomes a character in the action. Thus the portrait is a very intimate one. One can only give a few examples from the many incidents Noah credits him with.

As Bishop St. Palm, Ford, who is light-skinned, convinces his followers that the blond girl who is his accomplice is his sister. He chooses her carefully, ensuring that she is from a well-established family, one the law-enforcing authorities would not dare to embarrass.

Above the pulpit of the church, which the girl as slumlord owns, is a golden coffin that Ford enters by way of a fishnet ladder, while a steel guitar plays religious songs. Underneath the pulpit is an Egyptian cobra "in a veiled water tank," and below that are the stills in which Ford brews the moonshine that he peddles to his congregation as divine wine. Forty days before Easter, Ford begins a feast, remaining in the coffin until Easter morning, when he will rise to give the congregation "the word on the wine 'as it is revealed to me, through me, and through our Lord and Divine Savior, Jesus Christ' " (*Orphans*, 327).

Ford also knows how to exploit the old myths, particularly those of Genesis. On one such occasion he has the blond declare that she is Eve, who had been rescued by Ford after Adam (who is drugged and asleep nearby) had deserted her. Following this he serves the people fruit and jugs of milk and honey. Several days later, in an Oral Roberts' style crusade, he arranges with Noah to enact miracles and to command God to action.

The following passage depicting Ford is a brilliant emulation of the techniques of the Afro–American oral tradition:

Try as they might to subdue him, Ford toppled and darted and bopped about, like a half-mad fish on a hook—and goddamit if that old slick-swine wasn't beating back snakes with a graveyard snake and an Egyptian cobra now, with Gay-Rail high upon his shoulders; her blond tresses storming the breeze like a fleet of warring snakes; ...climbing up into one of the highest trees and then leaping and now flying with her atop his shoulders, from one tree to the next, with his tuxedo tail tucked under her bottom to cover her lilac drawers and outfit of seven veils.... The tree commenced to climb off the ground! ... The very roots striking out, like furious snake-heads, as several group members shot at the tree and the preacher and my girl, until the tree actually took off and then they all hit the ground as if under military siege. You never heard such praying going on (*Orphans*, 336–37).

There are numerous sources from which Noah culls his impressions to create his Ford. There is the serpent from the Garden of Eden, Milton's Eve, Elijah, Noah and the Flood, Moses—especially Cecil B. De Mille's movie version—, the Gorgon, Jonah, the various hoodoo personages in Hurston's *Mules and Men* (193–256), Tarzan and Jane, and Jesus Christ. His story is replete with satire against ignorant whites, blacks, himself, who are in search of a savior figure and who unwittingly make themselves Ford's victims.

While he creates or recreates his portrait of Ford, Noah makes several throwaway comments that imply why the confidence man and mythic figure he depicts Ford as being thrive: "Young rookie, you don't know the half of Ford. And, son, until you do, you don't know a thing about life and liberty. For his shifting soul is laced within the very spirit of the economy" (287). Here one is reminded of La Donna's description of his color-changing eyes, providing as it were a microcosm of Ford's self. The colors of his hat are those of the American flag. The feathers are reminiscent of Yankee Doodle and therefore of the War of American Independence. The green cape evokes fertility, the land of possibilities that America was/is perceived to be. The miniature globe connotes the magnitude of the American dream, and reminds one of another folk expression that recurs frequently in the novel: having the world in a jug and the stopper in one's hand. La Donna's description of Ford makes us think of Karl Shapiro's poem "Boy-man," which articulates a concept of America as a country of adolescents, devoid of values and tradition (La Donna remarks that Ford looks no more than eighteen). For the American, states Shapiro's narrator, "Time like a panama hat sits still... / The word has just begun, / And every city waiting to be built..." ([1953] 1978, 104). Ford, too, is the American melting pot: he is Amer–Indian, black, and white. What we perceive as his ruthlessness is the American national spirit stripped of its many disguises; his more fantastical elements are related to the wishful elements of the American dream. Take, for example, Noah's remark after Ford is narrated to have served honey and milk and fruit: "Ford was basing his replenishment theory on the Edenic land found after the Flood.... Old Ford was bringing heaven to earth without consulting Mao or Marx" (332). In Noah's story that the people chased him as he attempted to tell them the truth about Ford, the notion is implicit that Ford functions as a savior-figure, and so great is their need of him that they could not risk finding out that he is not what they wish him to be.

Having seen all three accounts of Ford, we still find him an elusive figure; furthermore Noah, whom Nathaniel at the outset thinks is Ford, seems to be Ford in another guise, the tall tale-teller. It does not matter, for all the characters who are depicted as outwitting the system incorporate elements of Ford. He is a very complex personification of cunning.

Forrest's trickster is radically different from those we have seen so far. There are some resemblances to Ellison's Invisible Man in that Nathaniel's encounter with Ford is part of his survival quest; but while the quest of Ellison's protagonist brings him to a full understanding of his invisibility as well as the means of employing it for his survival, the quest of Forrest's Nathaniel takes him to a concrete prison and forces him to develop mechanisms to subvert the intent of that imprisonment. Ford's portraiture should not be seen apart from the other characters nor, it should be added, from the series of black rituals cleverly telescoped into one another to form the novel's skeletal structure. Robert Lee writes that "*The Bloodworth Orphans* is conceived on the scale of *Ulysses* or Faulkner's Snopes Trilogy. Forrest ranges over a wide canvas which requires equally patient unravelling" (1980, 247). Both of the writers to whom Lee alludes are cited by Forrest as writers whose works he admires, studies, and teaches as great literature (1977, 631). And regarding his artistic vision, he states, "One of my visions as a black artist is the sense of ancestral responsibility, of purifying language to get our eloquence rounded, felt-like in the centre of the arena" (1977, 636). While that purity of language is not fully achieved in *The Bloodworth Orphans*, it is certainly a powerful novel, with the chameleon Ford, whose tentacular force extends in and out and around everyone, accounting for much of its power.

The trickster-preacher is a common occurrence in American literature. Alice Childress and Langston Hughes are among the Afro–American novelists who treat the trickster-preacher. Hughes' Laura in *Tambourines to Glory* (1958) and Childress' Mountain Seeley in *A Short Walk* (1979) are both satirical portraits. They share many of the traits we have already seen in Titus, Rhinehart, and Ford. Both portraits are firmly anchored in the "other" notion of the black preacher. The extent to which the black population was suspect of its preachers' intentions is documented in a sociological study conducted by Atlanta University in 1913 (DuBois [1914] 1968, 108).

One point that Hughes makes, as he shows Laura peddling "holy water" and divining numbers, and as we overhear the Harlem residents commenting on her sexual affair with Buddy, is that Laura engages in the duplicity with the complicity of her congregation. Raised in an amoral environment—her schooling was paid for with "bathtub likker"—Laura's morality is different from that of mainstream America. Hughes drew on his real-life experience with Dr. Becton, the parasite preacher, who was often a guest preacher in the church pastored by Countee Cullen's father, to create his portrait of Laura (*Big Sea*, 275–78). But regardless of the community's feelings toward Laura, Hughes dramatizes his disapproval for this form of duplicity by showing that it holds little salvation for Afro–America. In fact, he removes her from the stage to make place for Essie, for whom religion is the provision of social services for impoverished blacks.

Mountain Seeley is an all-out confidence man, who goes from city to city offering to perform miracles for a fee. The musical apparatus of the trickster-preacher, his ostentatious dress, his lechery, the word games he plays in defense of his lifestyle are all present in Childress' portrait. Because similar traits help to delineate Laura's character, we can safely assert that Hughes and Childress drew from a common lore.

Within the world of Childress' novel we encounter a wide array of characters, all of whom have little choice in what they do but are nevertheless very creative in their limited spheres of activity. By putting Mountain into this survival perspective, Childress implies no condemnation of him; he simply uses those talents he possesses to survive in the areas of the American jungle where his cunning is able to make a clearing.

In looking at these several portraits of the trickster in the Afro–American novel, we are, as it were, observing John in postslavery America. The work of art could easily be a ritual in which we are all participating, except that we witness the performance alone. Most of the portraits we see here suggest that John is definitely not getting the better of massa, for since Abolition, massa's weapons have grown deadlier. John's techniques too are decidedly postemancipation, for he has incorporated many of massa's mores: his tricks, like massa's, are played on blacks; in some instances, his contempt for blacks almost equals massa's. Some writers suggest that his practices are debilitating for himself and the black struggle for justice in America.

4

Rituals

DEFINING RITUALS

While the inclusion of archetypal figures from black folklore in the Afro–American writer's character portraits gives added significance to his work, it is in the rituals of his characters that we see the values, profoundest beliefs, and existential outlook of the black folk. Furthermore, it is frequently through the characters' response to certain rituals that the author succeeds in conveying essential character traits or in nuancing traits elsewhere portrayed. Besides, for the creation of an Afro–American ethos no other aspect of Afro–American reality is as potent as the ritual. It is inevitable, then, that in works where the characters embody very definite traits from black American legendary heroes, Afro–American rituals also abound, for the one complements the other.

Before discussing specific rituals in selected Afro–American novels, we need to define what is meant by ritual. According to Margaret Mead, "we do not normally talk about the things that people do everyday, although they are patterned and habitual, as ritual" (1973, 19). In this chapter ritual refers to those forms of behavior devised by a people over long periods of time to reinforce the key values of their culture and to promote social harmony and individual and group confidence. This definition implies that ritual is a way of ordering the chaos of existence or a way of programming the individual within the society so that he or she does not fall victim to that chaos. Thus E. R. Leach tells us that "ritual action and belief are alike understood as forms of symbolic statement about the social order" (in Skorupski, 1976, 19). To take an example from the Afro–American context, up to two decades ago when a state of inequilibrium occurred between the black and white segments of southern communities, it was customary for blacks to gather at their church and pray before facing the practical aspects of their plight. To some people such an act may appear passive; but on close reflection, we can see that the prayer ritual relieves tension and leaves the participants with better mental control to plan strategies for dealing with the crisis. The meeting at a central location serves also to unite the community against the anticipated ferocious brutality. In the case where they fail to avert it, the grief becomes communal and therefore less heavy on the individuals directly afflicted. If we add to these practical aspects the belief, explicit in black folk sermons and prayers, that God intervenes on behalf of those who serve him faithfully, what seems to be a passive reflex is in fact a courage-promoting exercise.

In spite of the earlier statement by Margaret Mead, deciding which action we include under ritual and which we exclude is not a simple matter. Skorupski argues that the breaking of a bottle of champagne at the launching of a ship, the cutting of a ribbon to open a new road, or burning the effigy of an unpopular figure are simply "ceremonial embellishments" (1976, 172). The cutting of the ribbon perhaps is, but if the champagne is intended to appease maleficent forces of the sea—especially where it is sanctioned by legends of harm coming to the ship where the custom had been omitted—such an act could qualify as ritual; and if the burning of the effigy of an unpopular figure serves to dissipate the people's anger against him or for that matter prevent the people from burning him, one could argue that this act has a ritual function. S. P. Nagendra implicitly supports Skorupski's position with his statement that ritual is "an expression of primordial existential urge for integration with the whole that transcends and transfigures it" (1971, 7). For both of these scholars ritual is decidedly religious. Jung implies a far more liberal interpretation in his linking of ritual to man's fluid, instinctual urges that reveal themselves only in symbols ([1964] 1968, 58).

My classification of rituals in the Afro–American novel inclines towards the Jungian view. I consider, for example, a practice like playing the dozens among Afro–Americans to be ritual. One knows of no myth that sanctions it; however, to the extent that it is an exercise in which feelings that could erupt into physical violence are transformed into poetic obscenity, that it contributes to an adolescent's acquisition of verbal dexterity in a context where verbal dexterity is considered a survival asset, that it confers status on those who excel at it, the dozens may be said to have a "transcendental" function. To take another example, is the carnival festival a ritual? What is its transcendental function—if we accept transcendental qualities as integral to the definition of ritual? Yet when one considers "the denial of the flesh" that comes with the Lenten season, carnival seems to be an adequate compensation for such asceticism. The festival, then, is a psychologically equilibrating ritual.

According to Brian Wicker, "a society that...ceases to believe with any conviction in the old established rituals" that sanction it "must inevitably be faced with a crisis on a global scale" (1973, 16). Rituals are therefore inevitable in human society. When the old ones die new ones, sometimes less satisfactory than their predecessors, take their place.

In this attempt to provide some idea of what is ritual, there is no conclusive definition of what is essentially a noumenal phenomenon. We therefore need to bear in mind, as we come to examine Afro–American rituals, E. R. Leach's remark that "no interpretation of ritual sequences in man is possible unless the interpreter possesses detailed knowledge of the cultural matrix which provides the context for the rite in question" (cited in Quinn 1973, 104).

What the rituals imply about Afro–American experience, to what extent they are part of an author's dialectic, how they affect the characters immediately and remotely, and how the author adapts an essentially oral form to a literary one are the principal foci of this analysis. These will not necessarily appear as pure categories of discussion but will nevertheless form the key bases. For the most part this inquiry will be limited to the content of the novel in question.

UNCERTAIN TRANSMISSION: JAMES WELDON JOHNSON

James Weldon Johnson was among the first black American writers to recognize the fictive potential of black religious rituals. This is not at all to imply that Johnson was the first novelist to employ black rituals: In *Blake or the Huts of America* (1859), Martin Delaney's Henry exploits for political and psychological ends a ritual of "good luck conjuration" that includes Christian elements. In many of his short fictional pieces Dunbar makes sparse use of Afro–American rituals. Chesnutt too makes use of them in his short fiction.

I feel, along with Houston Baker, that Johnson's decision to examine black folklore in *The Autobiography of an Ex-Colored Man* (1912) (cited hereafter *Autobiography*) was influenced by W. E. B. DuBois' cogent discussion of the spirituals and Afro–American folk religion in the *Souls of Black Folk*, which appeared a decade earlier (Baker 1974, 21–22). Johnson's unnamed protagonist mentions that he was greatly moved by DuBois' book. Moreover, much of Dr. DuBois' material is condensed and delivered by the protagonist as part of his own reflections. I do not mean to suggest that Johnson was unaware of black American folklore—he was born in Jacksonville, Florida, where such folklore thrived, as is evidenced by the work of a fellow Floridian and friend, Zora Neale Hurston. He himself notes in his preface to *God's Trombones* (1927) that the seven poetic sermons that comprise the work "were suggested by rather vague memories of sermons I heard preached during my childhood" (5).

In *Autobiography* the protagonist, who is raised outside the black tradition and eventually assumes a white identity, chances upon black folklore as he had earlier stumbled on ragtime. But whereas he masters the art of ragtime, he rarely gets beyond being an awed spectator at, and commentator on, black religious rituals. Because the protagonist presents the "Big Meeting" in terms of theories determined beforehand, the presentation is overwhelmingly expository.

This meeting which I was lucky enough to catch was particularly well-attended; the extra-large attendance was due principally to two attractions, a man by the name of John Brown, who was renowned as the most powerful leader for miles around; and a wonderful leader of singing, who was known as "Singing Johnson." These two men were a study and a revelation to me. They caused me to reflect upon how great an influence their types have been on the development of the Negro in America. Both these types are now looked upon generally with condescension or contempt by the progressive element among colored people; but it should never be forgotten that it was they who led the race from paganism and kept it steadfast to Christianity through all the long, dark years of slavery (*Autobiography*, 490).

Up to "Singing Johnson" one could accept this description as acceptable for fiction; the rest is essayistic writing, information which, if it is to be successful fiction, should be implicit in the interactions of the characters.

Following the pattern established above, Johnson's description weaves in and out of direct presentation, summary, and interpretation of the "Big Meeting" ritual. The protagonist tells us that John Brown "was a jet-black man of medium-size with a voice like an organ peal" as well as star-preacher who gave the culminating sermon every night "after several lesser lights had already done so" (490). Concerning the sermons, the protagonist tells us that they were all alike: "Each began with the fall of man, ran through various trials and tribulations of the Hebrew Children on to the redemption by Christ, and ended with a fervid picture of the judgment day and the fate of the damned" (490). So expository are these passages that many of them are repeated *verbatim* or in only slightly altered phrasing in the preface to *God's Trombones* and in Johnson's own autobiography, *Along This Way*.

Of John Brown's preaching we are told that he "possessed a magnetism and an imagination so free and daring that he was able to carry through what the other preachers would not attempt. He knew all the arts and tricks of oratory..." (490). Because of the difficulties of reproducing on the printed page the vocal and physical aspects of ritual, parts of this description are acceptable; but the "free and daring imagination" of John Brown should have been dramatized.

It is only when Johnson comes to portraying "the Heavenly March" that his writing becomes truly fictive. The congregation immediately began...a tramp...in time with the preacher's march in the pulpit, all the while singing....Suddenly he cried: "Halt!" Every foot stopped with the precision of a company of well-drilled soldiers, and the singing ceased. The morning star had been reached. Here the preacher described its beauties....The description of the imaginary march continues in similar fashion to "the evening star,...the Milky Way,...the gates of heaven," and into heaven itself, where the preacher greets well-known patriarchal members of the Church. The whole culminates with a march around the great white throne (490–91).

This is ritual depiction at its best, for it enacts a particular people's most cherished and life-sustaining belief—that at the end of this painful life a glorious existence awaits them. In Eurocentric sects a preacher would be taxed to convey such an affirmation all by himself, nor for that matter would his congregation expect him to attain the performance of a John Brown. Here the black preacher makes the audience active participants in the ritual. With a folk audience still rooted in the tradition of the *cante-fable*, a preacher who did otherwise would risk losing its interest. It is for this reason as well, though Johnson excludes it from his ritual, that the "Amen Corner"—which affirms the veracity of the preacher's statements, encourages him to be candid, and encourages the congregation to shout—is an established part of the black folk church.

The glories that the preacher depicts here are in sharp contrast to the congregation's lives of poverty, crudity, and ignorance very briefly hinted at by the narrator. Far more poignant in throwing this ritual into relief is the lynch scene, which is described later. Still, we are not sufficiently informed about these people; and because their lives are only an infinitesimal part of the novel's drama, the ritual loses much of the significance it could otherwise have had.

Johnson wants the reader to appreciate the vital role of the spirituals to the success of "Big Meeting." In the narrator's opinion "Singing Johnson" is as important as the preacher. He must understand the mood the preacher wishes to create and evoke it in his choice of spirituals. We see too that he is vested with the power of curtailing the preaching time of a dull preacher. Thus there seems to be an understanding that the message is lost when the preacher is poor, much as a play suffers when the actors are incompetent. One of "Singing Johnson's" roles is to ensure that such preachers quickly leave the platform. Because he alone knows all the words to the spirituals and he can carry the tune way over the voices of the others, the unity of the ritual rests with him. This safeguard surely compensates for the rampant illiteracy of the congregation; or, put another way, prevents any lag in the singing from a people unconditioned to memorize a large body of songs. Again, his role is to hold the ritual together. As composer of the popular songs that his brother Rosamond put to music, Johnson certainly understood the emotive power of certain lyrics. The samples of song that he includes in the ritual reinforces the sermon that enacts the "heavenly march" all the way to the New Jerusalem. They are taken from "Swing Low, Sweet Chariot," "Steal away, Steal away to Jesus," etc., songs that express a deep yearning to flee this life, to begin the after-death life of triumph. One of the functions of these songs is to provide strategic breaks for the preacher to rest, while his message is repeated in song; the singing too activates the congregation.

The foregoing are the key aspects of Johnson's presentation of the "Big Meeting" ritual. Because he chose reportage by way of a fictive autobiography to convey the events of the novel, the drama of the work is severely muted. It is worth noting that Ernest Gaines' *Autobiography of Miss Jane Pittman* (1971), written some sixty years after Johnson's novel, is also a fictive autobiography, but its ideas are inherent in the drama of the episodes themselves. It is obvious, then, that Johnson had much trouble submerging his ideas in fiction. He shared such problems of form with other black novelists before and after him—Chesnutt, Cullen, Hurston—who did not quite know how to adapt black folklore to fiction. If we look at Johnson's attempts to deal with key aspects of black American folklore in various works—*The Book of Negro Spirituals* (1925), *The Second Book of Negro Spirituals* (1926), and *God's Trombones* (1927)—it is clear that he felt he had something important to say about the fundamentally ritual aspects of Afro–American folklore. In an Afro–American literary tradition that makes extensive use of folklore, Johnson's value lies in alerting future novelists to the rhetorical value of Afro–American rituals.

THE PEOPLE'S IDIOM—
THE HARLEM RENAISSANCE: HUGHES

Langston Hughes was more aware of literary technique than Johnson was. But this consciousness was largely the result of the groundwork that had been laid by Johnson, just as Johnson had been influenced by DuBois. Hughes was even more fortunate in that he did not create in the silence that had been the lot of earlier black writers.

Regarding his *Not Without Laughter* (1930), Hughes felt that he had failed to do justice to the survival traditions of black people, who are the subject of the novel (1940, 305). Hughes' feelings aside, it is on the saving nature of black American rituals that the novel concentrates. Harriet and her brother-in-law Jimboy obtain relief from the pain of prejudice in the blues. The rituals of the black church provide Aunt Hager, Harriet's mother, with parallel relief. But while Hughes dramatizes the blues rituals in the novel, those of the church are only mentioned. Their effect on Hager's life, however, are very clearly shown.

Not Without Laughter (cited hereafter *Laughter*) begins on the note of Hager's faith in a God that intervenes to help his faithful followers when they call upon him. This is the only way we can explain her certitude that God intervened to prevent her from being caught in the cyclone that blows away her front porch and kills the white Gavitts. Hager continues this line of thought as she sets out to "see what mo' de Lawd has 'stroyed or spared" (*Laughter*, 7). Thus we are introduced to Hager's relationship to the world and God, who for her is both terror and benevolence.

Her grandson Sandy, about ten years old at the beginning of the novel, remarks that "all the neighbourhood, white or colored, called his grandmother when something happened. She was a good nurse, they said, and folks like to have her around. Aunt Hager always came...Sometimes they paid her and sometimes they didn't" (9). Hager's deeds, therefore, demonstrate the Christian creed that one should serve one's fellow men altruistically. Moreover she makes no distinctions between whites and blacks, in spite of the former's rampant bigotry throughout the novel. How then does she deal with the pain caused by prejudice?

A conversation between Hager and Sister Whiteside, a fellow church member, provides some insight into where Hager's hostility goes. Sister Whiteside affirms that being a "born-again Baptist" is a remedy for the woes that beset black people, and Hager feels that she could not belong to any church "so full of forms an' fashions that a good Christian couldn't shout" (24). Hager is echoing almost the identical words of a line found in at least three different spirituals, "I believe that every Christian has a right to shout." This shouting, which can be traced back to the field hollers of slavery, is no doubt part of Hager's release mechanism for the pain that comes from white bigotry. During their conversation Sister Whiteside informs Hager of the "big revival due to come off dis year...Great colored tent meetin' with the Battle Ax of de Lawd, Reverend Braswell preachin'! Yes Sir!..." Hager replies, "Good news!...Mo' sinners than enough's in need o' savin'! I's gwine take Sandy an' get 'im started right with de Lawd; and if that ornery Jimboy's back here, I gwine make 'im go, too, an' look Jesus in the face" (*Laughter*, 27). Very soon, therefore, Hughes gets the reader to understand that the source of Hager's strength (and narrowness of attitude to the blues) lies in her devotion to Afro–American Christian rituals and their underlying beliefs.

Hughes never shows her incorporating the dual personality that one sees, for example, in Cullen's Aunt Mandy and in the lore surrounding Afro–American Christians. To her, pleasure is sinful. In fact, Hager at times seems to exaggerate, fortunately without malice, her puritan inclinations. Her discomfort with her son-in-law comes not only from his being a blues singer and poor provider but from his being "illegitimate." That resentment, however, is only spoken; it is never shown and, together with the calm way in which Hager accepts the rejection by her social-climber daughter, Tempy, serves to illustrate the absence of a rancor-creating force in Hager. We see her day after day washing and ironing white folks' clothes, in the wet season hanging them in the house to dry; trying to balance a meagre budget; and never failing to find time to minister to the sick. Hughes attributes the patience with which she accepts his life to the deep commitment to her Christian creeds. Today we question whether religion by itself could exert such a controlling force on a person's life. It would seem that an individual must be temperamentally disposed to such stoicism before Christian doctrines could act upon him.

Black psychiatrists William Grier and Price Cobbs write in their study *The Jesus Bag*:

They have survived an attack aimed at their lives with guns and at their secret selves with the weapons of religion. They have refined and built a morality on that which has been their greatest danger. And they stand now the most moral of Americans, the most democratic of Americans and the most courageous of Americans.

They have taken a Jesus Bag shaped like a noose and refashioned it into a black cornucopia of riches (1971, 180).

How else could one explain Hager's reproof of Harriet for expressing her hatred of white people? "Harriet, ... if you don't like 'em, pray for 'em, but don't feel evil against 'em. I been knowin' white folks all ma life an' they's good as far as they can see—but when it comes to po' niggers they can't see very far, that's all" (*Laughter*, 76). Or her response to her grandson who had been refused admission to the amusement park for the simple reason that he is black? "Looking at the stars, Hager began to sing, very softly at first: 'From this worl o' trouble free / Stars beyond! / Stars beyond!'" The narrator tells us that in Hager's song Sandy "heard a great chorus out of the black past—singing generations of toil-worn Negroes, echoing Hager's voice as it deepened and grew in volume." It is on a note of triumph that she ends the spiritual—"There's a star fo' you an' me..." (213–14). Such is the power of these ritual-enforced beliefs to contain sorrow and inspire hope beyond earthly pain. Grier and Cobbs feel that such defenses have "much less to do with Christianity than Christians think." They are "rather the creative responses of a tortured, driven people" (1971, 179).

It is unfortunate that Hughes never shows Hager participating in the church rituals. Perhaps he felt that the availability of James Weldon Johnson's poetic sermons made this familiar ground. In his story "Big Meeting," Hughes shows how he would have described those rituals. In that story he focuses on the drama of catharsis inherent in black church worship. He reveals also the communal bonding that exists between the individual member and the congregation. In the sermon of Reverend Braswell he depicts how the sufferings of Jesus are made to reflect black suffering in America. Thus, in religion, blacks have various escapes by which to escape the prisons where institutionalized racism seeks to trap them.

But the religious outlook is only one response to pain in *Laughter*. Harriet, in the words of Grier and Cobbs, is one of those blacks whose "patience wears thin under the grossness of mistreatment" (1971, 168). Where Hager's vision, which is to some extent white-derived, is heavenward, Harriet's is terrestrial. She feels no need to spurn the dwellers of the Bottom, whom Hager fears, but rather feels a kinship with them. Her ritual of catharsis, then, the blues, is indigenous to her people. While Hager's piety and selflessness represent the acme of the religious intent, Harriet, too, in becoming a blues priestess, is equally effective in ministering to the secular realm. What seems initially like Harriet's desire to drown the pain of racism in hedonism turns out to be no more than part of her apprenticeship for her later role as blues priestess.

The blues concert in which Harriet, Jimboy, and the neighbors participate in Hager's backyard is a ritual of catharsis that produces a purging
of pain. According to blues scholar Albert Murray, the dance and the
rhythm are what effect this purgation (1976, 138–39). Here Harriet
dances and sometimes sings while Jimboy plays the guitar and sings.
Hager objects to the concert but remains a member of the audience until
the performance ends; periodically she prods Jimboy to play something
"decent-like." The Johnsons participate *ad lib* and at times everybody
sings the choruses, which shows that Hager is not as averse to the blues
as she thinks she is.

Through blues lyrics that tell of unfaithful love, abandonment by one's
sweetheart, etc.—fundamentally sad lyrics—Hughes lets the characters
empathize with suffering that is outside themselves. Thus the first stage of
the catharsis is obtained principally through sympathy with another. The
principle is somewhat like the aspects of reality that the ego shunts aside
during the day but which surface in various guises during sleep. This moves
on to somewhat brutally frank lyrics:

> O, I done made ma bed,
> Says I done made ma bed.
> Down in some lonesome grave
> I done made ma bed (*Laughter*, 37).

These lyrics are inherently suicidal and as such confront the death-wish
present in many spirituals and ridiculed in many black jokes and folktales.
By singing away the suicidal urge one is less inclined to yield to it.

Hughes wishes the reader to understand the communal bonding that
such a ritual produces, and so the neighbors are included. Tom Johnson
shouts approval from across his yard. His wife Sarah adds, "minds me o'
de ole plantation times, honey! It sho' do" (52). Johnson asks Jimboy to
sing "Casey Jones...so the ballad of the immortal engineer with another
mama in the Promised Land rang out promptly in the starry darkness,
while everybody joined in the choruses" (52). Why "Casey Jones?" From
what we know the ballad of "Casey Jones," a hybrid of black and white
musical styles, is about a white engineer who died in a train to make up
for lost time. The ballad highlights Casey's love for his machinery and the
sadness his death produced in his family. The tone is an extremely sad
one. The identification with Casey Jones comes in his failure to attain his
goal, much as Tom Johnson had to abandon a prosperous life in his
southern hometown because whites, jealous of the prosperity of the black
community, had burned everything the community possessed, including its
livestock. Casey Jones is a victim of his schedule, Johnson of whites—and
both are tyrannical. In singing the plight of the engineer, Johnson and
others present exteriorize their suffering by projecting it onto Casey

Jones; they can feel sorry for him, which is to say for themselves, without having to confront their plight directly; he symbolizes their suffering.

The lyrics "Here I is in dis mean ole jail..." put Johnson in a confessional mood, not unlike the church sisters in "Big Meeting." He gets as far as "Now when I was in the Turner County Jail..." before his wife commands him to shut up. Indeed the blues concert is "mass" confession—mass in both senses of religious and widespread. To borrow a term from Albert Murray's *Stomping the Blues*, one gets it out so that one could "stomp" it. It is this stomping we see Harriet doing as the ritual comes to a close.

The music continues, sometimes imitating the "hallelujahs, the moans and amens of the Sanctified Church" until an orgasmic pitch is reached: "Then with rapid glides, groans, and shouts the instrument screamed of a sudden in profane frenzy, and Harriet began to ball-the-jack, her arms flopping like the wings of a headless pigeon, the guitar strings whining in ecstasy, the player rocking gaily to the urgent music" (60). The analogy to an orgasm here is Hughes's attempt to convey the emotional intensity of the music. This is common in many Afro–American writers for essentially the same purpose; we shall see it again in Wright and Baldwin.

Hughes addresses the problem of theatrical effect by conveying as much as he can in metaphor and simile: "In the starry blackness the singing notes of the guitar became a plaintive hum, like a breeze in a grove of palmettos; became like a moan, like the wind in a forest of live-oaks strung with long strands of hanging moss" (*Laughter*, 56–57). Not only is the tone of sadness evoked in the hum and the sound pictures of the oak, but, using the technique of repetition from the blues compositions themselves, Hughes focuses on the crying that the guitar does for Jimboy. Since it is difficult for Hughes to reproduce the onomatopoetic sounds of the instrument germane to blues music, he simply tells the reader that those sounds are there.

This backyard ritual is a microcosm of the "Jam Session" Harriet defies her mother to attend, taking along the ten-year-old Sandy whom she is left to babysit.

"Aw, do it Mister Benbow" [the name of the band leader], one of his admirers shouted frenziedly as the hall itself seemed to tremble....

"Whaw, whaw, whaw," mocked the cornet—but the steady tom-tom of the drums was no longer laughter now, no longer even pleasant: the drumbeats had become sharp with surly sound, like heavy waves that beat angrily on a granite rock...Cruel, desolate, unadorned was their music now, like the body of a ravished woman on the sun-baked earth; violent and hard, like a giant standing over his bleeding mate in the blazing sun. The odor of bodies, the stings of the flesh, and the utter emptiness of the soul when all is done—these things the piano and the drums, the cornet and the twanging banjo insisted on hoarsely to a beat that made the dancers move, in that little hall, like pawns on a frenetic checker-board.

"Aw, play it, Mister Benbow!..."

"It's midnight. De clock is strikin' twelve."

"Aw, play it, Mr. Benbow" (*Laughter*, 97–98).

This intense depiction, including in many instances the lyrics of the songs, is carried on for twelve pages. This is both a naming-of-devils ceremony and a people's affirmation of its unwavering faith in the devil-exorcising power of its musician-priests. Hughes puts the sounds into images, painful pictures of rape, of powerlessness to defend those closest to one's heart. He thus implies that the musicians bring the dancers face to face with the horror of their lives and hold them there to gaze upon these images—like "pawns on a frenetic checker board." Whereas in the church the people do the confessing, here the music does it. Hughes' description is in line with Sartre's remark that "in order to understand [the] indissoluble unity of suffering, eros, and joy, one must have seen black men dance frenetically to the rhythm of the blues which are the saddest songs of the world" (1948, 31). In the way in which Hughes resorts to images to convey the emotional intensity of black rituals, he begins a tradition that has been picked up and expanded by Ellison, Baldwin, Murray (in *The Train Whistle Guitar*, 1974), and Forrest.

After her sufferings in the South and life of prostitution in Stanton, Harriet becomes a priestess of the blues. One of the persons she helps find catharsis is her sister Anjee, whose loneliness overpowers her as she thinks of Jimboy, who has fled the pain of America to embrace the pain of war. Again, the essentially religious call-response pattern is present at Harriet's concert, only this time it is decidedly more religious: "Lawd, Good Lawdy Lawd." This response is a common one at such concerts. It is out of the refrain from the "If I Had My Way" spiritual, perhaps the most militant of all the spirituals in that it enumerates Samson's feats in stanzas that express the revolutionary wishes of Afro–Americans.

Hughes understood that blues and religion were in essence similar in their cathartic and ritual effects on their audiences. Like religion to Hager, blues give meaning to Harriet's life. But there are radically different implications for each ritual. If we pursue Hager's ritual-enforced philosophy, we note that should it be practiced on a global scale—especially the singing of spirituals when one's innocent children are bruised by the wheel of bigotry—the subjugation of the black race by the white would be totally assured. The turning-the-other-cheek reality of Christianity is completely absent from the blues as are the after-death rewards. As far as the amelioration of the political and economic situation of blacks is concerned, Hager's rituals are weak, and both Harriet and Sister Johnson note it. Harriet intuits as well a connection between Hager's Christianity and white designs over black life; she therefore turns to a ritual that is indigenous to her people. In the end, Harriet is as much a minister to her people, as stoic, and generous as her mother was.

One cannot conclude this discussion of *Not Without Laughter* without looking closely at the "verbal blues," oral history session in which the older characters reflect on their "wanderings" in the wilderness" and the younger characters born *en route* to the Promised Land pour forth their complaints of bitter treatment. The episode also provides the reader with an explicit account of the painful experiences that require ritual exorcism.

The meeting place is Hager's porch. The ritual begins with the older women's inquiries about each other's health, followed by their comments on the difficulty of the white folks' work. Both women talk about their huge washload and attribute it to white folks' wickedness. This sets the tone for what is an implicit contrast throughout the session of white folks' material superiority and black folks' moral superiority.

Harriet's expression of her dislike for the church gives Sister Johnson the opportunity she needs to declaim against the black church as well as the confidential environment in which she can express her wishes for white people: "'Cause if de gates of heaven shuts in white folkses faces like de do's o' dey church in us nigger faces it'll be too bad.... One thing sho', de Lawd ain't prejudiced" (75). Sister Johnson's hope, like that of many blacks during slavery, is for retributive justice. This wish is graphically captured in the "Rich Man Dives" and "Go Down Moses" spirituals. Hager injects into the discussion her doctrine of universal love and subtly reminds Sister Johnson of the uncharitable nature of her wish. But Sister Johnson can see nothing but universal evil in the white race, and here as elsewhere she knows that they "will burn." Moreover, "White folks is white folks an' dey is mean. Ain't I been knowin' crackers sixty-five years, and ain't dey de cause o' me bein' here in Stanton.... Ain't I nussed t'ree of 'em right up from babies like ma own chillens, and, ain't dem same t'ree boys done turned round an' run me an' Tom out of town?..." She begins to tell again the tale she had told a dozen times, with Harriet and Jimboy assuring her that she had never told it, and Sandy and Willa-Mae ceasing their play to listen. The story concludes with the white section of town becoming extremely alarmed over the prosperity of blacks at the turn of the century:

Den dey say dey gwine teach dem Crowville niggers a lesson, all of 'em, paintin' dey houses an' buyin' cars an' livin' like white folks, so dey comes to our do's an' tells us to leave our houses—git de hell out in de fields.... Well, sir! Niggers in night-gowns an' underwear an' shimmies, half-naked an' barefooted, was runnin' ever' which way in de dark, scratchin' up dey legs in de briah patches, fallin' on dey faces, scared to death. Po' ole Pheeny, what ain't moved from her bed wid de paralytics fo' six years, dey made her daughters carry her out, screamin' and wall-eyed, an' set her in the middle o' de cotton-patch. An' Brian what was sleepin' naked, jumps up an' grabs his wife's apron and runs like a rabbit with not a blessed thing on.... Den looked like to me 'bout five hundred white mens took torches an' started burnin' wid fiah ever' last house, an' hen-house, an' shack, an' barn, an' privy, an' shed, an' cow-slant in de place.... When it were done nothin' but ashes. [One of the white men said]

'Well, after dis you'll damn sight have to bend yo' backs and work a little.' But we didn't—not yet. 'Cause ever' last nigger moved from there dat Sunday mawnin'.... We ain't had not even a rag o' clothes when we left Crowville—so don't tell me 'bout white folks, Hager, 'cause I knows 'em.... Dey done made us leave our home (76–80).

It is a familiar story in Afro–American history and literature. However, the twists that Hughes puts into Sister Johnson's recounting of it emphasize the Afro–American will to survive. Her telling of it is not devoid of humor, reflecting an attitude similar to the blues. The recounting of her relationships with white folks is a ritual reminder to all present of the victimization blacks have suffered; it is equally an affirmation of psychic triumph over white brutality and an opportunity to demonstrate moral superiority. At length Jimboy and Harriet tell stories of white prejudice, almost as harrowing as Sister Johnson's. The elementary school children, Sandy and Willa-Mae, who listen to such woe, learn what the white world holds for them. They already are made aware that they cannot expect just treatment from white people.

Together these rituals form the core of Hughes' novel and the basis of his characters' survival mechanisms. Because he never divorces the rituals from the oppression that is ever-present in the lives of the characters but rather shows the rituals as tools for surmounting oppression, for building community, for attaining psychic wholeness—Hughes conceives of black rituals as key factors in Afro–American survival. Nor is he hesitant to use them as structuring devices for his novel. Because the rituals are presented dramatically, their impact is immediate. Hughes is a long way from James Weldon Johnson's mostly passive, expository presentation, and he begins a long tradition of dramatic presentation of black rituals within the Afro–American novel, a tradition that endures to this day.

ENLARGING THE PERSPECTIVE:
WRIGHT, WALKER, ELLISON, BALDWIN, MARSHALL

Richard Wright's attack on the "minstrelsy" in Hurston's works is an indication of his youthful views of folklore (Hemenway 1977, 241). At this same period he wrote that the black writer has the responsibility of educating himself about his people's culture. "In order to depict Negro life in all of its complex relationships, a deep, informed and complex consciousness which draws for its strength upon the fluid lore of a great people, and moulds this lore with the concepts that move and direct the forces of history today" is an absolute necessity ([1972] 1937, 321). The intent of Wright's statement is not fully clear, but it is obvious that he perceives folklore to be one of the necessary tools that a black writer uses to do his task. Because Wright operated within theoretical perspectives, it is relatively easy to relate the folklore in his work to his general opinions of black life. In the previous chapter we saw a relationship between Bigger and the toast hero as well as the insufficiency of Tyree's trickster qualities to ensure his survival. Where Wright uses folklore in his works, it is mostly this insufficiency—the irrelevance of black beliefs and traditions to the solutions of black problems in America—that emerges. *Lawd Today*, Wright's first novel, published only after his death, contains his most extensive use of folklore. There are examples of the dozens, the blues, and the folk sermon—all used to add an element of pathos to the protagonist's existence. *Lawd Today* (the title is a blues exclamation) was written concurrently with the novellas that comprise *Uncle Tom's Children* (1938), for we know that Wright was working on it in 1937 (Walker 1973, 17). As early as "Big Boy Leaves Home" (*Uncle Tom's Children*) Wright shows a profound understanding of the psychological function and the irrational nature of ritual as well as an ability to use ritual to develop his theme and reveal the motives of his characters.

Wright uses a muted form of the dozens at the beginning of "Big Boy Leaves Home" to establish the bantering wordplay that evokes the boys' innocence. The dozens function as they ought to: they promote solidarity among the youngsters and establish Big Boy, the "man of words" among them, as the leader. Beyond that the humor inherent in the exercise relaxes the youngsters enough for them to suppress whatever fears surface about their decision to swim in Hervey's water hole. Essentially, Wright employs the dozens to establish the youngsters' innocence and to heighten the brutality visited upon them—two of them shot dead by Hervey's son merely because his wife sees their naked bodies and instinctively screams. Big Boy acts the leader's part and wrestles the rifle away from Jim and shoots him. If, Wright goes on to show, a white woman's chancing upon the naked bodies of pubescent boys justifies their being shot, how much more heinous is a black boy's killing of a white man in self-defense? The act creates a crisis of order in the white community, which then needs its own ritual to restore order.

The lynch scene becomes therefore such a rite. The ejaculatory description that characterizes the climactic moment may be seen as an ejaculation of fear, which brings the feeling of relief that once more they are in control. The very act of lynching someone, with the victim's community unable to defend him, is a potent affirmation to the lynchers of the power they exert over the captive community. That the release occurs at the moment the victim, now a human torch, screams—says something important about a community that allows itself to engage in such acts. Moreover, the situation is described in terms of a picnic.

When the rituals of blacks, as Wright describes them in his works, are contrasted with the ritual of lynching, they appear quite pale. In *Lawd Today*, in addition to the blues, religion, and the dozens, Jake also makes wife-beating into a ritual. Describing the forces that impelled him to write,

Wright states, "I hungered for a grasp of the framework of contemporary living, for a knowledge of the forms of life about me, for eyes to see the bony structures of personality, for theories to light up the shadow of conduct" (*American Hunger*, 26).

These statements are central to *Lawd Today*, where Wright shows materialism to be the pivot around which all—including the lives of Jake and his friends, their dreams, their superstitions, even their entertainment—spins. With the exception of the dozens, all the black rituals in the novel are adapted to the service of materialism, and even the dozens contain some traces of materialism. In a sense, then, one could say that Wright turned to black rituals to find a spark or two to reveal something about the effects of materialism on American blacks.

In *Lawd Today* ignorance, blind materialism, entrapment, and folly are all terms that could be used to delineate Jake's plight. Black rituals in this novel are more like poison tentacles than "the channels of racial wisdom" that Wright terms them in "The Blueprint for Negro Writing" (318). Jake is so programmed by American expectations that every act, including his dream, enriches someone else. In order for Jake to obtain the self-importance he thinks procures respectability in America, he needs to have a wardrobe with ten suits and matching shoes. It little matters that every store in the area has cut off his credit and is demanding payment, that he owes the doctor $500 and his wife's pending operation will cost another $500, and that he earns $2,100 annually. It is more important that he look successful. Consequently he must be a lavish consumer, must exhibit expensive tastes. To show that he can enjoy the life of the wealthy, he borrows $100 at 20 percent interest to have "one night on the town." We soon see that Jake gives himself a sense of power through wife-beating, even though her reporting his behavior to the post office, where he works, results in his having to pay enormous bribes to keep his job. Moreover, by showing Jake's and his friends' opinion on current affairs to be no more than a résumé of unsophisticated bigotry, Wright reveals the complete absence of personal input in Jake's and his companions' thoughts—they are merely programmed.

Wright sets the action of the novel on February 12, Abraham Lincoln's birthday, and uses intrusions from a radio broadcast about Lincoln's life and the American Civil War with ironic intent—to imply that the Civil War ended one form of slavery and materialism began another. Insofar as every character fails to confront reality and blames someone else for his plight or loses himself in a ritual of forgetfulness or is exploited by the purveyors of paradise, the novel presents a bleak and unbalanced picture of black life.

Turning to the religious rituals in the novel, we see Jake's wife, Lil, resigning herself to a childlike acceptance of naive Christian creeds. She is either reading about God's miraculous power, calling on God for help, or falling asleep on her knees. Because her life is composed strictly of her husband's physical and verbal abuse and the afflictions of her body—

related to such abuse—it is a strange solace that she derives from the fairyland type of Christianity she believes in.

Wright's *tour-de-force*, unquestionably the highlight of the novel, comes from a clever adaptation of the folk sermon to the needs of the confidence game. The two are not unrelated in that they both rely on stagecraft. The deliverer of the sermon is dressed in a checkered suit with a red tie and sets off a shower of sparks each time he moves. With a rattlesnake around his neck he beckons the crowd to him, and his antics are sufficiently clever to draw them. He assures them, "Ah got all the powers of evil in mah control." For a people conditioned to see the snake as evil, the image of a rattlesnake around his neck is more convincing than his words. In his delivery are all the syllabic accentuations and pauses of the folk sermon that James W. Johnson perceived as having the ability to move an audience to ecstasy. The comments of the impressed audience function as a veritable "Amen Corner." But it is in the flattery of his audience that he seems to be most clever:

LAdees 'n' Gen'meeeeens: Ah'ms the SNAKE MAN! Ah wuz Bo'N 'bout FOR-TEEEEEEY YEars erGo on the banks of the FAMous NILE in the COUNtreeeeey of AFRIker, yo' COUNtreeeeey 'n' mah COUNtreeeeey—in tha' LAN' where, in the YEars gone by, yo' FATHER 'n' mah FATHER rule suPREME! In mah FATHER'S day the PRINCES 'n' CROWNED heads of YOURpe came t' his feets astin' fer advice, astin' t' be tol' things they couldn't TELL themselves, astin' t' have things DONE they couldn't do themselves. The CROWNED heads of YOURpe respected mah FATHER—he wuz the WISE man of the NILE (*Lawd Today*, 99).

This passage is only the setting of the stage for deception. One sees the rough parallels between this medicine man's references to his father and those of Jesus, especially in the Gospel of John, to His Father.

The medicine man goes on to tell about having inherited his father's wisdom and techniques, the benefits of which he has come to share with the crowd. He proves his singular power with two rings that the audience is invited to unlock and naturally fails to do so. Of course, he succeeds.

Using the identical verbal techniques he moves on to phase two of the deception game by putting acid in rain water, which naturally turns dark. This is explained to the audience as defilement of the body which the leaf of a herb (obviously alkaline) makes clear again. Of course, this is God's secret revealed to him through his father. "WHUT THESE LITTLE HERBS DID FER THIS WATER THEY KIN DO FER YUH! THEY'LL DO THIS FER YUH IF YOU'LL ONLY LET 'EM 'N' THA'S THE GOSPEL TRUTH" (*Lawd Today* 103). This passage parodies the statement always present in the folk sermons that talk about the miraculous power of salvation, provided the listener is willing to give "God" a chance.

In the reactions of the crowd Wright shows how easily ignorance is manipulated, for the audience is deeply impressed and convinced about this "African's" powers. They have been primed for phase three which corresponds to the altar call:

LADees 'n' Gen'meeeeeeens, mah UNIVERSAL HERB CUREALL MEDICINE CURES NERVOUSNESS 'N' PNEUMONIA, MEASLES 'N' MENINGITIS, CORNS 'N' CANCERS, CONSUMPTION 'N' WHOOPIN' COUGH, RINGWORM 'N' RHEU-MATISM, CARBUNCLES 'N' LUMBAGO, 'N' ALL THE DIVERS AILMENTS OF THE HUMAN BODY. It prevents as well as cures, so if yuh ain't got nothin' t' matter wid yuh right now, git a bottle anyhow, jus' t' make sho'.... They's only one dollar... (*Lawd Today*, 103).

As in the folk sermon, the medicine man relies on the traditional metrical tricks. Each of the categories is the equivalent of a well-balanced line, and assonance and alliteration, adding to the hypnotic quality of the appeal, are plentiful. Apart from "The Sermon on the Mount" nothing in western tradition offers so much deliverance.

An intelligent person not seeking a miraculous existence could easily see the deception here, especially in the diseases cataloged; but for someone like Jake (and by implication the listeners of folk sermons that promise an after-death delivery), who has been raised on a literal interpretation of Christianity and whose mind is disposed to superstition, the confidence man is able to lay his hypnotic trap, and, like the folk preacher, sell de-liverance to his trapped audience. The degree of his success is shown in the large number of clients and the even larger number that leaves names and addresses for a mail order. Jake wants a bottle, which he is sure will cure Lil of her tumor and save him the $500 doctor bill.

The confidence man's approach suggests that he has studied the black man's psychology to such an extent that he knows which religious ex-pressions can sedate him. He imitates the preacher's oratorical style, espe-cially its incantatory aspects. Instead of painting the New Jerusalem he invokes a benevolent God who does not afflict His children without provid-ing them the necessary cures. Instead of the peace and bliss that come after yielding the soul to the "Maker" and the assurance of everlasting life in heaven, he offers everlasting health and freedom from medical bills. He effectively promises heaven on earth. Thus what Wright does here is to extract the rhetoric of the folk sermon and use it as a building base for the confidence game.

We see therefore in Wright's fictive use of religion a focus on its illusory nature—Lil uses it to avoid confronting life, the confidence man to "dupe" those seeking a magic formula to transform their lives. In the benefits that this ritual procures the confidence man Wright simply gives another twist to the role of materialism in American religion. An important aspect of the puritan covenant has always been material rewards from God in return for a life of devotion to His will. For the slave master the essential function of black religion during slavery was to dissipate anger and discontent, thus leaving the slave less rebellious and more profitable (Holt 1972, 189). The black confidence man here merely continues in a more colorful form a tradition that is the very soul of America.

The dozens ritual, a welcome scene in the novel because of the tedious card games that precede it, is both entertaining and revealing: entertaining because of its inherent humor, revealing because the insults the players direct against their ancestors imply a disrespect of their origins and consequently of themselves. That all present look forward to the dozens and enjoy it immensely reflects the extent to which they are delighted to see "feces hurled in the ancestors' faces." The purpose of the ritual is to underscore Jake and his friends' psychological arrestation and self-hatred. This performance and a few snatches of blues songs represent the totality of Jake's artistic appreciation. H. Rap Brown, a frequently cited authority on the dozens, remarks that adults do not play the dozens (1969, 27); and Grier and Cobbs perceive it as an initiation rite for the purpose of demonstrating self-control in early adolescence (1971, 5–6). Following are excerpts from the game:

"Listen, nigger," said Jake, "I was wearing shirts when you was running around naked in Miss'sippi."

"Hunh, hunh," said Al. "That was the time when you was wearing your hair wrapped in white strings, wasn't it?"

"White strings? Aw Jake! ... Hehehe!" Bob could not finish the idea tickled him so.

"Yeah," said Jake, "when I was wearing them white strings in my hair Old Colonel James was sucking your ma's tits, wasn't he?"

"Jesus," moaned Slim ... "I told a piece of iron that once and it turned *redhot*. Now what would a poor *meat* man do?"

Al glowered and fingered his cigarette nervously. "Nigger," Al said slowly, so that the full force of his words would not be missed, "when old Colonel James was sucking at ma's tits I saw your little baby brother across the street watching with slobber in his mouth..."

Slim and Bob rolled on the sofa and held their stomachs. Jake stiffened, crossed his legs, and gazed out the window.

"Yeah," he said slowly, "I remembers when my little baby brother was watching with slobber in his mouth, your old grandma was out in the privy crying 'cause she couldn't find a corncob...."

The ritual insults go on until they reach far back into the African ancestry:

"Yeah," drawled Jake, determined not to be outdone, "when my old greatgreatgreat grandmother was smelling them porkchops, your old greatgreatgreat*great* grandma was a Zulu queen in Africa. She was setting at the table and she said to the waiter: "Say waiter, be sure and fetch me some of them missionary chitterlings...."

"Yeah," said Al. "When my greatgreatgreatgreat grandma who was a Zulu queen got throuth eating them missionary chitterlings, she wanted a sewer ditch to take away her crap, so she went out and saw your old greatgreatgreatgreat*great* grandmother sleeping under a coconut tree with her mouth wide open. She didn't need to build no sewer ditch...."

"Jesus!" yelled Slim, closing his eyes and holding his stomach. "I'm dying!"

Jake screwed up his eyes, bit his lips, and tried hard to think of a return. But for the life of him, he could not. Al's last image was too much; it left him blank. Then they all laughed so much that they felt weak in the joints of their bones (*Lawd Today*, 93–95).

Bob and Slim provide the appreciative audience necessary to spur the verbal sparrers on. Essentially they all wanted an activity to fill the oppressive hours, and the humor of the dozens, for as long as it lasts, provides it. These men eschew thought; consequently the images in these insults emerge as from a dream they would never contemplate. The final laugh of all four welds again the friendship and affirms that no violence had been done to this community of four. Since this is the sort of behavior we obtain from adults whose duty it is to evince leadership, reinforce and transmit a cultural heritage, the future holds little promise. This is destruction rather than building of community, a smearing of the ancestral past that holds a community together. Self-targeted as these insults are, they convey only thinly-camouflaged self-hatred.

The blues ritual culminates the day before Jake returns home to beat Lil. Prior to this we see him before the "Review Board," which fires him and later pardons him on the postmaster's intervention. Since the men talk all day about the "night out," and Jake borrows $100 at 20 percent interest to make it possible, we await the event eagerly. Their mindless work at the post office, where they move around to the rhythm of machines and commands over intercoms, leaves us sympathetic to their desire to engage in some recreation that would heal such nerve-chafing employment. Moreover, as black men, they are aware that their positions as menial postal clerks represent the apex of their achievement within the post office hierarchy. In his own life Wright turned to Marxism in search of a solution to such social ills and was deeply disappointed (*American Hunger*, 130–33 and *Atlantic Monthly*, June 1940, 826–28). Jake, who early in the novel mocks a proselytizing Trotskyite, does not consider Marxism as a solution. In fact, to be a "Red" is to be a traitor to America, and to even agree that large numbers of people are unemployed is to be a "Red." For Jake and his friends one solves such painful situations by going to a "boss" blues dive where the music and the food and the women are good.

When we witness the ritual it is as imprisoning in its material aspects as is the confidence man's appropriation of the folk sermon. Gluttony and sex-conditioned responses—animal behavior—sum up Jake's and his confreres' actions, but the sex is never had because long before Jake gets to that point the prostitute he has selected helps another man steal Jake's wallet.

In the manner in which the audience discourses with the music and shouts and stomps out its pain, Wright's depiction of the blues resembles Hughes'. But while Hughes makes the blues into a ritual of communal wail, Wright never lets his go beyond being a prelude to sex. We notice that upon the ecstasy produced by the music a woman bites her man's ear, and at that point Jake must take Blanche off to the rooms, except that his wallet is stolen. Theft and exploitation are the axes around which Wright's portrayal of the blues revolves; and blues and sex, essentially beautiful phenomena in themselves, are made ugly because he stamps them with the profit motive.

There is nothing in Wright's depiction of the blues here to qualify them as "the spirituals of the city" that he calls them elsewhere (cited in Fabre, 1973, 238). For although happiness is what Jake and his buddies desire from the blues, they are merely taken to the foot of the Promised Land. Because Jake is beaten into unconsciousness for protesting the theft of his wallet, and his friends are forced to revive him on a snow bank in a deserted alley, the reader is left with a grim impression of something the black man, according to *Lawd Today*, mortgages his soul for. The reader does not miss the irony that earlier that day Jake left his wife without food but spends twelve dollars feeding his friends and their prostitutes and gives Rose the hostess a 25 percent tip.

The blues as Wright depicts them here take secondary importance to Jake and his friends' need for them. The emphasis is on the conversion of the blues into a tool for exploiting the unwitting. The jam sessions, the funeral dances, the communal spirit, and the celebration of triumph over defeat that nourished the blues and the people who needed the blues—are all absent here. One is reminded of W. C. Handy's story that he paid a band out of his own pocket to return to Mound Bayou to celebrate with the people "the grand opening of their oil mill" (Bontemps 1941, 91). Handy, who sang of the hopes and despair of black Americans, felt a compulsion to celebrate with them whatever social and economic progress they made. But Jake mortgages his future to quest after that something he thinks the blues contain and is merely lured to a place where he is further diseased. Here, then, the blues are simply a part of the money-making faculty of America and a part of the black man's destruction. Wright has pared them to his purpose, which is to show that the black man is a lost creature in America, and his folklore is a reflection of that confusion and meaninglessness. It is unquestionably a simplification that Murray has commented on at length (1970, 176). In *Black Boy* Wright recounts poignantly his father's desertion of his family and humiliation of Wright's mother when she tried to obtain money from him to feed the children (33–34). Writing about his father twenty-five years after this incident, Wright reflects on how chained were his father's "actions to the direct, animalistic impulses of his withering body." As Wright saw it, his father, circumscribed by peonage, had never had "a chance to learn the meaning of loyalty, of sentiment, of tradition"; he had no regrets and no hopes and did not know the heights of joy or the depths of despair. "There had come to me through my living the knowledge that my father was a black peasant who had gone to the city seeking life, but who had failed" (*Black Boy*, 43). Jake and his friends are from Mississippi, and it is a life of desperation that they lead in the city.

Altogether Wright's manipulation of these three Afro–American rituals results in his showing them either as destroying the black heritage or as being an adjunct to enslaving materialism. In "The Back-to-Africa" parade he hints at the political use to which black rituals could be put. Here is a consolidating myth of Africa as the Promised Land. And here is a people united by that symbol. In the novella "Fire and Cloud," religion is fused with politics and is used to unite the black community of a small southern town to challenge the white authorities, to withstand the inevitable brutality, and to gain eventual justice. Except where the black man manipulates folklore to gain justice in America, Wright shows folklore as a millstone around black people's necks.

It should be added that Wright did not seek to get *Lawd Today* published; he considered it an apprentice work. However, this fact does not invalidate this discussion of its folklore, for in his later works he followed through on these trends.

Apart from *Black Boy* where Wright holds up black religion to ridicule, little overt use of folklore is made in his work until his final novel, *The Long Dream*. And having already expressed his view that black folklore, which he saw as a hindrance to black success, should be suppressed by military means where possible (*Black Power*, 1954, 342–51), he is determined to show the bankruptcy of folklore in *The Long Dream*. Although the reader knows that such is Wright's intention so dramatic is his presentation of the folk sermon that one is able to see, in spite of Wright, its value to the congregation.

The Long Dream is full of desperate characters and depicts a ghetto whose residents seem to have already been ferried across the Styx. But insofar as black rituals are concerned, there is only the folk sermon (and snippets of others too insignificant for analysis). Since the novel is about the value of black life in the South, the funeral sermon for the forty-two victims of the Grove fire and Tyree is thematically central to the novel, for it is here that we see the black community, whose lives the white world holds cheaply and terminates with impunity, dramatizing its philosophy of death.

The narrator draws attention to Tyree's body as a reminder of the limits of trickery; black trickery is simply laid to rest by a bullet from a white man's gun. What will the folk preacher say about that? Reverend Ragland is supposed to have the formula to heal the wound left by the Grove fire. His function, Wright shows, is to bring his acting skills to the interpretation of what is essentially a preconstructed drama of the folk. We note that

Ragland's sermon bears many resemblances to James Weldon Johnson's in *God's Trombones*, for essentially such sermons are the property of the black American folk.

Like Johnson and Hughes, Wright emphasizes the role of song in the religious ritual. After a very vivid description of the ritual space, that is, the church, Wright focuses on the music:

There rolled forth a deep-vowelled hymn of melancholy sound in which the audience and the choir joined:

> "Sunset and the evening star,
> And one clear call for me!
> And may there be no moaning at the bar
> When I put out to sea..."

Amid the singing and the organ's roll a few black women gave forth crying sobs.

> "For though from out our bourne of time and place
> The flood may bear me far,
> I hope to see my Pilot face to face
> When I have crossed the bar..."

Deep-bassed "Amens!" rose and mingled with screams; several black women were escorted by ushers out of the church... (*Long Dream*, 321).

Two and one-half stanzas of the hymn are cited for their evocative quality, and are interspersed with the narrator's description of the congregation's behavior. We note that there is a build-up in the emotional intensity of the reactions. The third stanza of the hymn is interrupted to describe the entry of Reverend Ragland. The theatrical antics he is accorded have been studied by students of the folk sermon.

He lifted up his two long arms into the air and stretched them dramatically wide. Silence gripped the black brothers and sisters.

Reverend opened his mouth and emitted a rich carrying baritone: "Death!"

He moved agilely to the left of the pulpit and bellowed: "*DEATH*!" He glided to the right of the pulpit and leaned over the upturned faces in the coffins and screamed: "DEATH!"

Reverend now strode briskly to the pulpit and lifted his eyes to the soaring ceiling and announced in slow, ringing tones of sad amazement... (322).

This description of Ragland's entrance compares well with Grace Sims Holt's description of the black preacher's entrance: "The preacher's beginning is slow-moving (funky) to get the audience physically involved. The preacher walks, body-swaying from side to side, from one end of the pulpit to the other... He waits until he gets to one side, stands straight and makes a statement about sin" (1972, 191). Wright's preacher's preoccupation is death; it is therefore requisite that his statement be about death. James Weldon Johnson calls such movements of the preacher a rhythmic dance ([1927] 1969, 6). These are carefully calculated actions, as carefully calculated as the hypnotist's.

Ragland moves next to the incantory statements, which, in the repeated words, bear many parallels to the blues stanza:

Death's been a-riding through this land! I say Death's been a-riding through this old world! Lawd God Awmighty, Death's been a-riding through our hearts! And now you just look, look, LOOK, I say, at what Death's done done! Death's been a-riding and He done left his fingerprints! Lawd Gawd Awmighty, I can hear old Death's rustling black robe stealing softly away! (322).

When he interrupts his delivery with a hymn, the ritual takes on the same form as Braswell's in "Big Meeting." The song performs several offices: it consolidates the moving lyricism Ragland has started to build up, brings back those who might have strayed into inattention (highly unlikely here), unifies the congregation by virtue of the singing, articulates an aspect of the congregation's creed, and reinforces the sermon's central theme. Instead of interrupting each sentence with the congregation's cries, the way Hughes does, Wright masses for the most part the responses of the congregation and presents them between paragraphs of Ragland's delivery. This technique allows the full impact of Ragland's statements to reach the reader unimpeded by the congregation's cries. At the same time it destroys the illusion of spontaneity of response between the preacher and his listeners that Hughes's technique manages to convey.

Various sections of this folk sermon are interesting for their theological implications. The following is one such passage:

"Now, don't be a fool and go blaming Death!...Death ain't nothing but Gawd's special messenger! His Pullman car is the cyclone! His airplane is the wind! His streetcar is the thunderbolt! There ain't but one thing you can say when Death taps on your door: 'May the Good Lawd have mercy on my soul!'" Reverend waved for silence, advanced to the edge of the platform, stared down at the coffins filled with mute, black faces and spoke in quiet, matter-of-fact tones:

"Some folks in this town talking about trying to find out who's guilty of causing these folks to die. They even talking about sending folks to jail." Looking out over the sea of black faces, he gave forth an ironic laugh: "Ha, ha! Don't the fools know that no man can kill 'less Gawd wants it done? Not a sparrow flies 'less Gawd lets it fly. Not a raindrop falls 'less Gawd says, 'Yes, rain, you can fall!' You think you so powerful that you can kill another man? You a fool! You kill and call it killing but you only putting a name on something that Gawd's done done! When Gawd's a-working, you shut your big mouth and keep still! When Gawd calls you it's for your own good!..." (*Long Dream*, 324).

This passage suggests that the black folk's understanding of God is infantile. Wright burlesques the often-cited passage of faith in God's personal caring for the individual disciple by extending the examples to God's use of murderers as His personal agents of death. The passage is equally designed by Ragland to persuade the listeners into believing that whatever happens to them is the will of God (When later he castigates the dead for their sinful acts such statements appear contradictory to this belief, but logic is neither Ragland's interest nor his forte). Taken literally such statements absolve a murderer for his acts, since he is merely obeying a God-inspired command. A people prepared to accept such a theology must be powerless indeed. This goes beyond the blaming-of-the-victim that was common in the South when whites lynched blacks—it blames the individual for only those acts that jeopardize the "salvation" of his soul. The implication is that it is easier to do this than to look at the facts, which could lead to self-hate, madness, suicide, or simply revolt.

Because of the manner in which he uses hymns to underscore his point, Ragland is either a trickster or an "ignoramus." But from the staged tenderness and compassion that he showers on Tyree's widow, we are inclined to the trickster viewpoint. Such hymns include:

> God moves in a mysterious way
> His wonders to perform!
> He plants His footsteps in the sea
> And rides upon the storm.

> Ye fearful saints, fresh courage take!
> The clouds ye so much dread
> Are big with mercy and shall
> Break in blessings on your head (322–23)

> We give Thee but Thine own,
> Whate'er the gift may be:
> All that we have is Thine alone:
> A trust, O Lord, from Thee ... (324).

These are *bona fide* Christian hymns that all but a tiny minority of white Christians have long ceased to take literally. But here they suit Ragland's and his congregation's purpose—to relieve themselves of any responsibility for what is going on in the community and to rationalize their cowardice in not taking counteractive measures. Used thus such songs and scriptural passages would over the long run destroy objective perceptions of terrestrial reality and inhibit black people from seeking the earthly justice that should be their due.

Ragland moves on to a public proclamation of transgressors, a practice we shall again encounter in Baldwin's Father James. Since this custom exists in many of the African-derived Caribbean cults, it may be an African retention. Nevertheless such public proclamations do not occur when nonmembers are present at the gatherings of the Caribbean sects. The excommunication element of the Christian church no doubt reinforced this tendency among Africans of the diaspora.

We note that Tyree transgressed because he owned the dance hall, the musician because he lured others with his "horn," the nondescript dead because they were present. In language that is paced with an erotic, whip-lash tempo with the audience reacting in kind—as though receiving a pleasurable whipping from God, by way of Ragland—the congregation is told, and it accepts, that God ordered the Grove Fire deaths:

Who understands the Divine Plan of Justice? on the Fourth Gawd reared back and said:
    "Death, come here!"
    "Wonderful Jesus!"
    "Death, go down to that place called America!"
    "Lissen to the Lawd!"
    "Death, find that place they call Mississippi!"
    "Gawd's a-talking!"
    "Death, go to a town called *Clintonville*!"
    "Lawd, Lawd, Lawd!"
    "Death, find me a man called *Tyree Tucker*!"
    "Gawd's king!"
    "Death, I want you to tell Tyree Tucker that I want to see 'im."
    "Have mercy, Jesus!"

Expectedly an orgasmic release follows: "A black woman gave a prolonged scream and began leaping about; ushers rushed to her and led her bound-ing body out of the church" (*Long Dream*, 324–25). One could also see this as a frenzy resulting from the blows of Ragland's sermon. In the usual "Go Down Death" folk sermon, the passage on which this part of Ragland's sermon is modeled is usually comforting; Death is sent by God as an emis-sary of relief and as pilot for some sufferer home to God's kingdom (see Johnson 1927, 27–30).

Here Wright returns to the actual preacher-congregation antiphonal drama of the folk sermon. He keeps the commands short and, excepting slight changes, the structure repetitive. There is a seesaw effect between the preacher and congregation. The total effect comes in the sounds of a blow and its somewhat altered echo. There is sadism in the preacher's state-ments and masochism in the congregation's agreement. Perhaps the erotic tempo is intended to soften the harshness of the message; it is more likely Wright's way of transmitting what he feels to be the essential sadomasochis-tic quality of black American religion as he describes it in *Black Boy* (113).

After such ecstatic heights Reverend must inject humor into his de-livery—in terms of Tyree's telling death that he is busy. This is again a possible influence of the African trickster tale, in which tricksters often try to and frequently succeed in outwitting divine forces. In song and spectacle-wiping tidbits Reverend allows the congregation time to catch their breaths before he again picks up the cudgel, this time on Charlie Moore, the "horn" player.

As is to be expected from Wright, the time comes when Ragland decides to "cash in" on the disaster. In fact, he has been psychologically preparing the congregation for this all along. His specific aim is to increase his church membership, and along with this will come an increased "collection." Verbally he dethrones the white power structure—Cantley was God's agent to bring about Tyree's death—and enshrines the omnipotence of a merciless God (Wright interrupts the sermon at this point to introduce details about the intrigue surrounding Tyree's death and additional news about Tyree's partner Dr. Bruce and Gloria, Tyree's mistress, who have fled to Detroit—not to escape "Gawd" but police chief Cantley).

When the sermon is resumed Reverend reassures those who have resigned themselves to God's sway by telling them of the wonderful joys of heaven: "There ain't no death *hunh bomp* we all a part of the living Gawd *hunh bomp* and Gawd said: 'I go to prepare a place for you!' *hunh bomp* 'If it wasn't so I wouldn't have told you!' *hunh bomp* we all go sleep in Gawd *hunh bomp* but we all rise again *hunh bomp* and no man can kill you..." To the unsaved he says: "Gawd sees all things *hunh bomp* His eyes spy out your smallest secret thought *hunh bomp*..." (329). And to reinforce the situational irony Wright has set up is Fishbelly's desire to scream, "Naw, it ain't Gawd I feel; it' the white man" (329).

On paper the *hunh bomp* with which Ragland punctuates his utterances appears comical. The usual interrupting remark is in most cases *ha*. Ragland's is a head-knocking or kicking sound, which underlines the sadistic strain present throughout the sermon (The narrator uses the word "sadistic" to describe the delivery). Ragland's insertion of a second negative into the words of Jesus (taken from the Gospel of John) is deliberate on Wright's part and is expected to be comical, if not condemnatory—condemnatory in the sense that Ragland's words imply that he is dishonest. Wright's interruption of the sermon to focus on Fishbelly's fear is intended to invalidate the sermon.

There remains a haunting question in the entire novel, not just in the funeral rite: What option do these people have? They are shown to be powerless against lynch mobs and against all schemes, black and white, to defraud them. Their rituals, Wright would have us believe, are empty and delusive. Of course, on the last Wright is wrong. Ingrained in the sermon are profound beliefs in the uselessness of human struggle (a strange perversion of the predestination doctrine) and in the glorious life after death—a compensation for the black man's usual state of poverty. Without this last belief, most blacks would be unable to go on living.

What we therefore see in *Lawd Today* and *The Long Dream* is an attempt to denigrate what others have seen as valuable rituals. Wright implicitly favors political action. In *White Man, Listen* he praises Calvin and Luther for having begun the process of "emptying human consciousness of its ancient, infantile, subjective accretions" ([1957] 1964, 55). This work, published only a year before *The Long Dream*, conveys Wright's views on religion quite clearly: "The teeming religions gripping the minds...of Asians and Africans offend me. I can conceive of no identification with such mystical visions of life that freeze millions in static degradation, no matter how emotionally satisfying such degradation seems to those who wallow in it" (*White Man, Listen*, 48–49). But—and this goes back to Wright's earliest work on lynching—the "white man, having lost his mystic vision of a stern Father God, a dazzling Virgin, and a Dying Son who promises to succor him after death, settles upon racism" (49). Of course, the facts of the American South, where primitive Christianity is very powerful and racism nightmarish, contradict Wright's theory. Be that as it may, Wright's vision of religion deeply influenced the way he presented Afro-American religious rituals.

When Wright commented on the dozens, it was the "Dirty Dozens" that he addressed, and he saw them as an inversion of all that is highly prized by white America—they are therefore extolling of incest, broken homes, promiscuity, etc.—"What can you expect from men and women who have been driven out of life?" ([1957] 1964, 90–92). Concerning the blues, he saw them as "representing the apex of sensual despair," for many blacks "knew that their hope was hopeless" ([1957] 1964, 88). Since the blues and dozens are Jake's art forms, it is not difficult to see why his life is so empty and he is so hateful of his wife.

Before Wright no serious black writer ever accepted these rituals as being all good. But prior to him none had categorically rejected them as being desperate, infantile, and irrelevant. The historical element that the black American writers of his era infused into their use of black folklore is notably missing in Wright's fiction. Wright represents a sort of watershed, for after him those Afro–American writers who chose to use black folklore employ it as a politically unifying force, as incorporating an alternate reality to materialism, or as a source of racial strength.

Margaret Walker and Richard Wright should be examined together, if only because they influenced each other and were products of similar forces, though they produced radically different fiction. When *Jubilee*, the novel that Walker began writing in 1940, was published (1966) it was not surprising to find that behind it was an attempt to dramatize the survival techniques of black people during the final decades of slavery and the early years of Reconstruction. Walker's collection of poems *For My People*, which won the Yale Poetry Prize in 1942, shows her deep interest in Afro–American folk beliefs and heroes, and the relevance of these to the survival of black people.

The world that Walker creates in *Jubilee* is one that the slaves and ex-slaves order with their religion and folklore. Walker admires the work of Zora Neale Hurston for its use of black folklore (1975, 7) and employs a few of Hurston's techniques to create a black ethos through the medium of folklore.

With the atrocities of slavery and the Reconstruction framing the world of the characters, Walker's rituals for the triumph over pain emerge quite forcefully. They are linked essentially to religion, which in turn is linked to a struggle for freedom. Brother Zeke, the secretly literate preacher is as close to a Martin Luther King figure as slavery could have produced. He devotes himself selflessly to his congregation, coordinates meetings among the white abolitionists, free blacks, and slaves, and is one of the Underground Railroad's vital links. These meetings take place at the Rising Glory Baptist Church, deep in the swamps and a long way from the "Big House."

The novel begins with an epigraph from the spirituals—"Swing low, sweet chariot / Coming for to carry me home"—and a conversation about the screech owl being a sure sign of death. Sis Hetta lies in her cabin dying. Walker uses this death to point out the cooperation that existed among the slaves: Caline fans Hetta, Granny Ticey (midwife) administers drugs, Aunt Sally relieves Calline, Granny Sukey aided by Brother Zeke brings Vyry from massa's distant plantation so that Hetta can see her before she dies. Brother Zeke fuses the communal feeling in the spiritual he sings, "Soon one morning / Death come knockin' at my door..." (*Jubilee*, 9). To this he adds a prayer. It is a curious prayer insofar as it does not ask God to spare Hetta's life but rather to facilitate her access to those after-death blessings the slaves deemed their reward for a difficult life:

This here sister is tired a-sufferin', Lord, and she want to come on home. We ask you to roll down that sweet chariot right here by her bed, just like you done for Lishy, so she can step in kinda easy like and ride on home to glory. Gather her in your bosom like you done Father Abraham and give her rest. She weak Lord and she weary, but her eyes is a-fixin' for to light on them pearly gates of God. She beggin' for to set at your welcome table and feast on milk and honey. She wants to put on them angel wings and wear them pretty golden slippers... (*Jubilee*, 11).

One is first struck by the gentleness of the prayer which reflects the calm faith of the slaves in their theology. In fact many of the statements either paraphrase or echo several lines from the spirituals. The description of heaven as a place to escape to after a life of suffering makes death a positive experience. Death is almost a form of subversion. The promise of God's word, in the citation of Elijah as an example of the faithful who had been rewarded, is emphasized. Being able to "set at the welcome table" expresses that secret knowledge that after death slave and master will be equal. In making death a positive phenomenon, Brother Zeke seeks to cheer up Hetta so she would abandon any regrets she may have about dying. For those remaining as slaves he not only diminishes their sorrow but reminds them that they have death to look forward to, that is, if a Moses does not appear before. Whites writing about the ecstasy songs of heaven produced in slaves could not understand why (Kilham, 128). Here Walker indicates the reason.

The sorrow that comes with Hetta's death is also ritualized. Granny Ticey throws her clothing over her head and sets up the death wail; Brother Zeke takes it up in the death chant, and the residents of all the cabins join in. Because the sorrow is communal, unified in the chant, "Soon one morning / Death come knockin' at my door," its weight is borne by the entire community, not just the immediate relatives. It is in essence a ritual of unification and emotional purgation.

The religious worship at the Rising Glory Baptist Church is inherently subversive. The songs of comfort the slaves sing are obvious enough. But in the sermons, which are often based on Moses' leading the Hebrew Children out of Egypt, Brother Zeke counsels the defiance that Moses' mother practices. Moreover, since God had liberated the Hebrew Children and punished the defiant Egyptians, the implication is that He would come to the aid of these His other children. Walker dramatizes parts of the sermon and the animated responses of the slaves, but her chief concern is to reveal the ritual reinforcement of the faith in eventual freedom: "Brother Zeke admonished his flock to have faith in God and He would send them a Moses, a deliverer to free His people and prove to the world what the Bible says about a servant being worthy of his hire" (*Jubilee*, 39). The rationale for such a church lies in the prayer of deliverance and the hope for "Pharaoh's" death. Walker, unlike Wright, wishes her reader to be impressed by the genuine, dignified, and universal cry for freedom that lies behind this ritual, and whatever distracts from this she excludes from her presentation—whether or not it is characteristic of the ritual.

We are presented with other scenes at this church where the purpose is not to pray but to plan resistance, to be informed of abolitionist news, and to discover new stations on the Underground Railroad. Thus while the preaching functions to reiterate the slaves' hope for freedom, Walker shows a basic political function to the black church. That resistance sometimes went very far, as in the case of the two women who poison their masters and hang, convinced that they had done no wrong.

Walker merely comments on the grief-alleviating function of the spirituals. In Aunt Sally's use of them Walker shows the effectiveness of their icons, hope, and built-in shouts in providing psychic pillars and escape vents in the dreariest moment. On days when Aunt Sally is irrational with grief it is by singing the spirituals that she regains her equanimity. When her kinsman is killed by the slave driver Grimes and she herself, already an old woman, is sent off to the auction block, it is the belief in a coming Moses that gives her the courage to go on living.

The beliefs that underlie these rituals have little to do with white preaching to the slaves that they should submit to their masters' authority, should not steal, or sabotage his property. In fact the slaves do the opposite. They pry into every crevice for whatever is available to bring a sense of dignity and triumph to their life of servitude.

Walker also wishes the reader to understand that the slaves considered themselves the moral superiors of their masters. Because of this moral superiority they respond compassionately to the sufferings of their oppressors. Thus Jim carefully brings back the wounded Johnny to die at home despite Jim's knowledge that Johnny had been "fighting against all colored peoples"; Vyry puts aside everything else to take care of Miss Lilian after she loses her immediate family and her sanity to the Civil War. Toward the end of the novel Vyry tells both her husbands, "I honestly believes that if airy one of them people what treated me like dirt when I was a slave would come to my door in the morning hungry I would feed 'em. God knows I ain't got no hate in my heart for anybody" (*Jubilee*, 406). Clearly, then, the rituals enabled the slaves to avoid the pitfalls of vengeance, of righting wrongs by creating new wrongs.

At the core of Walker's work, then, is the "folklore that embodies [the black man's hopes] and struggle for freedom" that Wright saw as the central focus for the creative black artist (1937 [1972], 318), but which becomes a cudgel in Wright's work. Walker is in the tradition of Hughes, Bontemps, and Ellison, who use folklore in their fiction to reveal the psychology of black American survival. In an interview Walker stated that she admires Langston Hughes for precisely this reason (1975, 13). Walker's forte is not in the creation of new techniques for the incorporation of ritual into fiction. She merely borrows those techniques that are already present. It is moreso in the quiet ease with which the ritual beliefs exert a positively controlling force on the lives of her characters. Because of those rituals her characters have an identity quite apart from that which their masters seek to impose on them.

By virtue of his age, his conditioning by the Depression, and his association with Wright, Ralph Ellison could easily be linked to this period. As with Margaret Walker, the role of folklore in the psychological history of the black American is Ellison's preoccupation. Whereas Wright shows such lore as valueless, Ellison's protagonist in *Invisible Man* discovers that no other weapon is as potent for dealing with racial injustice in America.

Regarding ritual in Ellison's work, there are, among several essays on the subject, two that I recommend to the reader: Susan Blake, "Rituals and Ritualization in the Works of Ralph Ellison" (1979) and Robert G. O'Meally, "Riffs and Rituals in the Work of Ralph Ellison" (1980). Two subjects fleetingly addressed by the critics are the unifying ritual role of the "prologue"—which is in itself an iconographic blues ritual—and the jive session that culminates the Harlem riot. A third, which I shall not pursue here, is the function of the protagonist as Afro–American *griot* in the story-telling role dramatizing the history of the tribe; the "I" point of view is a technique borrowed from the blues singer and represents the tribe's collective self. Consequently in reading the novel one is in fact in attendance at a prolonged ritual.

The reefer that removes the repressions of consciousness to let the racial wisdom embodied in the blues surge from the protagonist's being can be likened to the shouts that chase away all inhibitions at a blues concert and let the music filter into the deepest recesses of the listeners' souls; it can equally be compared to the "Amen Corner" of the black church, which breaks down all barriers blocking the flow of "the spirit." The reefer makes the protagonist receptive to the meanings of Louis Armstrong's rendition of "What did I do to be so black and blue?" And he relives the vicissitudes of Afro–American existence, full of ambiguities and paradoxes that are either reconciled or contained in rituals like the blues to which he is presently listening. The images of the auction block and a sorrowful spiritual-singing mother, the chant of purgation cast in the form of the folk sermon that subtly deviates into the dozens, oral history, denial of pain, and self-hate are all present in the "prologue."

Upon emerging from the world of the blues song (an experience that is an underworld journey such as that of the epic hero, with Louis Armstrong being Tiresias), he promises never again to plunge too deeply into the unconscious, for the process takes him from the world of immediate survival where he needs to be vigilant. To some extent the protagonist is "signifying," for his home is now the underground made into the above ground as much as is humanly possible.

The power line from Monopolated Power (an ironic name since electricity is bipolar) is a unifying allegory for every survival technique enumerated in the novel, for in the white-dominated world, *to be,* that is, to assert one's self, one has to be white. Essentially, then, whatever power black people have is "stolen power." Moreover such power must be used invisibly (one is reminded of Richard Wright's uncle who was murdered and his wife chased out of town for being a prosperous saloon owner). Black rituals therefore, the protagonist sets out to show the reader, are about obtaining and using that "power." Every successful character—that is, every character who remains alive in this novel—steals power in one way or other and uses it invisibly.

In the jive session that culminates the Harlem riot we are presented with a resource we do not normally perceive as being a potent ritual. Against the intellectual protagonist, who confusedly perceives himself as some sort of Harlem savior, and Ras the Destroyer, who is convinced of his messianic mission, Ellison presents the wisdom of the folk and therein implies that the folk is its own savior.

The Harlem riot is coming to a close; everyone profits from it in whatever way he can—good old American wisdom. A group of men probably on their way home convert the riot into a festival: they pass a bottle from mouth to mouth. Each speaker brings his own perspective to the riot. Ras is seen as a madman: first because he shoots at the very people he purports to want to save, but even more so because "everybody else trying to git some loot and him and his boys out for blood" (*Invisible Man*, 550). Their assessment of Ras's conduct is good common-sense knowledge in America. One can cleanse loot and do something with it (That is the history of American capitalism), but what is the value of blood? In their recounting of what has already taken place there is a variation on the folk's readiness to act out the roles it must (Survival is a chameleon affair). One fellow becomes an instant businessman, selling liquor from a vandalized store: "Done gone into business, man!" (550).

The unifying sentiment is that the riot does not change the night from being one like all the others, "fulla fucking and fighting and drinking and lying" (549). In what the principal raconteur says, the folk's ability to penetrate Ras's regalia and rhetoric, into the void they seek to camouflage, is cogently communicated to the reader. The humor directed at his uniform, his horse, and his deportment is trenchant. They note his savagery to other blacks, his ineffectiveness against the "cops," and (what they would applaud him for) his running away from battle to save his life. They miss none of the contradictory details, and arrange them in such a way as to make them yield their maximum humor. Their perceptions penetrate where Ras's could not go, robed as he is in external trappings, and where the protagonist's had not yet dared to go.

The reader is left with a sense that the riot and Ras's behavior will be polished until it becomes another story in the Harlem folk repertory. The people are artists, Ellison suggests; to survive requires being an artist. The riot merely provides additional material for tooling. The two men listening to the principal raconteur are not fully convinced of the veracity of his story, but they know it is a good one. It is an artifact containing the hardnosed view of life evident in black oral literature; it is humorously told with blues onomatopoeia, resonance, metaphors, and rhythms; and it enthrones the *survival principle*. Meeting the riot with the resources of jive points to having a ritual in place to deal with such exceptional occurrences like riots. It is the folk's ritual for, among other things, rescuing them from the grandiose schemes of the brotherhood and semipsychotic "revolutionaries." For the protagonist, who is hiding behind a hedge, trying to get away from the hanging sentence Ras has ordered for him, overhearing this conversation begins the merger of the factors that finally give him an identity. In short he, the would-be leader, is rescued by the folk.

All the known survival rituals of black Americans are treated in Ellison's novel in one form or another: the longing for a Black Moses, the detonation of the unknown and feared through ridicule and jive, the vicarious conquests through empathy with folk tricksters, the catharsis provided by the black church, the paradoxically masochistic, healing blues—some intricately developed, others symbolically evoked, and for the most part their consequences probed. Ellison's novel is highly successful because he found, as he notes, the technique for incorporating these rituals into the form of the novel (*Shadow and Act*, 57). As far as the use of folklore is concerned, Ellison has a great deal in common with Hughes, at least at the level of intention. Both are convinced of the value of black American folklore in the survival of black Americans, because of the perspective and wisdom the folk find in such folklore. But already we see in Ellison that movement towards globalism, for which he is criticized by George Kent (1972, 161), and which expands in later writers like Forrest and Reed.

Baldwin's criticism of Wright for not depicting the institutions black folk evolved for their survival indicated the direction in which his own fiction would go. His first novel, *Go Tell It on the Mountain*, is unique in the sense that it is structured entirely around the rituals of the black church. This work will form the core of my analysis of Baldwin's rituals. I shall treat it in detail, for although Baldwin is a frequently studied writer, the discussion accorded his portrayal of the black church is scant and usually entangled with various aspects of Baldwin's vision of reality; it never gets treated for the unifying aesthetic principle that it is in *Go Tell It on the Mountain*. The attitudes of Baldwin's characters to the black church vary dramatically from novel to novel—from survival with a high price in *Go Tell It on the Mountain*, through social protest in *Another Country*, to all-out rejection in *Tell Me How Long the Train's Been Gone*, back to a saving or damning role, depending on the character, in *If Beale Street Could Talk*, to a decidedly political function in his last novel *Just Above My Head*. Despite these different viewpoints in the novels, James Baldwin the man knows that those who hollered in black churches paid a price that began the liberation of the present generation, and his role as writer is to "excavate the role of the people who produced" him (*A Dialogue*, 1973, 82).

The final picture of *Go Tell It on the Mountain* is of an island of people united by their common faith in a God who promised to reward them for obeying His edicts. Around them is the sea of ghetto filth that threatens to engulf them with the "vices of perdition." They are returning home after an all-night "tarry service" that had become an initiation ritual—a conversion event. The final picture encompasses the novel's principal preoccupations. During the hours preceding the "tarry service" we are witnesses to the Grimes' family battles that turn around guilt, poverty, wife-beating, and even sibling rivalry. These they leave to journey to the central location of "The Temple of Fire Baptized," to engage in rituals that affirm the beliefs that give meaning to their lives. The black church becomes a raft to which each of the characters clings. So central is it that Baldwin brings them to the church and begins the prayer ritual before taking the reader into the past of the senior Grimes.

A resonating word throughout the novel is *salvation*. Of course, for the characters theirs is a salvation from hell, which for them is a literal place. But the novelist uses the details of the characters' lives and the circumstances for which their religion is protection to show that such salvation is terrestrial. Saving one's self is the purpose of life, Baldwin states (*Dialogue*, 41), and this is what preoccupies the characters here. First, the need to escape Harlem's sordid life, the depression of poor-paying and insulting jobs they cannot leave, and the temptation to alcoholism; and, second, their quest for inner peace—become masked in their certain belief that they are God's children, which in turn requires of them rituals of reassurance.

Of foremost importance for Baldwin is to show the psychic reality behind the rituals of the black church; their inherent drama is secondary; he therefore links each aspect of the rituals to the characters' lives and the whole to Afro–American history. As we move from one to another of the characters' life histories we are treated to prose narrations of the blues; but since such characters equate the blues with damnation they find equivalent relief in its "sacred" counterpart. So intense has been their suffering that they surrender themselves to a system of beliefs that leaves no aspect of life unregulated. Furthermore theirs is a creed that promises reward for suffering. Every statement the "saints" make to one another is a Biblical quote or fragment from the spirituals reminding themselves of how difficult "the way" is, how clever the Devil, but how easy God promises to make the journey, how plentiful the rewards for faithful service, how dire the punishments reserved for the "unsaved." The irony in these beliefs is dramatized in Gabriel's life.

In matters of technique, Baldwin's presentation of the rituals in *Go Tell It on the Mountain* (cited hereafter *Mountain*) is mostly narrative with episodes of dramatic intensity. His writing is, however, not the bland expository prose of James Weldon Johnson, for throughout one hears thunderous echoes of the folk sermon. The language therefore carries a transcendent tone, is incantatory, and is quite appropriate for portraying religious rituals.

Baldwin makes the conversion ritual the pivot of the novel. The reader journeys with the characters to the ritual before he discovers each character's past. From there he journeys backwards. Where that past is long, Baldwin brings the reader back to the ritual before resuming the journey. The method is used with every member of the Grimes family present at the ritual. In doing so Baldwin dwarfs the characters and elevates the ritual to omnipotence (as every society does with its core beliefs). Each return to the ritual brings the reader back to the drama of singing, praying, and exhorting which the saints engage in all night. Such singing and praying become as it were a container, if not a narcotic, for all the characters' pain.

One dramatic episode (even though it is narrated)—and this is before we get to the "tarry service"—is the cathartic section of the Sunday morning service as John remembers it. Much of its mobile quality is conveyed in similes reminiscent of Hughes' descriptions of similar phenomena:

Something happened to their faces and their voices, the rhythm of their bodies, and to the air they breathed; it was as though wherever they might be became the upper room, the Holy Ghost were riding on air....

While John watched, the Power struck someone, a man or woman; they cried out, a long wordless crying, and arms outstretched like wings, they began the Shout...and the music swept on again, like fire, or flood, or judgement. The church seemed to swell with the power it held, and, like a planet rocking in space, the temple rocked with the Power of God.

Further on, the description focuses on Elisha's ecstasy and culminates in a milder version of the orgasmic explosions we have seen in Wright (*Mountain*, 15–16).

In the journey back into Gabriel's past Baldwin dramatizes the sermon of the youthful, recently converted Gabriel, but not to show its drama, since he only inserts token response from the congregation. Rather it is to reveal the puritan framework in which Gabriel conceives of man's relationship to God, and to set the trap that will later paralyze the rest of Gabriel's psychic life with the guilt that accrues from his failure to abide by the dictates he articulates. Baldwin therefore dramatizes this sermon both for its advancement of his theme and the motivation it provides his character.

The longest dramatic episode in the novel is John's conversion experience (twelve pages long in the 1971 edition cited). Baldwin chose to present this scene dramatically for he wished the reader to see that the conversion experience is a trap, a psychic net woven of fear-eliciting Biblical threads. Lying on the floor, John experiences a dream-like journey that is a combination of dream-metaphor illustrations of Biblical injunctions and several dramatic variations of the folk saying that unless a soul has been suspended over hell on a spider's web it would not seek salvation. According to Sister Price and Praying Mother Washington, John's being struck down by the Holy Ghost had been carefully orchestrated by the Lord; they had been given the signs a week before.

In having John's soul react immediately to the psychic paraphernalia of conversion, Baldwin employs a different technique from that of other novelists who have used the conversion ritual in their works. In her autobiography and in those essays where Hurston discusses the conversion ritual, and in Gaines' *Autobiography of Miss Jane Pittman*, the conversion experience is recounted after the person has arisen from the mourners' bench (Hurston, *Negro*, 32–33; *Dust Tracks*, 280–83; Gaines, 133–38). It is usually one of a number of stock tales that relate a horrifying vision of impending damnation from which the would-be convert is rescued by one of the popular allegorical depictions of Jesus Christ. Baldwin's prolonged dramatization of this aspect of the conversion rite embodies much implicit commentary and is therefore closer to fiction than folklore, in the sense that it is Baldwin's unique creation.

The following are samples of Baldwin's presentation of John's experience:

"Then Death is real," John's soul said, "and Death will have his moment."

"Set thine house in order," said his father, "for thou shalt die and not live."

And then the ironic voice spoke again, saying: "Get up, John. Get up, boy. Don't let him keep you here. You got everything your daddy got."

John tried to laugh—John thought that he was laughing—but found, instead, that his mouth was filled with salt, his ears were full of burning water. Whatever was happening in his distant body now, he could not change or stop; his chest heaved, his laughter rose and bubbled at his mouth, like blood (196).

Here John's conscience speaks in three different personae. His past sins and sinful wishes crowd the stage of his conscience and flagellate him; his ambivalence towards his father assumes a voice and disputes with him. Providing as it were a reverberating background music to these events are various lines from the spirituals and Biblical passages in the original or in the paraphrased language of the folk sermons—in short a merging of the fifteen years of programming that had prepared John for this moment.

But as is likely with any group that interprets the Bible too literally, John and, by implication, the other "saints" are trapped in the Manichean framework in which whites cast their religion—blackness representing sin and whiteness purity. Baldwin subtly works this in with John's tortuous reflection on that time he had looked upon his father's nakedness and had been thereafter haunted by the possibility of being cursed. He shifts the story from himself to Ham and back to himself. Of course, this is a reference to the explanation whites frequently gave for enslaving blacks—they were the descendants of Ham and were fated to be servants to their white brethren. Conversion among blacks, many of whom believe the Ham myth, is bound up with the "Ham curse," Baldwin implies.

All the temptations of perdition abundant in the city confront him, as do the inevitable "Valley of Despair," the throngs of filthy despairing humanity destroying themselves and futilely trying to cross "the Jordan," and finally the light of triumph: the sign that he is "saved."

When he rises from the floor the matrix of the church's creed, which he had heard described all his life—it is one of the lesser folk sermons common to black and white preachers—hems in his entire consciousness:

They wandered in the valley, forever; and they smote the rock, forever; and the waters sprang, perpetually, in the perpetual desert. They cried unto the Lord forever, and lifted up their eyes forever, they were cast down forever, and He lifted them up forever. No, the fire could not hurt them, and yes, the lion's jaws were stopped; the serpent was not their master, the grave was not their resting-place, the earth was not their home. Job bore them witness, and Abraham was their father, Moses had elected to suffer with them rather than glory in sin for a season. Shadrach, Meshach, and Abednego had gone before them into the fire, their grief had been sung by David and Jeremiah had wept for them. Ezekiel had prophesied upon them, these dry bones, these slain, and in the fulness of time, the prophet, John, had come out of the wilderness, crying that the promise was for them. They were encompassed with a very cloud of witnesses: Judas, who had betrayed the Lord; Thomas, who had doubted Him; Peter, who had trembled at the crowing of a cock; Stephen, who had been stoned; Paul who had been bound, the blind man crying in the dusty road, the dead man rising from the grave. And they looked to Jesus, the author and finisher of their faith running with patience the race He had set before them; they endured the cross, and they despised the shame, and waited to join Him, one day, in glory, at the right hand of the Father (*Mountain*, 205).

Here, then, are enumerated those Biblical heroes whose lives of holiness they were to emulate, and whose faith in God had guided them safely through life. But it is in those events that affirm that everything the Bible promises is fulfilled—except, of course, heaven, which they have not yet experienced—that their faith is anchored. Their ramparts of faith are thick and seem impenetrable to self-doubt, especially if the holders' lives, like the lives of so many of these characters are empty.

When, prompted by Elisha, John rises from the floor on which he had wrestled with his guilt all night, he is unable to speak for the "joy that rang in him this morning." Fear of hell and sin and guilt have been exorcised, and he truly feels "newborn." But from what Baldwin shows in Gabriel's inconsistencies, in the comic outlook of the pastors Gabriel rebukes, in Florence, and even in John's own observations of his parents' lives before he falls to the church's hypnotic power, the reader knows that John's joy is naive.

Having seen John's conversion experience and the conditioning that produces it, Baldwin's reader is well prepared to understand other aspects of the rituals of the black church hinted at before or not yet introduced. One such aspect is the protection from aloneness that the body of saints provide one another. While John is on the "threshing floor," the entire congregation is on its knees conjuring up the communal strength to pray his soul through the agonies of despair and indecision. Earlier that night they had failed to pray Florence through. Somehow she could not make herself into the little child she needed to become to let their praying power propel her into the kingdom of heaven. With John, however, they succeed. When he rises they accord him a great deal of importance, partly because his experience on "the threshing floor" is incontrovertible evidence that the spirit of God is in and among them, and partly because his conversion is a fulfillment of visions two sisters had been having. His experience is an occasion for much self-congratulation among the congregation. This is therefore a bonding ritual. In *No Name in the Street* (1972), a biographical work, Baldwin refers to his participation in the "praying through" of a friend and the consequent guilt he feels for the events that had alienated them (17–18). In *The Fire Next Time* Baldwin implies that John's conversion experience was similar to his own (17–18).

A second aspect of these rituals comes through in the advice various members of the congregation give to John. Their Biblical citations stress the difficulties that beset Christians and emphasize God's promise to assist the willing. Moreover, they declare that they will always be praying for his triumph. Because the reader has already seen the enslaving and destructive impact of these beliefs on Gabriel's life, these statements have a hollow sound. But the reader is also strategically placed to understand that those characters who cannot conceive of life outside the rituals are imprisoned by them. In effect the congregation implies that should John backslide it would be because he failed to heed God's promise or trust in the power of their prayer. Since their prayer had taken him through the Valley of Despair all the way to God's forgiving throne, they would be very disappointed were he to abandon the journey which with their help he has started.

To prevent such backsliding, however, the congregation takes its role much further. It relates to the pastor what it perceives to be various members' sinful or potentially sinful conduct, and it becomes the pastor's responsibility to give the offenders a public warning. At the beginning of the novel John reflects on such a warning that had been given to Elisha, whom John admires, and Ella-Mae. John later finds out that Elisha is grateful for the public castigation. Elisha's reaction underscores the solid entrenchment of this practice and suggests it was born out of the fear of backsliding. There is, of course, another side to such rigidities. Such expectations force violators of the creed to conceal their lapses and often with monstrous results—as in the case of Gabriel's sacrifice of Esther and Royal.

Baldwin treats extensively the role of visions in the rituals of the black church. We have already seen his incorporation of the traditionally recounted conversion vision into the drama of conversion itself. But long before we get to John's conversion we are told of Gabriel's conversion vision, which is cast in images of guilt and fear—guilt over his fornication and drunkenness, fear of hell instilled by his mother. Gabriel's conversion is not in a church, and his vision is simpler for he has not John's ambivalence for his father or doubts about the power of salvation or for that matter John's overall powers of introspection. But the final sign of salvation and the fullness of joy within that terminates the vision are identical. As Hurston states, this function of the vision is a conventional aspect of conversion—part of that intractable need for a sign, a practice modeled on the behavior of various Old Testament characters, Caleb, for example.

But Baldwin shows that the element of prophecy—God speaking directly to the saints in visions—is fraught with danger. Frequently such visions come to the saint who is looking for a sign to confirm one or another decision. Baldwin makes one such desire for a sign a vital element in Gabriel's tragedy. Either to prove his capacity for sacrifice or his sympathy for the saintly but physically repugnant Deborah, who has been psychologically injured by a white gang rape and who is much older than Gabriel, he has a notion to marry her. But before Gabriel can do so he needs a sign. He gets it: first, a dream of naked women followed by a nocturnal emission; next a dream of ascent to a precipitous place described in images of clouds, mist, thorns, and Gabriel with bleeding hands and feet and legs trembling from fright and fatigue. The scene changes to one where Gabriel is "wearing white robes," and is standing "in the sun like God all golden" watching "the elect" appear; finally God's voice tells him not to touch them for His "seal is on them"; moreover, "so shall [Gabriel's] seed be" (111–12). For Gabriel this is the approving sign he seeks, and he marries Deborah, whom he comes to hate intensely but silently.

We already know what happens to Esther and Royal. But for Gabriel this is a literal promise. Whenever he reflects on Roy's delinquency and on John's (the bastard's) moral ways, he sees God's unfulfilled promise and proof that God is scourging him for having sent off "Hagar and Ishmael" to die in the "Chicago wilderness." In marrying Elizabeth with her bastard, John, he had thought that his meeting her was the sign that he had been forgiven and God was then going to give him an Isaac. But it is Ishmael who will inherit the kingdom. Because Gabriel is trapped in his Old Testament beliefs, God's "unfulfilled promise" leaves him a hateful man who victimizes his household with his guilt-derived anger. He comes to see his marriage to Elizabeth as a continuation of God's scourge. The novel ends with Gabriel still seeking a sign. To sacrifice one's psyche and others' happiness for a promise made in a dream is indeed pathetic. Gabriel's fate must be extended to all those who engage in a literal interpretation of the Bible and who seek to live in conformity with its impossible demands. Baldwin felt that among the things that drove his father mad was "his unreciprocated love for the Great God Almighty" (*No Name in the Street*, 5).

One of Baldwin's reasons for including Florence in the novel is to show that there are those American blacks who manage to escape the pitfalls of the black church. Florence confronts what is a black existence of pain, poverty, and lovelessness with an endurance that comes from within. It is only as she nears death that she panics. However, in including sanctified religion among the magical cures by which Florence seeks to avoid death and in showing her rejection of them all, Baldwin points out that there are those who can suffer and confront life in its nakedness without the additional burdens (or defenses) of religion.

Baldwin is equally intent on showing that there are factors that perpetuate this religion. One of them is historical. It is Baldwin's way of saying that the black church played a saving role during slavery. Gabriel's mother links her commitment to the rituals of the black church to the fact that when a slave she had prayed for a Moses to come to Egyptland and she had seen that Moses come. Thus the deliverance from slavery with which blacks linked their religion, as we have already seen in Bontemps and Walker, appears in Baldwin's work. But Baldwin is sure to link the fervor with which Gabriel's mother held her Christian beliefs to the fear that motivates Gabriel to convert and the fear that momentarily overcomes Florence as she nears death. In other words, besides providing a rationale for enduring an oppressive life, the black church owes a great deal to the transmission of its beliefs over several generations.

In the character of Deborah, Baldwin implies that occasionally an individual, as a result of temperament or psychological trauma or hatred of the world or any combination of factors, succeeds in achieving the total self-abnegation that the black religious creed demands. The existence of such characters among those psychologically or physiologically incapable of attaining such self-abnegation nevertheless bolsters the feeling that such doctrines are tenable. Of course, the majority fails and is guilt-laden; it in turn requires scapegoats to bear the blame for its failure or is consumed by feelings of guilt and inferiority.

The offices in the church and the ritual roles of various members also play a factor: they invest the lives of otherwise insignificant people with great importance. There is as well the certitude of being "saved," which gives the holder a feeling of superiority over the "unsaved." Being "saved" they then become the "Lord's instruments of salvation." Of Sister McCandless the narrator tell us:

She was an enormous woman, one of the biggest and blackest God had ever made, and He had blessed her with a mighty voice with which to sing and preach, and she was going out soon into the field. For many years the Lord had pressed Sister McCandless to get up, as she said, and move; but she had been of timid disposition and feared to set herself above others. Not until He had laid her low, before this very altar, had she dared to rise and preach the gospel. But now she had buckled on her travelling shoes. She would cry aloud and spare not, and lift her voice like a trumpet in Zion (*Mountain*, 57).

She did not look then like the Sister McCandless who sometimes came to visit them, like the woman who went out everyday to work for white people downtown, who came home at evening, climbing, with such weariness, the long, dark stairs. No: her face was transfigured now, her whole being was made new by the power of her salvation (*Mountain*, 144).

As a preacher at fifteen in this type of church, Baldwin knew of the value such ritual roles accorded the "saints," and has written about their value to him (*The Fire Next Time*, 49–50).

Baldwin's characters here are inseparable from the black church. The conversion ritual, since it is the central event in every character's (except Florence's) life, is given prominent focus. Fear of eternal damnation is made the major motivation of the characters. The rituals are pared to respond to these fears and to alleviate them. The fears are further intensified by the lack of an alternative, for without the hope of heaven these would be lives of despair. Strand by strand Baldwin weaves these hopes and fears together at the altar scene. It is as if the altar is the place where all aspects of the characters' lives crystallize. But if Baldwin had ended his novel there it would have been a mediocre work. Instead he makes the perennial human emotions of jealousy and feelings of inadequacy as well as the problems of racism—all of which could in one way or another imperil the salvation that is the *raison d'être* of these characters' existence— function as an antagonistic force. The battle between the "ideal" and the "natural," which is never clearly decided despite the surface reality that Gabriel presents to the public, makes the novel profoundly interesting, for it is a paradigm that parallels the lives of individuals and groups. As such the actions and their outcome engage the reader and lead to further introspection.

To date Baldwin is the only black American novelist to write a serious novel exclusively around the rituals of the black church. For him as for Bontemps and Walker the black church was a mystical body during slavery, but he goes beyond that to show that what was essentially beneficial in slavery had been transmitted unchanged to a nonslave era, with damaging results. The exorcism of pain and the promise of the glories of heaven treated in Hughes and Wright are also evident here. But the moral strength of a Vyry or an Aunt Hager is missing—even in a character like Deborah. Baldwin waited until *The Fire Next Time* and his later novels to express much of what he felt was negative about the black church. In *The Fire Next Time* he feels the black race would be better served if, instead of holding Sunday school classes and calling on the Lord, blacks organized rent strikes (57). Having been a preacher, he realized that what was deemed to be the Holy Spirit was simply theatrical conjuration; moreover the preachers knew it. It was only the congregation that was fooled (*Fire*, 55). He chose, however, not to show these feelings in *Go Tell It on the Mountain*. In *Just Above My Head* (1978) Baldwin focuses on the political possibilities of the black church, especially in its use of the spirituals to strengthen the determination to fight injustice, just as in an earlier era those same spirituals had helped blacks to surmount injustice.

Paule Marshall's triple heritage: Barbadian, Afro–American, and American, has profoundly enriched her vision of human reality and equipped her with a broad perspective that so enriches her characters that it is not as Afro–Americans, Carriacouans, "Bournehillians" or white Americans that we respond to them but as people with a deep need to survive and for whom ritual is primordial to survival. Part of Marshall's perspective comes undoubtedly from her close observation of the interdependency, com-

munalism so to speak, that characterizes Caribbean village life; in black
America it is a phenomenon that can be seen only in small rural communities where values derived from African communalism and transported via
slavery have managed to withstand the corrosion of materialistic culture.
But the interest that Marshall holds for many readers is also rooted in the
ontological circumstances of her characters, as Mary Helen Washington
notes in her afterword to *Brown Girl, Brownstones* (1981, 319).

There are several critics who have analyzed Marshall's exceptional talent
for incorporating ritual into her fiction. Eugenia Collier points out how
ritual, in *Brown Girl, Brownstones*, inducts Selina, even against her will, into
the Brooklyn Barbadian community, and how it holds that community
together; how it functions via carnival in *Chosen Place, Timeless People* to
dramatize history; and how it brings Avey Johnson in *Praisesong for the
Widow* to her psychic center (Collier 1984). In his analysis of ritual in
Marshall's work, John McCluskey's conclusions are similar to Collier's
(1984). Hortense Spillers provides the most detailed analysis yet published
of ritual in *Chosen Place, Timeless People* (cited hereafter *Chosen*). Her essay is
replete with explanations that establish the theoretical vantage from which
she analyzes the novel. Occasionally they impede rather than enhance her
analysis (1985). Barbara Christian's analysis of *Praisesong for the Widow* is
particularly good for its probing of Marshall's use of ritual to convey theme
(1983). Keith Sandiford accomplishes for *Praisesong for the Widow* what
Spillers does for *Chosen Place, Timeless People*. He too employs a great deal of
anthropological theory to get at the core of the novel's meaning (1986). My
own analysis will focus on areas ignored by these and other Marshall scholars. I shall focus on the interrelationship of folk hero, ritual and character
in *Chosen Place, Timeless People*.

Cuffee Ned, as he is presented in the novel, is a historical figure and a
folk hero in the Black Moses tradition. Through ritual enactment of his
deeds at carnival and daily arguments over details of his triumphs and
defeats, the Bournehills community achieves an extraordinary communal
and psychic triumph not comprehensible to outsiders. It is a world where
Kingsley and Sons, British absentee landlords, own everything that is of
material value. Because Kingsley uses his power to keep Bournehills folk
slightly freer than slaves, one expects to find among them a white interpretation of history and a veneration of white values; because of the bleakness
of the landscape one is inclined to expect an emotional void. None of these
obtains in the novel. In fact, a fierce battle is being waged by outsiders to
"rescue" Bournehillians from material deprivation and a quiet but effective
counteroffensive by the latter to remain unchanged. Folk hero, myth, and
concomitant ritual provide the strength for the Bournehills struggle. Percy
Bryam, the white planter whom Cuffee Ned, a slave, defeated for a time,
represents one dialectical extreme of the novel's forces; in the world of the
novel Bryam is metaphor for Kingsley and Sons and the Bourne Island elite

that are their managerial servants. The other extreme is encapsulated in Cuffee Ned; his *de facto* priests, Delbert and Fergusson; and their indefatigable followers, the Bournehills people. In the battle for survival that the Bournehills folk must fight every day against those sent to alter their landscape, to conquer them with television, radiofusion, jukeboxes, and irrelevant industry, a microcosm of the Pyre Hill revolt is enacted.

Striking parallels exist between the villagers and Cuffee Ned. Most noticeable is that Bryam had made Cuffee Ned his most trusted servant, so completely ignorant was he of Cuffee's designs. We see Saul, Harriet, and Allan never getting to know the Bournehills people, for, like Cuffee, they will not reveal themselves to the "conquering" race. Instinctively they understand the Grecian quality of foreign gifts, coming as they do from the allies of Kingsley and Sons and negotiated for by their hirelings. Careful planning, secret organizing—these had been the hallmarks of Cuffee's beginning. Keeping the secret of their spiritual sustenance from probing outsiders is one way to be like Cuffee.

But this faithfulness to Cuffee's memory extends further. Long before we witness the enactment of the deeds of Cuffee's life, we are told by Fergusson that Cuffee will return. In fact, the second coming of Christ and Cuffee's return become so syncretized that the one is indistinguishable from the other in the people's minds. They do not want, if I may use an analogy from the Christian myth, to be found serving alien gods when he returns.

It is in Leesy Walkes that Marshall best captures the invincible silence to outsiders. Much of Leesy's commentary never exceeds "Ha." When Vere comes back from America (where, in the words of the novel's protagonist Merle Kibona, his head becomes full of the nonsense of car racing), Leesy disapproves of the time he spends on his car, for instinctively she knows, presumably from animist tradition, that "things such as cars had human properties . . . and were constantly plotting against those whom they served" (*Chosen Place, Timeless People*, 185). In her vision of reality, having a decent house in which to put a woman and buying land for that purpose are the pivots of a man's reality, not investing in "tyrannical" machinery. So great is her distrust of machinery that she refuses to have her canes transported by truck to Brighton and capitulates only when her donkey cart is unable to do so.

As if to clinch the indirect portrait of Leesy as one deriving her wisdom and survival from nature and as one seeing corruption in the nature-altering machinery of man, Marshall effects a physical oneness between Leesy and the Bournehills landscape: "She was slight and dry, a mere husk, but for her hands, which were as large as a cane cutter's" (*Chosen*, 8).

That it is her sow that is slaughtered to provide meat for the cavalcade that goes to New Bristol to relieve the Pyre Hill revolt is significant; for she is an earth mother, a fact clearly shown when she accepts Vere's death with a stoicism equal to the earth's accepting a corpse. But the slaughter of the sow in her yard (at which time the reader learns of the villagers' respect for all forms of life and witnesses the bonding ritual implicit in the communal biting of the sow's tail) makes her yard a shrine to the values of pantheism and community, and probably makes her priestess of both.

Marshall knew that the "inextinguishable fire" and "inner light" with which her narrator characterizes Leesy and Merle could not exist within a vacuum. She accounts for it largely by the Cuffee Ned myth and its ritual enactment and constant evocation. Cuffee is referred to as an "obeah" man, implying that like the Moses of Reed's *Mumbo Jumbo* and Hurston's *Moses Man of the Mountain*, he possessed the ability to employ cosmic force to achieve superhuman feats. Cuffee knew who his enemies were. Cuffee had left them a promise. Since Cuffee had conquered, he had left them a legacy of possible conquest. Under Cuffee they had been a people; enacting the ritual in New Bristol, they are a people, complete with god and rituals.

Part of the Bournehills people's otherness is their refusal to play carnival according to the rules of the colonial lackeys. Such rules would have been quickly understood by Leesy as being part of "the machine," a ploy by white merchants and their lackeys to make carnival commercially profitable. Nor can the scorn poured on them by the New Bristol elite in anyway inhibit them; we are submitted to pages upon pages of it to alert us to the fact that it is a form of reaction formation. The real reason, one suspects, is that the Pyre Hill revolt succeeds in unmasking those people who had long joined the Bryam camp. Each time it is performed it quietly calls the Bourne Island elite traitors. It further implies that Bryam's fate, when the appropriate moment arrives, awaits the traitors. In a sense, the enactment of the ritual is a political act; it is a ritual statement about those who sold out for power and prestige.

The ritual creates embarrassment for the black and brown elite who has failed in its mandate to impose Euro–American mores on the population; the Pyre Hill revolt proclaims Bournehills residents as possessing a self-sufficient history, philosophy and religion. Thus Lyle Hutson, one of those entrusted with bribing capitalists into exploiting Bourne Islanders, feels the need to call the ritual "sport."

The wisdom from nature that made Cuffee an obeah man and gives Leesy her special assurance about reality is pictured generously, some will say too generously, in the novel by Marshall. The rhythms of nature parallel those of the Bournehills community. There is that time of year when the Atlantic boisterously spews forth seaweed, when it is said to be cleaning itself, and when, as Merle says, it also lectures. This alternates with its calm period. The analogy finds expression in the lives of the Bournehills folk. In crop time Stinger, Ten-ton, and their gangs cut the cane, completely oblivious to the sun, and Gwen and the other women transport it to the waiting trucks. Saul, from another society (one where air conditioning destroys summer), gets vertigo from merely standing in the sun and looking at them. But these characters do what they must do and understand their actions as an extension of nature. When the crop season is over and the "dead" season takes over (along with mass unemployment and hunger), that too is understood and contextualized. Merle, who is outside of the crop cycles, marks the changes in the flowering of her caccia tree as well as in the moods of the sea. The vignette in which she and Harriet discuss the blooms of the caccia tree is present as part of the dramatization of the opposing worldviews of Harriet (Euro–American) and Merle (more or less African). Harriet would rather have the tree bloom in perpetuity; Merle is opposed for she knows that in perpetual bloom it will cease to be beautiful.

This circularity of time inadvertently lends credence to the Cuffee myth. For if time is circular, if the sea cleanses itself periodically and alternates between calm and boisterousness, then too at the appropriate moment Cuffee's time will come. The people's annual acting out of the Pyre Hill revolt in the same costumes and with the same dialogue is their self-implantation into the circularity of time.

Like Baldwin and Hughes, Marshall uses ritual to mirror character. As far as character traits go, Cuffee Ned is alive in Merle Kibona. We receive hints of this throughout the novel: in her self-description as an obeah woman, i.e., that she is a repository of the race's wisdom and powers, in her incorporation of all religions, and in her uncompromising quality to confront others with truth (in her inability to be diplomatic she has none of Cuffee's trickster qualities). Her function in the novel is to interpret; in fact, she is the community's bard—rationally expressed in her role as historian but more profoundly present in her psychic tentacles that both draw and impact sustenance. This function is conveyed iconically in her role of pole bearer at the Pyre Hill Revolt drama. I have already alluded to her conflation of Euro–American reality into the machinery that kills Vere. She is an uncontainable character, vacillating in the roles of castigator, enlightener, madwoman, and giver of language to other people's feelings, a provider as it were of form for the inchoate. But for her very human frailties she would have been a mythic character—a Legba, for example.

She is a matrix, since she is the link between Bournehills and the world that despises it, and Bournehills and the expatriates: Saul, Harriet, and Allen; it is her vision that more or less puts these three worlds into perspective. In a physical, social, conventional, and intellectual sense, she respects no boundaries, not if they impede truth and justice. The triple heritage that formed Marshall's psyche (Marshall 1973, 106) is especially evident in the communication styles she accords Merle, who combines signifying and "tracing," the latter being a ritualistic form of discourse used only by "unschooled" Caribbean women. She employs these styles at all times to get to the heart of matters. We encounter it first in her "reading" of Lyle, later with Erskine Vaughan, and after that with Saul. It is ineffectual with Lyle and Erskine; both, as part of "the machinery," are outside the framework in which the ritual can be effective. But it works with Saul. He has acquired some insight into the dialectics of the Cuffee myth, and her words are the catalyst that moves him from the realm of observer to participant. As insignificant as those words may appear, they are crucial to the plan that is later developed and which, in the way it comes about and is carried out, is analogous to the Pyre Hill revolt. Collecting data, she informs him, will not repair the rollers at Cane Vale; he must use some of his "millions" to help the people harvest their canes.

Hers is like King Arthur's quest to restore health to the kingdom. The difference is that the morality of the one embarking on the quest is essentially African, where chastity is death and fecundity and sex are life; here the affliction is manmade: contempt by the powerful for the powerless; and the forces to be confronted are not changing phantoms (though indeed they are equally invisible) but the profit machinery.

The community's understanding of Merle's value is depicted in the protective ring the women form around her as they rescue her from the cursed surroundings of Cane Vale. At home Leesy and Carrington stand guard over her, and the villagers daily trek to her house to impart to her the communal strength that will return her sanity and to feed her.

But Merle is not Leesy Walkes. She knows in very close detail the inner workings of the oppressor's psyche, having lived in his country and studied at his universities. Further still, she is intimate with his power equations, having been enclosed in one of its brackets. And because the oppressor set the trap that destroyed her marriage when she no longer played according to the former's terms, she has on that account been permanently wounded. In a way of speaking, she has experienced her version of Bryam's oppression in the control-or-destroy approach to reality. Her difference from Leesy also lies in her ability to use the "machine" in its real and metaphoric sense; in the person of Saul and in the ownership of the departed governor's Bentley. She knows, however, that the machine must be adapted if it is to be incorporated into the physical and psychic landscape. The battered state in which Merle keeps the Bentley is part of Marshall's depiction of this quality in Merle.

Unlike Baldwin's characters in *Go Tell It on the Mountain*, who employ ritual strictly as escape from or compensation for a reality they are unable to negotiate, Marshall's characters evince a practical survival in their myth. In fact, the Cuffee Ned/Percy Bryam struggle is updated when Kingsley and Sons close the sugar factory and show indifference to the loss this will cause the small cane growers. As far as Kingsley's representative (a white Bourne Islander who makes no effort to conceal his contempt for poor blacks) is concerned, Bournehills folk are accustomed to crises and will be able to get over this one. What he is actually saying is that they are too unimportant to be ever worth consideration.

A collective Cuffee emerges to resolve this crisis. To create him the mythic Cuffee is invoked as an example of the possible, and the history Bournehillians annually enact is held up as containing the formula for the unity required to end the crisis.

Delbert, one of those always engaged in the contentious arguments over the details about Cuffee's downfall, and a key figure in the dramatization of the Pyre Hill revolt, tells the community that when Cuffee was live they were the ones "running things around here." At that time they did not fight one another because selfishness meant defeat. In the present crisis it has a similar meaning. The situation they are faced with is getting their canes to Brighton before they spoil. "We're going to see if the unity we achieved during Cuffee's reign cannot be achieved once more. Because if it's otherwise, 'everyman for himself and to hell with the other fellow,' we're going to lose out..." (*Chosen*, 394–95).

Delbert here takes over from where Merle, now ill, left off. He transforms the Cuffee Ned revolt into a metaphor that is analogous to the challenges inherent in the current crisis. The "we" in the song that is the matrix of the ritual and the "we" in Delbert's harangue remove the challenge from the passive past and put it in the present as a possibility.

Who could resist such a challenge? In a sense Bournehillians are already a community complete with connectors—the ritual eating of the roasted pig's tail, their work teams, their funerals, their collective nursing of the sick back to health, and certainly their invasion of New Bristol once a year to show the elite that they had not capitulated. In this role Delbert is the Apollonian counterpart of the Dionysian Merle, according to whom the people should invade Cane Vale and either burn it down or manage it (389).

In the people's collective action we begin to see an updating of the myth. It begins to take on the qualities of pride and confidence. There is also the implication that Cuffee can no longer be one man; moreover in the actual myth he could not carry out his exploits singlehandedly; nor, if we take Saul's role—directly resulting from his confrontation with Merle—can it exclude those who, while they look like the enemy, are sympathetic to the people's ideals and can offer nonenslaving, nonhumiliating assistance. Besides, in a technological era, however much people spur machines and fear becoming like those who have mechanized themselves by being over-reliant on the machine, the latter are nonetheless indispensable: donkey carts will get the canes to Cane Vale; only lorries will get them to Brighton.

Conditioned by the Cuffee myth but ashamed that they had not fully lived according to its tenets, the people as if by a convenant labor in concert, sacrificing all, to harvest and transport the canes to Brighton. Without the Cuffee myth to subordinate their selfish desires, without the memory of Cuffee's success to urge them on, without the communal spirit that the myth perennially engendered, one wonders whether the undertaking could have been possible. Cuffee Ned is the binding force of Bournehills.

Marshall by her own admission creates with a sense of the function of ritual. She recalls how the Barbadian women used talk "to exorcise the day's humiliations and restore them to themselves" (1973, 98). The model for passing on survival wisdom came from her mother and her mother's friends. In her view they had preserved the *griot* tradition blacks brought from Africa (1973, 104). Along with others—Ralph Ellison, Larry Neal, James Baldwin, and Amiri Baraka—they provided her the inspiration to create along this line.

Ritual, then, is neither accidental nor incidental to *Chosen Place, Timeless People*. In many respects this work is reminiscent of Hughes's *Not Without Laughter*, at least in its intention. Because, however, of the fusion Marshall effects in ritual and character, so that the one becomes at points indistinguishable from the other, and because of her intentions for doing so, this novel is a ground-breaker. In my estimation no new links were added until Morrison's *Song of Solomon* (1977), which embodies a large number of similar approaches to the question of black identity and survival, and Forrest's *The Bloodworth Orphans* (1977).

What we see then in Wright, Walker, Ellison, Baldwin, and Marshall is not only a mastery of various techniques for incorporating ritual into fiction, but a commitment to explore such rituals as a way of finding out what they imply about the hopes, beliefs, and day-to-day reality of black existence. Such writers, too, have unrestrainedly dramatized what they feel are the assets and liabilities of such rituals. There is no doubt that the Afro-American novelists of the post–Harlem Renaissance era who chose to make folklore an essential part of their creative material have contributed significantly to a deeper understanding of the role black folklore plays in the lives of blacks as well as new ways of adapting that folklore to the needs of fiction.

TOWARDS GLOBALISM: FORREST

Leon Forrest represents the contemporary phase in the use of Afro-American folklore. What one sees in his and several other contemporary novelists' use of ritual is a pulling in of elements from non–Afro–American traditions. The Afro-American tradition remains primary in all this and is certainly not diminished because of the alien elements. This is especially notable in the works of Ishmael Reed. The effect of such a change is to make the creation, especially in Reed's case, more fiction than folklore, and the rituals more symbols than mimesis. The writing as well ceases to be realistic.

Leon Forrest's Ford, whom we have already seen, inhabits a fictive world where ritual predominates. Though essentially Afro–American, Forrest's rituals incorporate beliefs and practices from Judaic and Hellenic myths. The result is that the actions of the characters resonate man's tragedy and triumph from the beginning of "imaginative" history. The eternal needs that create internecine warfare, scapegoats, and inordinate preoccupations with power underlie much of the novel's action. Not becoming a victim of these impulses is the protagonist's greatest challenge. The characters are trapped by the human condition and particularly the American chapter of that condition. The implication of *The Bloodworth Orphans* (cited hereafter *Orphans*) is, among so much else, that to escape permanent entrapment by these forces, one needs to understand the whole course of human history and to acquire the cunning to negotiate both long- and short-term reality. The novel itself is a sort of "genesis" that moves into an "exodus" of the few. The omniscient jive artist whose art is strictly defensive is shown to be superior to the trickster in that he escapes the latter's attempts to enslave him; he is also well-equipped for survival and for showing others the way to salvation. Apart from jive, all Afro–American rituals are shown to be inadequate to meet the needs that created them in the first place—unless one has the power to manipulate those rituals; i.e., has the skills of the jive artist.

The novel is cast in the form of a saga: the Bloodworth saga. Its language is for the most part epic. The principal characters are orphans or foundlings with little or no knowledge of their origins until probes lead to discoveries of incest among them. Such discoveries take the reader back to the incestuous deeds of the Bloodworth family; a symbol of white plantation morality. Along with incest comes a number of family curses that devolve upon the black branches of the family. Forrest is using an allegorical structure to "signify" on white America. It is not Ham's curse that is withering blacks but the curse of white lust. Forrest universalizes the devastating consequences of that lust by evoking its treatment in Greek and Roman mythology and in the Noah myth. Consequently the black self-hate and guilt that Afro–American rituals (according to this novel) seem intent on exorcising have their origins in the human depravity that is abundantly identifiable in Caucasian mythology (and I am sure in all other mythologies).

Most of the characters are consumed by their quest for identity, their craving for community, or their perpetual self-sacrifice. According to the novel's frequent refrain, excerpted from the spirituals, they are all motherless children, "a long ways from home"; or in the words of folk historian-midwife character Mama Lucia Breedlove, "children of the wreckage" (185). In *The Bloodworth Orphans* the foundlings always find a physical home among Afro–Americans but consume themselves in the attempt to be psychologically at home in America. But the foundlings are exaggerations of the essential homelessness that characterize all Afro–Americans. To find existence merely tolerable these characters must engage in numerous rituals of guilt-expiation and self-validation. Forrest provides them in the Catholic mass (rejected as being ineffectual), the blues, the dozens, lying/jiving, and the black church.

The first elaborate ritual that the reader witnesses is Packwood's exorcism of Rachel's evil. The evil consists of Rachel's murder of her white half-brother, who is also the father of her two children; she pushes him upon God's command into a fire that was intended to sacrifice a sheep. The murder left Rachel incapable of functioning. Packwood is an itinerant evangelist and an ex-blues prince; the last quality makes him an exorciser *par excellence*.

The entire ritual, although recounted years later by a malicious Sister Stella Wordlaw, is dramatized. Packwood employs surgical metaphors to describe his exorcising act. Urged on by the congregation, he performs a form of "logo-surgery" and with his "gospel knife" cuts out Rachel's guilt. In fact what he does is give her the courage to function once more.

The ceremony occurs during a torrential downpour and throughout, a sheep is, again, sacrificed. The roasting sheep returns one to a pre–Christian era and infuses the ritual with a primal quality. It is not difficult to see Rachel's guilt transferred to the sheep, which is in turn burned, as a rather concrete symbol of expiation. Forrest uses the ritual to tell Rachel's life story up to the murder. One aspect of the ritual is quite surreal, when Packwood takes Rachel up into the branches of a tree. It is probably Forrest's attempt to move back to the concept of the transcendental elements; thus he moves her temporarily from the base elements of earth and water into air. It lifts Rachel from the literal mud that the earlier flood had brought as well as the psychic mud in which she had remained stuck.

Forrest uses an aspect of Wright's technique in *The Long Dream* in that he too masses the responses of the congregation and inserts them between paragraphs of Packwood's delivery. The preacher's frequent calling for "a witness," a common device in the Afro–American folk sermon or "testimony" but not used in any of the sermons we have seen so far, is frequent in this work and in this ritual.

The exorcism begins for Rachel a life-long practice of the self-sacrifice she deems necessary for her salvation (It is as if she moves from "air," where Packwood had taken her, to her own form of "fire"). This need tyrannizes all aspects of her existence, even her choice of Money Czar Flowers, a repulsively gluttonous, malodorous, and sexually prepubescent man, as husband. To La Donna Scales, who administers insulin to him three times per day, Rachel says that she keeps him in her household as an everpresent reminder of the state of the nation's soul upon which God is preparing to operate and for which she, as "God's handmaid nurse," is preparing "the operating table" (*Orphans*, 68).

Regarding her sons, Rachel feels that they are irremediably tainted by the Bloodworth curse and are "the dead branches" that by Biblical injunction must be pruned away. The narrator adds that such should have been the fate of half the black population in the Mississippi county where Rachel lived in 1917. In other words Rachel, like so many blacks who interpret the

Bible literally, carry their religious beliefs to absurdity. But Forrest does not deprive her of maternal instincts, for she prays to God to give her sons, in return for the sacrifice she is prepared to make, a more humane fate. But the answer comes to her in a vision: "No deals!" The vision leaves her stuttering and so uncoordinated that her flesh crawls when she is asleep.

Together such details suggest that Rachel's religiosity becomes a sickness. This is understandable, since she approaches God in terms of what she perceives to be biblical absolutes regarding the inheritance of sins and curses. If she could have apportioned the blame to the Bloodworth clan, could have seen her children as victims who had to survive a horrendous heritage, she might have escaped this illness. But this central responsibility she never faces. Her blindness, which becomes complete shortly after the exorcism ritual, equally characterizes her intellect.

Visions, prayer-rituals, fasts—including the thousand-mile fast-journey following the death of her sons—her roles as choir leader, gospel singer, and social worker among orphans (yet with a contempt for all that is earthly) absorb Rachel completely. It is easy to see that she, subconsciously at least, does not believe that the Bloodworth curse in her has been expiated; in her acts of piety she leaves not the slightest chink in her armor of righteousness to allow God's wrath to enter and demolish her. Her piety discomforts others, especially the congregation of River Rock of Eden. But for the pastor there she is a useful tool.

Forrest implies what we have already seen in Baldwin—though more forcefully—that the rituals of the black church can be life-crippling and are designed to expiate curses that blacks did not originate. The implication is that blacks are not responsible for the existential problems of Americans, and yet they have allowed themselves to believe that they are and have adopted ghastly rituals to cope with the burden. Since Rachel's curse and its punishment derive from the white race—including the theology by which she interprets that curse—her psychic mutilation evokes deep pathos. Her similarity with Grimes is that both the curse that imprisons her and the religion that imprisons him derive from slavery.

The refusal by white fathers to acknowledge their children born of black mothers, the separation of children from their parents when they were sold to other plantations, the virtual defenselessness of black women, long after abolition, against lust-driven white men, the economic hardships that forced fathers to work long distances from home or simply to abandon the responsibility of fatherhood—fuse into a huge psychic wound in Forrest's work. The "foundling" is its metaphor. The desperate acts to compensate for, avenge, or accommodate the pain is dramatized in the lives of characters like Regal, Dolphin, La Donna, Thig-pen, Ironwood, and Bass. Each is a child of the "wreckage." Since Regal is the most important character as regards the discussion of ritual, I shall discuss him in connection with the role Forrest accords the masses. For our purpose Ironwood Landlord

Rumble, the blind, insane priest of the blues is important, since it is through him that Forrest communicates the meaning of the blues. The remaining aforementioned characters are more relevant to the working out of the Bloodworth curse.

Nathaniel tells us that sometimes he and Regal go to the Refuge Hospital *cum* prison to hear Ironwood play. On another occasion Nathaniel goes alone and is almost made a prisoner. Before this journey Rachel, in an overeffusion of religiosity, almost drowns him in a bathtub of water. The trip is therefore juxtaposed against Rachel's fantaticism to show the blues as a balancing factor, as an equilibrium for religious excess.

Before Nathaniel's imprisonment in the Refuge Hospital we are treated to a first-hand account of the ability of the blues to liberate him from the life-denying, antisexual injunctions of white Father O'Keefe. The blues provide Nathaniel with the verbal tool he needs to signify on O'Keefe as well as another vision of reality. Thus at the end of the confession Nathaniel resolves to leave the Catholic Church because of what he feels is Father O'Keefe's misunderstanding of human sexuality and hostility to the Black Baptists, "the babblers of confusion and witchcraft" (*Orphans*, 27). At this point he turns to the blues with a vengeance:

"Jelly, Jelly, Jelly...Jelly stays on my mind...Jelly roll killed my Pappy and ran my Mammy blind." Oh Father O'Keefe you don't put this jelly near your teeth (unless your nature's gone to your head), you roll it, man. You roll it all Night Long. And Nathaniel hummed:

> "You've got to whip it to a jelly,
> You've got to stir it in a bowl.
> You've got to whip it to a jelly
> If you want good jelly roll."

...Ah but not the dough roll of the Bread. But he'll think I'm signifying, trying to dilute Jesus, rolling bread into wine and getting only old funky-good yeast; trying to make Jesus walk the waters, where the grapes of wrath are stored....Bread and wine, your burden ain't as heavy. And him denying Magdalene's parts and J.C.'s body to make you forget the magic of Jesus. Roll Jordan, Roll. Yet thinking of old Foxworth [the Baptist minister and a fox in every sense of the metaphor] too, who said, "Young man, your arms are too short to box with God." Old Signifying Foxworth, up a tree, and old O'Keefe playing the dozens about the origins (*Orphans*, 27–28).

The blues, interwoven with jive and signifying, provide Nathaniel with a standard against which to measure false theology. Thus it is a ritual of salvation. Through the linguistic magic of the blues and jive he fuses sex (jelly roll), triumph (the roll of Jordan), and food. In prohibiting sex, Father O'Keefe is considered to be either awkward or impotent (wanting to eat the jelly with his teeth). Hence Forrest shows that Nathaniel is able to escape the fear trap of the rituals and beliefs of the church precisely because the blues and other folk attitudes have already immunized him against it. What we see here then is the saving quality of the blues.

One of the exercises that the inmates of the Refuge Hospital, where Nathaniel is eventually incarcerated, must attend is a routine concert given by Ironwood. The hospital *cum* prison setting that Forrest chooses for this scene evokes the restrictions within which black culture operates. Moreover, in this same room the bodies of slaves used to be brought for dissection, to further scientific knowledge. For many it was the last stop on the Underground Railroad, but not because they had reached Canada.

Forrest intends the description of the premises to evoke slavery and Ironwood to be a black but ineffectual Moses. It is around a number of axial emotions that Forrest portrays the concert. These emotions remain constant from one section of the ritual to another. Forrest achieves this through repetition of a number of similar feelings in altered phrasing or synonymous images, a technique he adapts from the blues lyrics. Such repetitions correspond to the riffs or repeated phrases in many spirituals, the blues, and jazz. Forrest resorts to synonymous phrasing to avoid the tedious repetition that Ostendorf notes in mere transcripts of the blues and folk sermons (1982, 8). We come to rely on the feelings of Nathaniel and the comments of the prisoners for the emotions and memories that the blues concert releases. There is in the wide spectrum of feelings released something of the experience of Ellison's Invisible Man listening to Louis Armstrong in "The Prologue." But what is communicated in single images in Ellison becomes a catalogue of images in Forrest.

The "mothering" of Ironwood's music is not enough, Forrest shows, to foster community and motivate the inmates to conquer the "prison"; that prison is largely within themselves, and is pictured in very ferocious outbreaks of the dozens whenever the music ceases. The suggestion is that unless they are being distracted they turn to destroying one another. Wherever Forrest employs the dozens in this novel it is such mutual destruction that he depicts. The role of the dozens in the blues concert will be excerpted and analyzed when we come to look at the dozens.

We cannot overlook the white authorities' rationale for having the inmates attend the blues concert. The reason is to propagandize the Euro–American vision of reality: science (The whole is arranged somewhat like the enticing programs on television so that the listeners could be presented with the sponsors' products). The inmates are encouraged to donate themselves to scientific experiments and by doing so attain wealth and fame—those "transcendental" American values. With few exceptions they respond to such blandishments with ridicule.

Looking at the blues ritual more closely, we note that Nathaniel's reflection on the blues before he enters the actual performance area sums up what the men are about to participate in. In a sense, then, like most rituals, the participants know what to expect and attend because of such expectations:

And now Nathaniel wondered was Ironwood an out-of-sight Warlock, a black-and-blue-splattered spook, a blizzard-driven Angel, or simply one of the yoked yet free-floating rib cages flocking and flouncing about like eagles: bartered, recycled, *decomposed*, then released within the asylum chambers to haunt our dehydrated days (like gutted pillows of fire and ice, hurled out of a windstorm) down into the anguished wailing wall about the bloody, dream-grasping, egg-shelled rivers, in the homeless, underground, hooded masquerade of carnivals, weaved out of their skins (*Orphans*, 293–94).

For Nathaniel the blues experience is so spiritual and nightmarish that he can only deal with it in images that evoke essentially mystical though fright-ful phenomena. It is largely in such images that the performance is portrayed.

Forrest adapts the repeated blues line with only slight alterations to the prose with which he portrays this ritual. We move from passage to passage and confront the same constellation of emotions. I shall explain this tech-nique by citing and analyzing three of over twenty such passages spaced over the twenty-four pages devoted to the blues ritual:

Then he commenced to transport his homeless patrons on out of that cellar kitchen. Ironwood "Landlord" Rumble, navigating blue-melted steel through a forest on fire, through Job's tear grass; wisteria; cotton fields and patches of maize; through the tumble-down razor strapped gospels and epistles of tracks to glory of chained stars; lost tar-babies gathering in the black berries, canceled notes, wigs, straight jackets, as abandoned rib cages, upon a ferris wheel, whirring, choking, raging; pinched-nerve abandoned children, foundlings, chalking the grotto black-board, tiptoeing up charred ladder rungs, arising from the blood of Niobe's children (295).

Bathing, baptizing, purifying Sound into the shape of the softly jangling tambou-rines in his left hand—washed pure in the Cross—fretful, blissful innocence, lamb-like on the skins of baying tide-tossed Sound, as the three bags of wool, wining-ballooning, kiting into nine circles, encompassing the voice of Styx and Niobe and now with bellowing steel-making resonance of a nine-pound hammer; lining track out the projected Soul, Ironwood flourished inside of an invisible moldering, or a stirring wakefulness, as the rib of Adam dancing into new singing shape riffed from his image-spieling, reshaped out of the valley of dry bones: humbled by the glorious harvest of her fire-scarred fingers upon the ladder fire escape, touching back into his essence . . . *a long way from home* (297).

Now from a tower burial lookout site, on the outskirts to the city, Ironwood became the high priest of the tribe, extemporizing upon his royal golden flute with a faint jangle of the whispering tambourine, a psalm of memory to Lady Day. Celebrating in tongues her time-freezing, prison love, muted hypodermic-jellied, sight-blinding, knocking-bones, lean-honed, aching vision, in the frigid, dehydrated valley of the bleached dry bones of love, Ironwood's rage-muted violin sounding flute; and behind *that*, talking, dancing spirit, meat shaking off their bones, Big Maybelle, like the huge-hearted felt flesh like, like Bessie inside the body and blood of Lady's delicate violin song of sorrows . . . Singing them all back to the foundling child of the path-road, tiny enough to fit into a mailbox . . . *Sometimes I feel I'm almost gone* (301).

Almost all of Forrest's writing depicting the blues concert is done in this surreal manner. One could talk on and on about who might have influenced Forrest, but the actual reality is that surrealism is native to the principal Afro–American rituals. They are so surreal that a camera would capture only the more visible aspects and a tape recorder the mere sounds. In blues concerts, comedy sessions, and church worship, the groans and moans at varying pitches jarring with one another and the body movements that accompany them or made instead of them create an apparent babel of sound. The atmosphere too is laden with these emotions that exert a hypnotic effect on the observer. In the case of the blues concert order is maintained strictly by the musician who leaves the exorcising spaces as demanded by the needs of the audience. This last, as we shall see, is evident in Forrest's portrayal of the blues concert—although it is only a token evocation that he manages to convey.

The references to the dead musicians reincarnated by Ironwood's playing are very much in keeping with African traditions of ancestor worship, reincarnation, etc. It is therefore requisite that Ironwood be described as a high priest. The effect of a train ride and hence of a journey, conveyed principally through assonance, elision, and the use of the present participle, as well as numerous journey metaphors, makes the music itself a vehicle for conveying the psychic history of the Afro–American people; this music is, as it was for Ellison's Invisible Man, a sound synthesis of Afro–American existence from slavery to the present. It is a journey back into the past that undergirds the present.

The references to Job, the rib cages, dry bones, the various religious images and forms, embody all the promises of triumph that will compensate for earthly suffering. Among blacks the "Dry Bones" sermon is well-known, and is perhaps their most poignant symbol of hope that they will eventually triumph over the forces that oppress them in America. The exercise in which Ironwood engages here is not unlike a "dry bones" reincarnation: giving life to the dead and hopeless. Rachel describes herself in Jobian terms—"Yet though Thou slayest me still will I trust Thee." Her thousand-mile fast could be likened to Job's sackcloth-and-ashes ritual of asceticism. The "fire-scarred fingers," "blood of Niobe's children," the motherless children combined with the various flood references not cited in these three passages, are emblematic of the permanent grief in the Afro–American community. The fire is both a reference to lynching and to the victims of "the kitchenette" so vividly described by Wright in *Twelve Million Black Voices* (1941). The river image never fails, because of the context of homelessness, to evoke the Jewish lamentation during captivity. It is pregnant too with personal memories: Many of the inmates have fled Mississippi, many of them have been victims of floods, and many of them, no doubt, look forward to crossing the metaphorical "Jordan."

But "Lethe," "Styx," "hypodermic riffs" (frequently repeated in other

passages) and the return to the state of the foundling infant connote, if not
a death-wish, the desire to return to a painless childhood (if such ever
existed for these characters). This return defeats the purpose for descend-
ing into the underground of ancestral wisdom, for it is essentially a repository of survival techniques. In the Graeco-Roman tradition, for Aeneas, for
example, it is a prelude to empire-founding. These images reinforce the
abundant self-destructive and group-destructive tendencies in the novel.
Forrest underscores "the descent," as I have already stated, with a liberal
interspersing of the dozens. Forrest wishes this group-destructive tendency
to be a central focus in this work and that is why he presents Regal's
nightmare, which serves as an encapsulating metaphor for these various
themes, at the beginning of the novel. In Regal's recurring nightmare he is
chosen to destroy all those barriers that prevent his brothers and sisters
from attaining "the treasure" (that is, he becomes a Black Moses), but he
finds that he is forced to slay his brothers. And after he kills "the boar" that
impedes access to the treasure and leads the sisters to it, they in turn
dismember him, except that the sprouting pieces come back to life. The
sisters extract only baubles from the treasure chest and run away in confusion, losing the treasure once more. Regal, a minor blues musician, gospel
singer, and before his demise, preacher, is a spiritual guide into past and
present Afro–American reality. It is largely with this internecine warfare
that the novel ends. These conflicts negate whatever possibilities of ethnic
solidarity the blues proffer.

But there are elements of terrestrial triumph in the music too. John
Henry (referred to in numerous ways), railroad, North Star, grotto black-
board, High John the Conqueror (abundant in the uncited passages) are
references to symbols of black defiance of white control during and after
slavery. The Underground Railroad and the North Star need no explanation. High John the Conqueror, as Zora Neale Hurston points out in an
essay of that name, is the mythic embodiment of the Afro–American cunning and will that defeated the dehumanization intended by slavery ([1943]
1958, 93–94, 102). The grotto blackboard is certainly a tribute to those blacks
who became clandestinely literate during slavery.

Forrest singles out especially the regeneration element of the blues.
There are frequent references to the "dry bones" and, more important,
Forrest's analogue of the Orpheus myth is woven into the ritual. Ironwood
is described as playing "Daddy Street," whose dead daughter he brings in
on his shoulder. It is Forrest's play on the words *child of the street*. It is also an
evocation of the Afro–American literary heritage—Ann Petry's *The Street*
and Baldwin's *No Name in the Street*. Ironwood's trombone is described as an
offering "of Almighty God Armstrong deep down in the wells of the impoverished wooden coffin of the Street child...shaped out of the magnolia
tree..." (*Orphans*, 297–98). Not only is Ironwood an agent of the deceased
Armstrong, i.e., his medium, but he must rescue the dead girl from the

"magnolia coffin," i.e., the death produced by slavery. A few paragraphs later we are given additional images of the raped child, her blood-stained dress ripped from her body and her "head dangling from a wheel barrow of human feces upon which the spirit of a pig rooted and lived and drove" (298). This is another variation on the Bloodworth horrors that the blues musician is called upon to sedate or exorcise. Thus Ironwood is portrayed putting into sound the suffering of defenseless black women in an environment of lust-ridden white men. Killens in *Youngblood* (1958) and Gaines in *A Gathering of Old Men* (1983) explore this feature of the South in their fiction. Ironwood succeeds in that Nathaniel recognizes the "visage of Street's older daughter and reincarnated spirit of the child on Ironwood's shoulder" (*Orphans*, 298–99). This type of portrayal is ironic, for as we shall see later, it is Ironwood who needs to be regenerated. Nevertheless, because Nathaniel uses the blues earlier in the novel to liberate himself from the life-denying religion of Father O'Keefe, the health-giving aspect of the blues is validated within the universe of the novel.

Forrest relies heavily on the inmates' responses to provide a focus for the experiences the music forces out of the listeners; thereby he shows its evocative and cathartic power. Some of the responses are of pure pain:

"Oh Lord a motherless child, and a long ways from home—don't I know about it. . . .

Bread and wine, bread and wine; child, your hurt ain't as heavy as mine. . . .

Flame of my life going up like a hole-ridden sock tied to a kite in a storm. . . . Lord, wondering would a matchbox hold my dreams. . . .

. . . And many thousands still peeled for the evening mail.

". . . Flood swam me out of my body, soon one morning, troubled my house down the river, like a natural man, with my woman and my child buried in my bed upside down, inside . . ." his fingers at work upon an imaginary guitar, which he cradled like a baby (*Orphans*, 297).

Painful as these utterances are, the pain is held in art—metaphors, similes, rhyme—stylized a long time before the men come to this concert. In fact, the expressions they employ are not unique to them but are the property of the folk. Hence even these responses are ritual. What is not ritual is their presence in the Refuge Hospital, which represents America's coercion of its black citizens.

Some of the responses are even more stock but not unrevealing:

Teach, preach deliver that mail, Ironwood . . . this here's the great-great-grand-daughter of High John the Conqueror . . . bringing back the good times. . . .

ALL NIGHT LONG. . . .

Others, reflecting the sporting element in the audience, are straight out of the toasts:

Here come I, old Beelzebub. About my neck I carry my club....

I'm the blood-stopper who rolls when icicles hanging off trees.
(*Orphans*, 298–301).

The dominant sentiment is of a nostalgic sadness. Memories of unfulfilled dreams, of a country—the American South—from which they have
escaped, of previous catastrophes, are the chief ingredients of these excla-
mations. That their plight has worsened is evident in their incarceration in
the Refuge Hospital in the ironically named city of Eden. For this reason
Ironwood addresses the topic of suicide. We are told when Ironwood plays
"'Good Morning Heartache'...many of the men were heard to weep
aloud... the scene became so overcast with gloom that Ironwood broke into
a few bars of 'Do Nothing 'til You Hear from Me'" before breaking for
intermission (306–7).

When Nathaniel enters the concert scene he reflects on Ironwood's role
as artist-priest leading back along the trails of the ancestral voyage, and also
as "skinned lamb"; i.e., reduced to the functions the hospital authorities
require of him. The energy required to flesh out in sound the psychic
history of the Afro–American tribe exhausts him and he staggers (He is no
Black Moses able to conjure power out of Jehovah). Three goons with
unsheathed sabres chain the staggering Ironwood to "an ancient-looking
rack." To the astonished Nathaniel the inmates say that such an act is
routine and executed for Ironwood's welfare, and that moreover Ironwood
is protected in such a state, for in the Refuge Hospital his music is appreciated and no one feeds him drugs to destroy him. The sabres, the goons,
and the chaining say something else, i.e., that someone with Ironwood's
power to move his people should be regulated. Such arguments, white
propaganda that the inmates have unfortunately come to believe, are
reminiscent of the arguments about the slaveholders' benevolence, since
the black man's supposedly childish nature requires white paternal supervi-
sion. If we miss the implications of the argument we do not miss those of
the "rack": an effective metaphor for all the permutations that slavery has
undergone in America (much as the blues are permutations of the original
"field hollers" but performing the same function of providing relief from
the pain of oppression (Le Roi Jones, 1963, 60–64). It is a very unclimactic
note on which to end the ritual, but it is Forrest's paradoxical way of showing that even those forms that Afro–Americans have evolved for their liberation have become corrupted by white propaganda and are ultimately still
under white control.

Before focusing on the dozens, I feel it is necessary to examine the role
that Forrest gives to "the masses" in this novel. In *Invisible Man* Ellison
shows the masses as being, on the one hand, victims of the confidence
games set up by the power seekers, and on the other hand, in possession of
a skepticism that rescues them from the delusions of grandeur proferred by

certain self-proclaimed, semisane leaders. In her novel *Their Eyes Were Watching God* (1938), Hurston portrays the black masses as destructive of one another. Forrest combines all three views. Regal's nightmare, summarized already, sums up Forrest's portrayal of the masses. In his depiction he wishes to show that Afro-Americans are devoid of national or group goals. Because the dozens is a ritual of verbal warfare it effectively dramatizes self-destruction among Afro–Americans. Since this self-destruction is highlighted in the behavior of the masses, an understanding of the one adds to the better comprehension of the other.

Rachel's domination of the church sisters comes from their ignorance of what motivates it, and for that matter, what motivates them. Of course, Rachel uses them to work out her own salvation. But we see how far the confusion goes when, at the Easter Sunday concert that Rachel and Regal give, the ecstasy the sisters are moved to comes from their desire for Regal's body. Rachel's illness becomes another focus for Forrest to show how Regal's traumatic existence serves the divisive politics of the church, and to reveal the eagerness of the congregation to rid itself of Rachel. To cope with the psychic disorder that Rachel's illness creates in him, Regal picks up her sacrificial quality by undergoing instant conversion, by deluding himself into thinking he is a preacher, and by finding in Sister La Donna Scales— his unknown triplet sister and a self-sacrificer on the scale of Rachel— Rachel's surrogate. Reverend Foxworth, who is experiencing the perennial difficulties of the black preacher with his flock, knows that Regal's behavior is grief-motivated and will be temporary. His determination, then, is to let Regal preach: that would bring the young sisters in and make the old ones happy; and when they grow weary of his preaching and his unattainability they would turn to ridiculing him, and Foxworth would again grow in their esteem. Foxworth, we see, is the politician that John Pearson was not. Like Wright's Ragland he knows how to exploit grief for his self-enhancement.

The storm that levels the community, including the building that houses River Rock of Eden, occurs around the same time that the community learns that Regal and La Donna's relationship is incestuous. And so a group of church members disguise themselves and hack Regal's body to pieces. Regal's incest among them is the reason they fix upon for God's not having spared *their* church. Forrest shows us Sister Stella at the site of the levelled church "resurrect[ing] the ashes," leading the pack in an expiation of Regal's curse. And how vehemently they urge her on!

LEAD US ACROSS THIS TROUBLED WATER, SISTER STELLA, 'CAUSE WE ARE PRONED TO PERISH! ... (252).

CLEAR THIS THING UP, DEAR SISTER, REGAL WAS A CURSE UPON US! ...(252).

CALL HIM TO THE JUDGMENT SEAT, SISTER, BRING THE DEEDS BEFORE HIS PEOPLE ... (252).

TALK ABOUT IT, DECLARE THE NEWS AND CLEAN REGAL'S LYING WAYS
OUT FROM AMONG US! (253).

The atmosphere of Genesis, not 1970 America, characterizes this ritual.
We think of Sodom and Gomorrah and of the Flood. We see the congregation tyrannized by its fear of God and the use to which Sister Stella puts that
fear. There are parallels here with Gabriel's understanding of his covenant
with God.

In the above we also see the congregation as being hardly more than
leaves spinning in the currents of each new breeze. There is potential here
for comedy, which Forrest quickly introduces when Nathaniel, given an
occasion to speak, announces that Regal had willed his estate of $33,000 to
River Rock of Eden; this news inspires the congregation to seek Sister
Stella's death. She runs to escape them. In treating the subject thus Forrest
makes of River Rock the primordial instrument resonating to each player's
voice. He is among a tiny minority of Afro–American writers, Wright and
Hurston among them, who treat the black masses thus. Forrest certainly
raises the question of whether Afro–Americans are a people unified around
a certain set of beliefs and rituals or a people confused about itself and its
rituals and prey to all exploiting forces. Confusion seems to be paramount
in the vision of reality Forrest portrays here, especially, as we are about to
see, in his use of the dozens.

Forrest's treatment of the dozens is principally to show the ritualization of
mutual distrust among blacks. It is another manifestation of the same forces
that cause Sister Stella to want to sacrifice Rachel or Regal or whoever
presents himself as an opportune victim. This tendency is also shown in
Saltport's experience with the Black Muslims to whom he goes seeking
salvation from narcotics and who "redeem" him and later destroy him. Such
self-destruction reaches its acme in the physical warfare we witness at the
end of the novel. Self-vindication in all these acts is so acute that each being
operates as though he were a nation at war with everyone else. That
Nathaniel, Forrest's commentator in this work, can deal with strange males
only through the dozens points to the depth of racial distrust. It is therefore
Rap Brown's perception of the dozens that come through in Forrest's
exploitation of them, i.e., that "you try to destroy somebody else with words"
(1969, 27). In Wright's *Lawd Today* we saw the dozens being shown principally as entertainment, albeit at the expense of what a healthy people
reveres; its heritage. As well, the ritual occurs among friends. In Forrest's
depiction, however, it is definitely verbal warfare, though lightened by
humor.

Upon boarding the bus that he hopes will take him to Bloomsbury Road,
Nathaniel becomes sidetracked by his reveries of Ironside's music. When he
breaks out of his daydreaming and addresses the driver a dozens bout
begins:

"This ain't no Midnight Train to Georgia, nigger, you've been standing there contemplating your half-ass for the last five minutes—mother-fucker, can't youall read? You've dropped your change, like a whore who's dropped her drawers, bent over and touch her toes, and then asks if my hard-on *Jones* is the wild blue-black goose that's gonna saddle a galloping ghost, and fly up the crack in the chimney."

"Are you the Lone Ranger? Or Batman?"

"I'm your mammy's backyard grocery boy.... I probably fed her the night you were fired from the flint of your sire.... But she useda to call me Mandrake the Magician, you butchered-up, quartered splib."

"If I washed your face with a watermelon rind, long enough, you'd be presentable to your mammy—but your blue-gummed pappy swear you ain't no cream out of his jar..." (*Orphans*, 85).

One sees where Roger Abrahams derived his theory that the dozens is a young man's way of cutting loose the apron strings (*Positively Black*, 41). The psychic energy, not to mention the physical energy, that pours out of this encounter bears no relationship to the question Nathaniel asks. The question becomes simply an excuse to expel anger that originated elsewhere. The tensions of the society—"the motherlessness"—probably make such explosions necessary. The anger is badly directed, against other blacks who did not cause it. Yet, as one student of the dozens observes, blacks know that it is safer to direct anger against members of their own race than against the whites who engendered it (Dollard [1939] 1973, 291–92). Both Baldwin and Poussaint write extensively about this anger (Baldwin, *Dialogue*, 41–42; Poussaint, 62–63, 71–74). It is rather obvious that in diverting the hostility created by whites to members of the black race, blacks only succeed in perpetuating discord among themselves. It is precisely this point that Forrest overtly makes in the second dozens episode in the novel.

This episode occurs when Nathaniel encounters Noah Grandberry for the first time at the Refuge Hospital in the room that they are to share. Nathaniel characteristically mistakes Noah for the Ford described in the news media and proceeds to attack him with a feces-laden bedpan. He misses and Noah responds straight out of the dozens: "Why I'll dangle your lower quarters out of this window until you curse your mammy-fouling hide" (283). But both men quickly realize that neither is the enemy. Here Forrest introduces the concept that Afro–American survival necessitates the abandonment of intragroup warfare, of which the dozens is a symptom. And in a novel that is rarely ideological, two statements by Noah and Nathaniel are outrightly so: "They've set us down here...in order to perish." Nathaniel responds: "They are hoping for our collective suicide or homicide...." And Noah advises Nathaniel that they should "unleash this energy upon the enemy, lest it absorb us in its brimstone black pitch" (283–84). Thus begins an impressive cooperation between the two men that makes their imprisonment easier, for jointly they are able to devise various techniques to defy the prison rules which singly they would have been unable to do. Through their joint effort they are able to *escape* altogether from the Refuge Hospital.

The final episode of the dozens comes at the Ironwood concert. We note that the insults become keenest at the intermission. The exchanges verge on violence at times, for many of the inmates are authentically insane. According to Albert Murray violence is a part of the blues concert, "What with the piano thumping and ringing and the singer walking and talking it like an evangelist at a revival meeting, somebody was forever getting *besides* himself and somebody else was getting maimed for life or killed right on the spot" (1976, 136). The maiming does not occur here; the attendants prevent it.

It is worth noting that despite Nathaniel's epiphany about infighting it is in dozens lingo, which brings him close to being beaten at one point, that he communicates. Since many of the inmates engaging in the dozens are intellectuals who consequently should be able to see into the destructiveness of the form, Forrest implies that their need for the dozens is stronger than the rational faculty that might control it.

Black psychiatrists Grier and Cobbs state that the dozens are "a highly evolved instrument of survival by means of which black boys are introduced to the humiliations which will become so intimate a part of life." But they also add that a promiscuous use of the ritual is engaged in "only by lost men who have no hope of redemption, who live already in hell and who have no further fear of punishment." This evaluation could be applied to the letter to describe Forrest's depiction of the inmates at Ironwood's concert. Moreover on a broader level the prisoners are "boys," America never having allowed them to become men. Grier and Cobbs go on to point out that the same folk culture that nourishes the dozens also esteems "The Signifying Monkey" as a cautionary tale about verbally-promoted discord (1971, 7).

A discussion of Forrest's use of ritual could not conclude without an examination of the role he gives Noah Grandberry, who functions as Forrest's evaluator *par excellence* of the actual function of Afro–American folklore and folklore in general. As his name implies, he is an allegorical figure. Moreover he literally rescues himself from an inundation of Bloodworth curses. His declared descent from "the Seer" (Tiresias), like the Bloodworth lineage, is allegorical. Noah understands that he is a child of perversion (mythologically speaking everyone is) and admits that he suffered from such knowledge. But from the tribulations of his grandfather, who adapted to his alternating male-female role every seven years and his blindness, and yet fulfilled his principal calling as dispenser of wisdom, Noah obtains excellent first-hand knowledge of survival. Furthermore, in seeing how his grandfather was tricked, Noah is determined that not even a professional confidence man like Ford should be able to delude him. Noah learns and demonstrates to Nathaniel that survival depends upon one's creative use of the wisdom of mankind, not just the wisdom of Afro–Americans. Therefore, he will not let a blood curse he had no part in creating, nor history, which is also not of his making, nor a white prison permanently disbar him from the life that he wills.

When, therefore, he procures the parachutes by which he and Nathaniel escape from the sixtieth floor, we are able to see this as an imagistic rendering of what is abstractly called survival. As they land in the schoolyard where rival gangs are murdering each other and the black mayor is burning, Noah's experience with the confidence man equips him to pilot Nathaniel through the destruction into safety. Two very interesting things happen: one is that they find a baby abandoned in a shoe box, another foundling; this suggests the continued cycle of motherlessness just as the intragroup warfare taking place suggests its unabating quality; two, they make their getaway from the scene in an empty police car whose engine was left running, which is to say one simply uses whatever tools are at one's disposal. However, in their insistence on taking the abandoned child, they affirm that whatever survival necessitates, it is not at the price of their humanity.

As a vision of Afro–American survival Noah is a "tall order." Too few people have the resources to deal with short-term reality to be able to find the extra resource to understand the historical plight of Afro–Americans and mankind in general and to convert such understanding into survival strategies. In the name of Forrest's character we get hints of a new order as well as the survivor of the old: Noah, survivor of the Flood, Grandberry, full of seeds to be planted in a new earth. If Noah's depiction is to suggest a fundamental cleansing of the old order, keeping only what is vital for the new, then the novel is quite optimistic. The Biblical story is also about human survival. However, the enduring internecine warfare in the novel undercuts that optimism.

CONCLUSION

This chapter has analyzed seven influential black writers' use of rituals. We can tentatively identify a tradition in the way Afro–American novelists treat the rituals of black Americans. These writers affirm their commitment to portraying Afro–American reality by way of black American rituals. Via such they dramatize the group's beliefs and survival techniques. They also set up a dialectical structure whereby they implicitly evaluate the positive and negative qualities inherent in the rituals. In making the ritual element of folklore a central part of their rhetoric, they establish a clear pattern in the broader domain of the Afro–American novel.

We have also seen that the question of how to integrate such rituals into fiction arises for each author, that the earlier writers greatly assisted the later ones to discover new portrayal techniques, and that, with few exceptions, each writer brings a degree of innovation to the manner in which the rituals are fictionally recorded. We note that with each epoch the perspective for discussing and portraying such rituals widens. Those novels that were published after 1950—*Invisible Man*, *Go Tell It on the Mountain*, *Jubilee*, *Chosen Place, Timeless People*, *The Bloodworth Orphans*—refer black rituals to the conditions and attitudes of, or that derived from, slavery.

Survival or damnation, triumph or resignation are the conceptual frameworks in which the characters are analyzed. Frequently the novelist has no clear answer about the functions of the rituals. Baldwin, for example, feels that the characters in *Go Tell It on the Mountain* would have better served themselves in active battles against injustice—organizing rent strikes, for example—rather than spending whole nights exorcising spurious guilt (*The Fire Next Time*, 57). But there is nothing in *Go Tell It on the Mountain* itself to indicate that Baldwin feels this way. If we turn to Richard Wright, it is clear that he has no answers for the victims of racism in *The Long Dream* despite the ridicule he pours on their rituals; in *Lawd Today* Garveyism is hinted as a possible lever for lifting Jake out of his morass, but even this option is characterized by profound ambivalence. Hughes, Walker, Ellison, and in a lesser way Forrest, take for granted the idea that a people survives as best it is able; and insofar as its rituals help it survive they are a positive force. Forrest reflects much skepticism about the number of Afro–Americans who are *truly* aided by their rituals. In the black preachers Foxworth and Ragland we see how they manipulate their congregations in order to consolidate their power. Increasingly we note that the rituals are tainted by materialism, a portrayal equally evident in Reed's, Morrison's, and Bambara's works (novelists untreated here but who make Afro–American folklore a central part of their aesthetics). All these writers dramatize in one way or another their awareness of the white prison walls that enclose, necessitate, and even caricature Afro–American rituals.

Conclusion

Now that we have seen what several novelists have done with Afro–American folk heroes and rituals, it remains for us to attempt to articulate a tradition for the treatment of this material. Or course, it would be impossible to try to abstract a set of features that apply to all the writers treated here.

The earliest writers were somewhat clumsy in the manner in which they integrated folklore into fiction. The folklore tended to be discrete or predominated at the expense of characterization or theme. Good examples of the former are James Weldon Johnson's *The Autobiography of an Ex-Colored Man* and Zora Neale Hurston's *Jonah's Gourd Vine*. Chesnutt's *The Conjure Woman* is a good example of the latter.

The earlier novelists were handicapped by what publishers demanded. The white public sought generous quantities of minstrel-type buffoonery; they received it from the white writers who interpreted black material, and if black writers did not provide such buffoonery, whites ignored their work. The challenge for the black writer was to appear to satisfy these demands while ensuring that he did not compromise the dignity of the black race; frequently he failed, and in the process his art suffered. During the Harlem Renaissance white America's quest for the "primitive" in Afro–America unbolted the doors of publishing houses and gave a much needed impetus to black writing (Bontemps 1972, 35). This freedom is reflected in the wide range of folk material that Langston Hughes explores in *Not Without Laughter*, material that would not have interested white readers in Chesnutt's and Dunbar's day. Excluding Hurston and Bennett, all the authors treated here are similar to Hughes in that they examine folklore seriously to discern its implications for Afro–American existence. Rituals are not allowed to remain a thing apart or as caricatured quaint antics; instead they are integral aspects of the characters' struggle to survive.

The folk heroes treated here are rarely removed from a realistic context. From the oral portraits of these characters the post-'thirties writers select what they are able to integrate into their plot and discard the rest. They have learned from the many failed experiments, including Hurston's Pearson, that in attempting to incorporate all the characteristics of a given folk hero into a fictive portrait one could easily vitiate the writing. The danger, they saw, was that faithfulness to folklore did not always produce the highly individualized characters that fiction demands. Thereafter each writer who chose to identify a given character with a folk hero selected only enough material to make his character identifiable; from there he proceeded to use that material as a catalyst or obstacle in his fictive world.

But over and above the writers' imaginations, how far they go with this material is largely determined by a folk tradition, in the main African-derived, that demands that black artists minister to their society. Thus art in Afro–America is expected to have a communal function, and the black writer who fails to respect this condition alienates himself from the black community. This accounts greatly for much of the negative criticism blacks directed at Baldwin for writing *Giovanni's Room*, *Another Country*, and *Tell Me How Long the Train's Been Gone*. The obvious option for the black writer, then, is to interpret the psychic and sometimes didactic value of these folk heroes to Afro–Americans. Closely related is the impact of American material culture on the values these heroes embody. Few writers could afford to avoid this subject.

Ministering to the community accounts as well, it seems, for the relatively few portraits of the black preacher of folklore and the Bad Nigger; it requires exceptional fictive invention to make these characters reflect the communal values of black Americans—already in the lore they are accorded an ambiguous status. On the other hand, this ministering function has caused the black novelist to be preoccupied with the trickster. His infinite potential for entertainment and moral instruction is strikingly evident in the lore and the written literature. The manipulation of language is at the heart of trickery; so is material survival. Both are assets for the writer who is himself a trickster of sorts. Even those writers who are chiefly concerned with other folk heroes cannot avoid enriching them with a trait or two from the trickster. It is as though his genes are pervasive in the family of Afro–American folk heroes. But beyond this it is in their trickster tales that Afro–Americans have best conserved the story of their psychological sojourn in America. Duplicity with honor salvaged and the appearance of acquiescence to an immovable force without loss of pride—manipulation that readily reveals the hollowness of white stereotypes about blacks—make these tales an enduring source of race pride.

Much that has been said about the folk heroes can be repeated for the rituals. Every writer analyzed in the ritual section wishes the reader to understand the implications of the rituals that are witnessed. The writers, for the most part, reproduce the humor inherent in many black rituals (they know it represents a resource for dealing with the unchangeable absurd within black American existence) and, with varying degrees of deftness, the tragedy or suffering such humor is intended to soften. This humor is rarely at the expense of the characters—this is the radical distinction between white and black authors' treatment of Afro–American folklore. Even in the case of Wright and Forrest, who sometimes caricature the rituals, the intent is didactic. The amount of reader participation in the rituals varies from author to author and from work to work. In Hughes, Marshall, and Forrest it is abundant; in Ellison, Walker, and Baldwin it is sparse. This is not to say that any of these writers excludes evocation or graphic depiction from their work. Each combines both.

Concerning technique, folklore becomes absorbed into realism. The most notable examples of these works are Bontemps' *Black Thunder*, Wright's *Lawd Today* and *Native Son*, Walker's *Jubilee*, and Gaines' *Of Love and Dust*. From the 1940s onward this became the preferred approach over a mere reproduction of unaltered folklore.

There is another competing approach, one that retains much of the stream-of-consciousness, surrealistic flavor of the folklore. It is exemplified in Morrison's *Sula*, Ellison's *Invisible Man*, and Forrest's *The Bloodworth Orphans*. As in the folklore the characters are weighted with symbolic significance. But the authors are aware that they are writing novels, and so they endeavor to establish a dialectic that comments implicitly on such symbols and that relates them to Afro–American concerns. Such a combination makes for very original writing.

This study brings us almost to the present, which, I feel, requires a study of its own. Not treated here are some of the experiments occurring presently in the Afro–American novel: for example, Toni Morrison's transformations of old folktales into entire novels that interpret contemporary Afro–American reality and that warn, as the folktales do, against the aberrations occurring in Afro–American communal values. *Song of Solomon* utilizes an old folktale that imbued the slaves with hope—the folktale tells of a group of slaves who conquered slavery by acquiring wings and flying back to Africa. In the novel the tale is converted into the Song of Solomon, which is sung at various points, reminding one of the *cante fable* tradition in Afro–American folktale performance. The meaning of Solomon's song is the principal point of the novel, and comes only when ancestral wisdom is relearned and ancestral obligations fulfilled. Timeless beings and unnatural births are part of the mythos; one is reminded of Homer and Coleridge, especially the latter's *Rime of the Ancient Mariner* and *Cristabel*. Moreover the quest for gold which consumes the protagonist and the inordinate preoccupations with racial vengeance of the antagonist must first be cast off if they are to acquire the psychic readiness needed to reestablish a oneness with the ancestral past. In *Tar Baby* Morrison also experiments with the Tar Baby tale. The results are different, but the end is to clear a pathway through the dense jungle of materialism back to the source of ancestral wisdom.

Ishmael Reed is another such writer. His approach reminds one of a painter. Hoodoo is his canvas. Whether one takes *The Freelance Pall-bearers*,

The Last Days of Louisiana Red, or *Mumbo Jumbo,* the black ethos comes together in a set of rituals, beliefs, behaviors, and attitudes to life, to which the term *hoodoo* is given. Hoodoo is derived from nonwestern forces and is always antithetical to western attitudes in that it is a threat to capitalism. In *The Last Days of Louisiana Red* capitalist interests are successful in creating internecine warfare among blacks as a way of appropriating the hoodoo cancer-curing properties of Ed Yellings' gumbo. They are unsuccessful. But while the battle is going on Reed profits from the occasion to comment on the discrete and conflicting aspects of western civilization and their inherent afflictions. He reflects equally on those blacks who have become webbed into them. In *Mumbo Jumbo* the "Jes Grew" phenomenon that threatens capitalist America is derived from hoodoo. The threat of "Jes Grew" is in its neutralization of the competitive urge, its power to impel people to sing and dance and celebrate the sensual. White intellectual and capitalist America seek its source in order to eradicate the threat it poses to puritan hegemony in America. The plots of these novels focus on the battles either to convert hoodoo into a tool of exploitation to increase the profits of the wealthy or to eliminate those of hoodoo's qualities that impede the production-consumption mentality of America. The plots are surrealistically constructed, and the black-white poles of the society remain. There are "close calls," but the hoodoo secrets are eventually preserved or rescued. Above all what informs the world picture in Reed's novels is derived from an African prewestern ethos.

Another writer experimenting with the African ethos is Toni Cade Bambara. She is a cross between Reed and Morrison. In Bambara's *The Salt Eaters* the concepts of illness and the approach to healing are nonwestern. The illness of Velma, the protagonist, is revealed to be the result of a disjunction between herself and the community. The folk healer and her supporting band reestablish that oneness via rituals in which several loa—various minor deities in the vodun tradition—are invoked and communal oneness dramatized for the purpose of opening once more the psychic ducts whose closings had brought about Velma's illness.

With *Praisesong for the Widow* (1983), Paule Marshall joins this group of writers. Gone is the contrasting dimension that white American reality represents in *The Chosen Place, The Timeless People* to which the Bournehills community must react. Great Aunt Cuney's role in passing on ancestral wisdom and Lebert Joseph's demonstration of the vitality of that wisdom are the forces that rescue Avey Johnson from spiritual anemia.

Points of reference, a community of values, and a communal haven carefully restructured with African ancestral wisdom are features common to this set of writers. For them folklore is not a compensatory mechanism, nor is it a reaction to racism, it is a *bona fide* philosophy. These authors are among the most technically audacious and interesting of contemporary

Afro–American novelists. They have all elevated the use of black American folklore in literature to another plane.

Even James Baldwin, so committed to integration in the 'sixties, returned to the exploration of the survival strengths within black American institutions. The vast majority of Afro–American novelists are concerned with exploring what is distinctly theirs within the American cultural matrix. In their quest for styles compatible with their subject matter, they borrow fictional techniques from all sources. But some have evolved styles from the material itself. Albert Murray and Gayl Jones have consciously adapted their prose to reflect the cadences of the blues. We explored that situation at length in our discussion of Forrest. But Murray's and Jones' approach extends as well to the philosophy of the blues. Their characters are not content with failure; rather they pore over it, examine it thoroughly, and use their findings as a basis to begin anew.

The long struggle by earlier black novelists to integrate form and content has resulted in a checklist of questions for those novelists who employ folklore in their creations. In their interviews and autobiographical essays they affirm that these questions weigh heavily on all they create: What techniques are there in the folk forms that can be incorporated into fiction? What techniques or materials are a hindrance to the creation of successful fiction? Are black Americans black first or are they American first? What is valuable in black folklore? What is in it that should be discarded? Or, put another way, what do black Americans desire as a people? And how does folklore aid or impede such aspirations? It is within the framework of such questions that there exists today a definite and crucial tradition of folklore in the Afro–American novel.

Bibliography

WORKS ANALYZED

Baldwin, James. *Go Tell It on the Mountain*. 1953. Reprint. New York: Dell Publishing Co., 1971.

———. *Just Above My Head*. New York: Dial Press, 1978.

Bambara, Toni Cade. *The Salt Eaters*. New York: Random House, 1980.

Bennet, Hal. *Lord of Dark Places*. London: Calder and Boyars, 1971.

Bontemps, Arna. *Black Thunder*. 1936. Reprint. Boston: Beacon Press, 1968.

Brown, Cecil A. *The Life and Loves of Mr. Jiveass Nigger*. New York: Farrar, Strauss and Giroux, 1969.

Chesnutt, Charles W. *The Conjure Woman*. 1899. Reprint. Ridgewood, New Jersey: The Gregg Press, Inc., 1968.

———. "Dave's Neckliss." 1889. In *The Short Fiction of Charles W. Chesnutt*. Edited by Sylvia Lyons Render. Washington, D.C.: Howard University Press, 1974.

———. "The Passing of Grandison." *The Wife of His Youth and Other Stories*. 1899. Reprint. Ann Arbor, Michigan: University of Michigan Press, 1978.

Childress, Alice. *A Short Walk*. New York: Coward, McCann and Geoghegan, 1979.

Cullen, Countee. *One Way to Heaven*. 1932. Reprint. New York: AMS Press, 1969.

Dunbar, Paul L. "Aunt Mandy's Investment." *Folks from Dixie*. 1898. Reprint. Upper Saddle River, New Jersey: The Gregg Press, 1969.

———. "The Ordeal at Mount Hope." *Folks from Dixie*. 1898. Reprint. Upper Saddle River, New Jersey: The Gregg Press, 1969.

———. "The Fruitful Sleeping of the Reverend Elisha Edwards." *The Strength of Gideon*. 1900. Reprint. Miami: Mnemosoyne Publishing, Inc., 1969.

———. "Jim's Probation." *The Strength of Gideon*. 1900. Reprint: Miami: Mnemosoyne Publishing, Inc., 1969.

———. "The Walls of Jericho." *Old Plantation Days*. 1903. Reprint. New York: Negro Universities Press, 1969.

———. "How Brother Parker Fell from Grace." *Old Plantation Days*. 1903. Reprint. New York: Negro Universities Press, 1969.

———. "The Mission of Mr. Scatters." *The Heart of Happy Hollow*. 1904. Reprint. New York: Negro Universities Press, 1969.

———. "Old Abe's Conversion." *The Heart of Happy Hollow*. 1904. Reprint. New York: Negro Universities Press, 1969.

_____. "The Promoter." *The Heart of Happy Hollow*. 1904. Reprint. New York: Negro
        Universities Press, 1969.
Ellison, Ralph W. *Invisible Man*. New York: Vintage Books, 1952 (1982 ed.).
Forrest, Leon. *The Bloodworth Orphans*. New York: Random House, 1977.
Gaines, Ernest J. *Of Love and Dust*. New York: W. W. Norton and Co., 1967.
Hughes, Langston M. *Not Without Laughter*. New York: Alfred Knopf, 1930 (1969 ed.).
_____. *Tambourines to Glory*. New York: John Day, 1958.
Hurston, Zora Neale. *Jonah's Gourd Vine*. Philadelphia: J.B. Lippincott, 1935 (1968 ed.).
Johnson, James W. *The Autobiography of an Ex-Colored Man*. 1912. Reprint. In *Three
        Negro Classics*. New York: Avon Books, 1965.
Killens, John O. *A Man Ain't Nothin' but a Man*. Boston: Little, Brown and Co., 1975.
Marshall, Paule. *The Chosen Place, The Timeless People*. 1969. Reprint. New York:
        Vintage Contemporaries, 1981.
Morrison, Toni. *Sula*. New York: Alfred A. Knopf, Inc., 1973 (1975 Bantam ed.).
Walker, Margaret. *Jubilee*. Boston: Houghton Mifflin, 1966.
Wright, Richard. *Uncle Tom's Children*. New York: Harper and Row, 1940 (1966
        Perennial Library ed.).
_____. *Native Son*. New York: Harper and Row, 1940 (1976 Perennial Classics ed.).
_____. *The Long Dream*. Garden City, New York: Doubleday and Co., Inc., 1958.
_____. *Lawd Today*. London: Anthony Blond, Ltd., 1965 (1969 Panther Books ed.).

WORKS CITED

Abrahams, Roger D. *Deep down in the Jungle: Narrative Folklore from the Streets of Philadel-
        phia*. 1963. Reprint. Chicago: Aldine Publishing Co., 1970.
_____. *Positively Black*. Englewood Cliffs, New Jersey: Prentice-Hall, 1970.
Achebe, Chinua. *Things Fall Apart*. London: Heinemann Educational Books, Ltd.,
        1959.
Aptheker, Herbert. *American Negro Slave Revolts*. 1943. Reprint. New York: International
        Publishers, 1969.
_____, ed. *Book Reviews by W. E. B. DuBois*. Millwood, New York: KTO Press, 1977.
Aubert, Alvin. "Black American Poetry: Its Language, and the Folk Tradition." *Black
        Academy Review*, 2:1–2 (Spring 1971): 71–80.
Baker, Houston A. "*Utile Dulce* and the Literature of the Black American." In *Singers at
        Daybreak*. Washington, D.C.: Howard University Press, 1974.
_____. "A Forgotten Prototype: *The Autobiography of an Ex-Colored Man* and *Invisible
        Man*." In *Singers at Daybreak*. Washington, D.C.: Howard University Press, 1974.
_____. "Black Culture, White Judgement: Patterns of Justice in the Black Narrative."
        In *Singers at Daybreak*. Washington, D.C.: Howard University Press, 1974.
_____. "A Note on Style and the Anthropology of Art." *Black American Literature Forum*
        14:1 (Spring 1980): 3–4.
_____. *The Journey Back*. Chicago: University of Chicago Press, 1980.
_____. "A Black and Crucial Enterprise." *Black American Literature Forum* 16:2
        (Summer 1982): 51–58.
_____. *Blues, Ideology, and Afro–American Literature: A Vernacular Theory*. Chicago: Uni-
        versity of Chicago Press, 1984.
_____. "Belief, Theory and Blues: Notes for a Post-Structuralist Criticism of Afro–
        American Literature." *Studies of Black American Literature Volume II: Belief vs.
        Theory in Black American Literature*. Edited by Joe Weixlmann and Chester J.

Fotentot. Greenwood, Florida: Penekill Publishing Co., 1986.

———. "Caliban's Triple Play." *Critical Inquiry* 13:1 (Autumn 1986): 182–96.

Baldwin, James. "Everybody's Protest Novel." 1949. Reprinted in *Notes of a Native Son*. New York: Bantam Books, 1972.

———. "Many Thousands Gone." 1951. Reprinted in *Notes of a Native Son*. New York: Bantam Books, 1972.

———. *The Fire Next Time*. New York: Dial Press, 1962 (1972 New Dell ed.).

——— and Giovanni, Nikki. *A Dialogue*. Philadelphia: J.B. Lippincott, 1973.

Baldwin, James. *No Name in the Street*. New York: Dial Press, 1972.

———. *If Beale Street Could Talk*. New York: Dial Press, 1974.

Ball, Charles. *A Narrative of the Life and Adventures of Charles Ball, A Black Man*. 1854. Cited in selection reprinted in *To Be a Slave*. Edited by Julius Lester. New York: Dell Publishing, 1968.

Bell, Bernard. *The Folk Roots of Contemporary Afro-American Poetry*. Detroit: Broadside Press, 1974.

Bischoff, Joan. "The Novels of Toni Morrison: Studies in Thwarted Sensitivity." *Studies in Black Literature* 6:3 (Fall 1975): 21–23.

Blake, Susan. "Modern Black Writers and the Folk Tradition." Ph.D. diss., University of Connecticut, 1976.

———. "Rituals and Ritualization in the Works of Ralph Ellison." *PMLA* 94:1 (January 1979): 121–36.

Bone, Robert. *The Negro Novel in America*. New Haven, Connecticut: Yale University Press, 1965.

———. *Down Home*. New York: G. P. Putnam's Sons, 1975.

Bontemps, Arna, ed. *W. C. Handy: Father of the Blues*. 1941. Reprint. New York: Collier Books, 1970.

———. Preface to reprint of *Black Thunder*. Boston: Beacon Press, 1968.

———. "The Awakening: A Memoir." In *The Harlem Renaissance Remembered*. Edited by Arna Bontemps. New York: Dodd, Mead and Co., 1972.

Botkin, Benjamin A., ed. *A Treasury of American Folklore*. New York: Crown Publishers, 1944.

Brawley, Benjamin. *The Negro in Literature and Art in the United States*. New York: Duffield and Co., 1930.

Brewer, John M. *The Word from the Brazos*. Austin, Texas: University of Texas Press, 1953.

Brewer, John M., ed. *American Negro Folklore*. Chicago: Quadrangle Press, 1968.

Brown, Claude. "The Language of Soul." 1968. Reprinted in *Mother Wit from the Laughing Barrel*. Edited by Alan Dundes. Englewood Cliffs, New Jersey: Prentice-Hall, 1973.

———. "Negroes of the Tenderloin." 1898. Reprinted in *The Paul Laurence Dunbar Reader*. Edited by Jay Martin and Gossie H. Hudson. New York: Dodd, Mead & Company, 1975.

Brown, H. Rap. *Die, Nigger, Die*. New York: Dial Press, 1969.

Brown, Sterling, Arthur P. Davis, and Ulysses Lee, eds. *The Negro Caravan*. 1941. Reprint. New York: Arno Press and the New York Times, 1970.

Brown, Sterling. "The Spirituals." In *The Book of Negro Folklore*. Edited by Langston Hughes and Arna Bontemps. New York: Dodd, Mead and Co., 1958 (1984 reprint).

———. "The Blues as Folk Poetry." In *The Book of Negro Folklore*. Edited by Langston

Hughes and Arna Bontemps. New York: Dodd, Mead and Co., 1958 (1984 reprint).

Brown, William W. *Clotel or the President's Daughter*. 1853. Reprint. New York: Citadel Press, 1969.

Bullins, Ed, ed. Preface to *New Plays from the Black Theater*. New York: Bantam Books, 1969.

Bullins, Ed. Preface to *The Theme is Blackness*. New York: William Morrow, 1973.

Burley, Dan. "The Technique of Jive." 1944. Reprinted in *Mother Wit from the Laughing Barrel*. Edited by Alan Dundes. Englewood Cliffs, New Jersey: Prentice-Hall, Inc., 1973.

Butcher, Margaret Just. *The Negro in American Culture*. New York: Alfred A. Knopf, Inc., 1956.

Byerman, Keith E. *Fingering the Jagged Grain: Tradition and Form in Recent Black Fiction*. Athens, Georgia: University of Georgia Press, 1985.

Carter, Bo, and Walter Vincson. "He Calls that Religion." Paramount 13142, July 1932. Lyrics cited in Paul Oliver. *Aspects of the Blues Tradition*. London: Cassell Ltd., 1968 (1970 ed.).

Carter, Harold A. *The Prayer Tradition of Black People*. Valley Forge, Pennsylvania: Judson Press, 1976.

Chapman, Abraham, ed. *New Black Voices: An Anthology of Contemporary Afro-American Literature*. New York: Mentor Books, 1972.

Chesnutt, Charles W. "Superstitions and Folklore in the South." 1901. Reprinted in *Mother Wit from the Laughing Barrel*. Edited by Alan Dundes. Englewood Cliffs, New Jersey: Prentice-Hall, Inc., 1973.

Chesnutt, Helen. *Charles Waddell Chesnutt: Pioneer of the Color Line*. Chapel Hill, North Carolina: University of North Carolina Press, 1952.

Christian, Barbara T. "Ritualistic Process and the Structure of Paule Marshall's *Praisesong for the Widow*." *Callaloo* 6:2 (Spring–Summer 1983): 74–84.

Clark, Kenneth B. *Dark Ghetto*. New York: Harper and Row, 1965.

Collier, Betty J., and Louis Williams. "Economic Status of the Black Male: A Myth Exploded." *Journal of Black Studies* 12:4 (June 1982): 487–98.

Collier, Eugenia. "The Closing of the Circle: Movement from Division to Wholeness in Paule Marshall's Fiction." In *Black Women Writers (1950-1980): A Critical Evaluation*. Edited by Mari Evans. Garden City, New York: Anchor Books, 1984.

Cook, Benjamin. "Non-Verbal Communication among Afro-Americans." In *Rappin' and Stylin' Out*. Edited by Thomas Kochman. Urbana, Illinois: University of Illinois Press, 1972.

Courlander, Harold A. *The Drum and the Hoe: The Life and Lore of the Haitian People*. Berkeley: University of California Press, 1960.

Courlander, Harold A., ed. *A Treasury of Afro-American Folklore*. New York: Crown Publishers, 1976.

Dagan, Esther. In Conversation with the Author. Montreal: 1983.

Dalby, David. "The African Element in American English." In *Rappin' and Stylin' Out*. Edited by Thomas Kochman. Urbana, Illinois: University of Illinois Press, 1972.

Dance, Daryl Cumber. *Shuckin' and Jivin': Folklore from Contemporary Black Americans*. Bloomington, Indiana: Indiana University Press, 1978.

Daniel, Walter C. *Images of the Preacher in Afro-American Literature*. Washington, D.C.: Universities Press, 1981.

Davidson, Basil. *The African Genius*. Boston: Little, Brown and Co., 1969.

Davis, Charles T. "Black is the Color of the Cosmos." In *"Black is the Color of the Cosmos:" Essays on Afro-American Literature and Culture 1942-1981*. Edited by Henry Louis-Gates, Jr. New York: Garland Publishing, 1982.

Davis, Gerald L. *I Got the Word in Me and I Can Sing It You Know: A Study of the Performed Afro-American Sermon*. Philadelphia: University of Pennsylvania Press, 1985.

Delaney, Martin. *Blake or the Huts of America*. 1859. Reprint. Boston: Beacon Press, 1970.

Dixon, Christa K. *Negro Spirituals: From Bible to Folksong*. Philadelphia: Fortress Press, 1976.

Dollard, John. "The Dozens: Dialectic of Insult." 1939. Reprinted in *Mother Wit from the Laughing Barrel*. Edited by Alan Dundes. Englewood Cliffs, New Jersey: Prentice-Hall, Inc., 1973.

Dorson, Richard M. *American Negro Folktales*. Greenwich, Connecticut: Fawcett, 1967.

———. "The Career of 'John Henry'." 1965. Reprinted in *Mother Wit from the Laughing Barrel*. Edited by Alan Dundes. Englewood Cliffs, New Jersey: Prentice-Hall, Inc., 1973.

Douglass, Frederick. *Narrative of the Life of Frederick Douglass*. 1845. Reprint. New York: Signet Books, 1968.

DuBois, William E. B. *The Souls of Black Folk*. 1903. Reprinted in *Three Negro Classics*. New York: Discus Books, 1965.

———, ed. *Morals and Manners among Negro Americans: Report of a Study Made by Atlanta University*. 1914. Reprint. New York: Arno Press and the New York Times, 1968.

Dundes, Alan. "African Tales among the North American Indians." 1965. Reprinted in *Mother Wit from the Laughing Barrel*. Edited by Alan Dundes. Englewood Cliffs, New Jersey: Prentice-Hall, 1973.

———. "The American Concept of Folklore." 1966. Reprinted in *Essays in Folklore*. New York: Mouton Publishers, 1975.

———. Introductory notes to "The Career of 'John Henry.'" By Richard M. Dorson. In *Mother Wit from the Laughing Barrel*. Edited by Alan Dundes. Englewood Cliffs, New Jersey: Prentice-Hall, Inc., 1973.

———. "Structuralism and Folklore." 1976. Reprinted in *Essays in Folkloristics*. New Delhi: The Folklore Institute, 1978.

Elder, Arlene. *'"The Hindered Hand:" Cultural Implications of Early African-American Fiction*. Westport, Connecticut: Greenwood Press, 1978.

Eliot, T. S. "Choruses from the Rock," *Collected Poems 1909-1962*. London: Faber and Faber, 1963.

Ellison, Ralph W. *Shadow and Act*. New York: Vintage Books, 1964. (1972 ed.).

———. *Invisible Man*. New York: Vintage Books, 1952 (1982 ed.).

———. "Study and Experience"—An interview with Ralph Ellison by Robert Stepto. *Massachusetts Review* 18 (Autumn 1977): 417–35.

Ensslen, Klaus. "Collective Experience and Individual Responsibility: Alice Walker's *The Third Life of Grange Copeland* (1970)." In *The Afro-American Novel since 1960*. Edited by Peter Bruck and Wolfgang Karrer. Amsterdam: B. R. Gruner Publishing Co., 1982.

Evans, David. "The Toast in Context." *Journal of American Folklore* 90:356 (April–June 1977): 129–48.

Everett, Chestyn. "Tradition in Afro–American Literature." *Black World* (December 1975): 20–35.

Fabre, Michel. *The Unfinished Quest of Richard Wright*. New York: William Morrow and Co., 1973.

Fanon, Frantz. *Black Skin, White Masks*. New York: Grove Press, 1967.

Ferdinand, Val (Kalamu Ya Salaam). "From "Blackartsouth Ms.'" In *New Black Voices*. Edited by Abraham Chapman. New York: New American Library, 1972.

Fiddle, Seymour. *Toasts: Images of a Victim Society*. New York: Exodus House, 1972.

Fisher, Miles M. *Negro Slave Songs in the United States*. 1953. Reprint. New York: Citadel Press, 1963.

Fisher, William A. *Seventy Negro Spirituals*. 1926. Reprint. New York: AMS Press, 1974.

Forrest, Leon. *There's a Tree More Ancient than Eden*. New York: Random House, 1973.

———. "If He Changed My Name." An Interview with Leon Forrest by Maria Mootry. *The Massachusetts Review* 18 (Winter 1977): 631–42.

Frazier, Franklin E. *The Negro Church in America*. Liverpool: Liverpool University Press, 1964.

Fuller, Hoyt W. "The New Black Literature: Protest or Affirmation." 1970. Reprinted in *The Black Aesthetic*. Edited by Addison Gayle, Jr. Garden City, New York: Doubleday and Co., Inc., 1972.

Gaines, Ernest J. *The Autobiography of Miss Jane Pittman*. New York: Dial Press, 1971 (1981 Bantam ed.).

———. "Characteristics of Negro Expression." In *Negro*. Edited by Nancy Cunard. 1933. Reprinted in an abridged version, edited by Hugh Ford. New York: Frederick Ungar, 1970.

———. *In My Father's House*. New York: Alfred A. Knopf, Inc., 1978.

———. *A Gathering of Old Men*. New York: Alfred A. Knopf, Inc., 1983.

Gallagher, Kathleen. "Bigger's Leap to the Figurative." *CLA Journal* 27:3 (March 1984): 293–314.

Garon, Paul. *Blues and the Poetic Spirit*. 1975. Reprint. New York: DeCapo, 1979.

Gates, Henry-Louis, Jr. "Introduction: Criticism in de Jungle." *Black American Literature Forum* 15:4 (Winter 1981): 123–27.

Gates, Henry-Louis, Jr. " 'The Blackness of Blackness': A Critique of the Sign and 'The Signifying Monkey'." *Critical Inquiry* 9:4 (June 1983): 685–723.

———. " 'The Blackness of Blackness': A Critique of the Sign and 'The Signifying Monkey'." *Critical Inquiry* 9:4 (June 1983): 685–723.

Theory. Edited by Joe Weixlmann and Chester J. Fotentot. Greenwood, Florida: Penekill Publishing Co., 1983.

———, ed. *Black Literature and Literary Theory*. New York: Methuen, 1984.

Gayle, Addison, ed. *The Black Aesthetic*. New York: Anchor Books, 1971.

Gayle, Addison. *The Black Situation*. Garden City, New York: Anchor Books, 1972.

———. *The Way of the New World*. Garden City, New York: Anchor Books, 1975.

Genovese, Eugene. *Roll, Jordan Roll: The World the Slaves Made*. New York: Pantheon Books, 1974.

Gerald, Carolyn F. "The Black Writer and His Role." 1969. Reprinted in *The Black Aesthetic*. Edited by Addison Gayle. New York: Anchor Books, 1972.

Gloster, Hugh M. *Negro Voices in American Fiction*. New York: Russell and Russell, 1948.

Gregory, Dick, with Robert Lypsyte. *Nigger: An Autobiography*. New York: Pocket Books, 1964.

Grier, William, and Cobbs, Price. *Black Rage*. New York: Bantam Books, 1968.

_____. *The Jesus Bag*. New York: McGraw-Hill, 1971.

Hansberry, Lorraine. *A Raisin in the Sun*. New York: Signet, 1958.

Hansen, Chadwick. "Social Influences on Jazz Style: Chicago 1920–30." 1960. Reprinted in *Mother Wit from the Laughing Barrel*. Edited by Alan Dundes. Englewood Cliffs, New Jersey: Prentice-Hall, 1973.

Harris, Joel Chandler. *Uncle Remus: His Songs and His Sayings*. New York: Appleton, 1881.

Harris, Leon. "The Steel-Drivin' Man." 1925. Reprinted in *Mother Wit from the Laughing Barrell*. Edited by Alan Dundes. Englewood Cliffs, New Jersey: Prentice-Hall, 1973.

Haskins, Jim. *Jokes from Black Folks*. Garden City, New York: Doubleday and Co., Inc., 1973.

Heermance, Noel J. *Charles W. Chesnutt: America's First Great Black Novelist*. Hamden, Connecticut: Archon Books, 1974.

Hemenway, Robert E. *Zora Neale Hurston: A Literary Biography*. Urbana: University of Illinois Press, 1977.

_____. "Are You a Flying Lark or a Setting Dove?" In *Afro–American Literature: The Reconstruction of Instruction*. Edited by Robert B. Stepto and Dexter Fisher. New York: Modern Language Association, 1979.

Herskovits, Melville J. *The Myth of the Negro Past*. 1941. Reprint. New York: Harper and Row, Publishers, 1970.

_____. *Dahomean Narrative*. Evanston, Illinois: Northwestern University Press, 1958.

Holland, Laurence B. "Ellison in Black and White: Confession, Violence and Rhetoric in *Invisible Man*." In *New Fiction Studies in the Afro–American Novel since 1945*. Edited by A. Robert Lee. London: Vision Press, 1980.

Holloway, Karla F. C. *The Character of the Word: The Texts of Zora Neale Hurston*. Contributions in Afro–American and African Studies 102. Westport, Connecticut: Greenwood Press, 1987.

Holt, Grace Sims. "Sylin' Outta the Black Pulpit." In *Rappin' and Stylin' Out*. Edited by Thomas A. Kochman. Urbana, Illinois: University of Illinois Press, 1972.

Howard, Lillie P. *Zora Neale Hurston*. Boston: Twayne Publishers, 1981.

Howells, William Dean. Introduction to *Lyrics of Lowly Life*. 1895. Reprinted in *The Complete Poems of Paul Laurence Dunbar*. New York: Dodd, Mead and Co., 1913. Reprint 1970.

Hubbard, Dolan. "The Black Preacher Tale as Cultural Biography." *College Language Association Journal* 30:3 (March 1987): 328–42.

Hughes, Langston M. "The Negro Artist and the Racial Mountain." 1926. Reprinted in *The Black Aesthetic*. Edited by Addison Bayle, Jr. Garden City, New York: Anchor Books, 1971.

_____. *The Big Sea*. New York: Alfred A. Knopf, Inc., 1940.

_____. "Fooling Our White Folks." 1950. Reprinted in *Black American Literature: Literary Essays, Poetry, Fiction, Drama*. Edited by Darwin T. Turner. Columbus, Ohio: Charles E. Merrill Publishing, 1970.

Hughes, Langston M., and Arna Bontemps, eds. *The Book of Negro Folklore*. New York: Dodd, Mead and Co., 1958.

Hurston, Zora Neale. "How It Feels to Be Colored Me." 1928. Reprinted in *A Zora Neale Hurston Reader*. Edited by Alice Walker. Old Westbury, New York: Feminist Press, 1979.

———. "The Sermon as Heard by Zora Neale Hurston from C. C. Lovelace, at Eau Gallie in Florida, May 3, 1929." In *Negro: An Anthology*. Edited by Nancy Cunard. 1933. Reprint. New York: Frederick Ungar Publishing, 1970.

———. "Conversions and Visions." In *Negro: An Anthology*. Edited by Nancy Cunard. 1933. Reprint. New York: Frederick Ungar Publishing, 1970.

———. "Shouting." In *Negro: An Anthology*. Edited by Nancy Cunard. 1933. Reprint. New York: Frederick Ungar Publishing, 1970.

———. *Mules and Men*. 1935. Reprint. Bloomington, Indiana: Indiana University Press, 1978.

———. *Their Eyes Were Watching God*. 1937. Reprint. Urbana, Illinois: University of Illinois Press, 1978.

———. *Moses Man of the Mountain*. 1939. Reprint. Urbana and Chicago: University of Illinois Press, 1984.

———. *Dust Tracks on a Road*. Philadelphia: J. B. Lippincott, 1942.

———. "Story in Harlem Slang." Reprinted in *Mother Wit from the Laughing Barrel*. Edited by Alan Dundes. Englewood Cliffs, New Jersey: Prentice-Hall, 1973.

———. "High John de Conqueror." 1943. Reprinted in *The Book of Negro Folklore*. Edited by Langston Hughes and Arna Bontemps. New York: Dodd Mead and Co., 1958.

Jackson, Bruce. ed. *The Negro and His Folklore in Nineteenth Century Periodicals*. Austin, Texas: University of Texas Press for The American Folklore Society, 1967.

———. "Circus and Street: The Psychosocial Aspects of the Toast." *Journal of American Folklore* 85 (1972): 123–39.

———. *'Get Your Ass in the Water and Swim Like me.'* Cambridge, Massachusetts: Harvard University Press, 1974.

Jackson, Bruce, and Dennis Wepman. Notes and Queries. *Journal of American Folklore* 88 (1975): 185–87.

Jakoski, Helen. "Power Unequal to Man: The Significance of Conjure in Works by Five Afro-Americans." *Southern Folklore Quarterly* 38 (1974): 91–108.

Jenkins, David. *Black Zion: The Return of Afro-Americans and West Indians to Africa*. London: Wildwood House, 1975.

Joe, Kansas, and Memphis Minnie. "Preacher Blues." Vocalion 1643, January 1931. Blues Classics, BC 13. Lyrics cited in Paul Oliver. *Aspects of the Blues Tradition*. London: Cassell Ltd., 1968 (1970 ed.).

Johnson, Charles S. "The New Frontage on American Life." In *The New Negro*. Edited by Alain Locke. 1925. Reprint. New York: Atheneum Press, 1975.

Johnson, Clifton A. *God Struck Me Dead*. Philadelphia: Pilgrim Press, 1969.

Johnson, Guy B. *John Henry: Tracking down a Negro Legend*. Chapel Hill, N.C.: University of North Carolina Press, 1929.

Johnson, James W., and J. Rosamond Johnson, eds. *The First Book of Negro Spirituals*. 1925. *The Second Book of Negro Spirituals*. 1926. Reprinted in one volume *The Books of American Negro Spirituals*, 1969. New York: Da Capo, 1981.

Johnson, James W. Preface to *Book of American Negro Poetry*. [1921] 1931. Reprint. New York: Harcourt, Brace and World, Inc., 1950.

———. *God's Trombones: Seven Negro Sermons in Verse*. 1927. Reprint. New York: Viking Press, 1969.

_____. *Along This Way*. New York: Alfred Knopf, 1933.

Jones, Bessie W., and Audrey L. Vinson. *The World of Toni Morrison: Explorations in Literary Criticism*. Dubuque, Iowa: Kendall/Hunt, 1985.

Jones, Coley. "The Elder He's My Man." Columbia 14489D, December 1929. Lyrics cited in Paul Oliver. *Aspects of the Blues Tradition*. London: Cassell Ltd., 1968 (1970 ed.).

Jones, Gayl. *Corregidora*. New York: Random House, 1976.

Jones, LeRoi (Baraka, Amiri). *Blues People*. New York: William Morrow and Co., 1963.

_____. *Home*. New York: William Morrow and Co., 1966.

_____. *Black Music*. New York: William Morrow and Co., 1967.

Jordan, June. "Notes toward a Balancing of Love and Hatred." *Black World* 23:10 (August 1974): 4–8.

_____. "Strong beyond All Definitions..." Lecture delivered at the 1987 Brown University Conference, "Poetry and Politics." Printed in *The Women's Review of Books* 4:10–11 (July–August 1987): 19–20.

Joyce, Joyce-Ann. "The Black Canon: Reconstructing Black Literary Criticism." *New Literary History* 18:2 (Winter 1987): 335–44.

Jung, Carl G. "On the Psychology of the Trickster Figure." *The Trickster*. Edited by Paul Radin. London: Routledge and Kegan Paul, 1956.

_____. "Approaching the Unconscious." *Man and His Symbols*. Edited by Carl G. Jung. London: Aldus Books, 1964 (1968 Dell ed.).

Karenga, Ron M. "Black Art: Mute Matter Given Force and Function." 1968. Reprint. *New Black Voices*. New York: New American Library, 1972.

Kaunda, Kenneth. "Interview." *Africa Now* 29 (September 1983): 39–52.

Kay, Shirley, ed. *Patterns of the Blues Romance*. New York: Crown Publishers, 1963.

Keil, Charles. *Urban Blues*. Chicago: University of Chicago Press, 1966.

Kelley, William M. *A Different Drummer*. 1959. Reprint. Garden City, New York: Anchor Books, Ltd., 1969.

Kent, George E. "Ralph Ellison and Afro–American Folk and Cultural Tradition." *Blackness and the Adventure of Western Culture*. Chicago: Third World Press, 1972.

_____. "Patterns of the Harlem Renaissance." *Blackness and the Adventure of Western Culture*. Chicago: Third World Press, 1972.

Kenyatta, Jomo. *Facing Mount Kenya: The Tribal Life of the Gikuyu*. New York: Vintage Books, 1965.

Kernan-Mitchell, Claudia. "Signifying." 1971. Reprinted in *Mother Wit from the Laughing Barrel*. Edited by Alan Dundes. Englewood Cliffs, New Jersey: Prentice-Hall, 1973.

Kilham, Elizabeth. "Sketches in Color: IV." 1870. Reprinted in *The Negro and His Folklore in Nineteenth Century Periodicals*. Edited by Bruce Jackson. Austin, Texas: University of Texas Press for the American Folklore Society, 1967.

Killens, John O. *Youngblood*. 1954. Reprint. Athens, Georgia: University of Georgia Press, 1982.

_____. "The Black Writer *vis-à-vis* His Country." 1965. Reprinted in *The Black Aesthetic*. Edited by Addison Gayle, Jr. Garden City, New York: Anchor Books, 1972.

Kochman, Thomas A. "Toward an Ethnography of Black American Speech Behavior." In *Rappin' and Stylin' Out*. Edited by Thomas A. Kochman. Urbana, Illinois: University of Illinois Press. 1972.

Labov, William; Cohen, Paul, *et al.* "Toasts." In *Mother Wit from the Laughing Barrel.* Edited by Alan Dundes, Englewood Cliffs, New Jersey: Prentice-Hall, 1973.

Leach, E. R. *Political Systems of Highland Burma.* 1954. Cited in *Symbol and Theory: A Philosophical Study of Theories of Religion in Social Anthropology.* By John Skorupski. Cambridge: Cambridge University Press. 1976.

———. "Ritualization in Man in Relation to Conceptual and Social Development." *Philosophical Transactions of the Royal Society of London.* Series B, CCL1: 722 (1966): 403–8.

Lee, A. Robert. "Styles of Innovation in the Contemporary Black Novel." In *Studies in the Afro-American Novel Since 1945.* Edited by A. Robert Lee. London: Vision Press, 1980.

Lee, Brian. "Who's Passing for Who in the Fiction of Langston Hughes." In *New Fiction Studies in the Afro-American Novel since 1945.* Edited by A. Robert Lee. London: Vision Press, 1980.

Leonard, Neil. "The Jazzman's Verbal Usage." *Black American Literature Forum* 20:1–2 (Spring–Summer 1986): pp. 151–60.

Levine, Lawrence A. *Black Culture and Black Consciousness: Afro-American Folk Thought from Slavery to Freedom.* New York: Oxford University Press, 1977.

Locke, Alain. "The Negro Spirituals." In *The New Negro.* Edited by Alain Locke. 1925. Reprint. New York: Atheneum Press, 1975.

Marshall, Paule. *Brown Girl, Brownstones.* 1959. Reprint. Old Westbury, New York: Feminist Press, 1981.

———. *Praisesong for the Widow.* New York: G. P. Putnam's Sons, 1983.

———. "Shaping the World of My Art." *New Letters* 40:1 (Autumn 1973): 97–112.

Mason, Ernest D. "Black Art and the Configurations of Experience: The Philosophy of the Black Aesthetic." *College Language Association Journal* 27 (September 1983): 1–17.

Mayer, Phillip. "Joking of Pals in Guisii Age Sets." *African Studies* 10 (March 1951): 27–41.

Mbiti, John S. *African Religions and Philosophy.* London and Nairobi: Heinemann, 1969.

McCall, Dan. *The Example of Richard Wright.* New York: Harcourt Brace Jovanovich, 1969.

McCluskey, John, Jr. "And Called Every Generation Blessed: Theme, Setting, Ritual in the works of Paule Marshall." In *Black Women Writers (1950–1980): A Critical Evaluation.* Edited by Mari Evans. Garden City, New York: Anchor Books, 1984.

Mead, Margaret. "Ritual and Social Crisis." In *The Roots of Ritual.* Edited by James Shaugnessy. Grand Rapids, Michigan: William B. Ferdman's Publishing Co., 1973.

Meriwether, Louise. *Daddy Was a Number Runner.* 1970. Reprint. New York: Feminist Press, 1986.

Mitchell, Henry H. *The Recovery of Preaching.* New York: Harper's Ministers Paperbacks, 1977.

Morrison, Toni. *Song of Solomon.* New York: Alfred A. Knopf, Inc., 1977 (1978 Signet ed.).

———. *Tar Baby.* New York: Alfred A. Knopf, Inc., 1981.

———. " 'Intimate Things in Place:' A Conversation with Toni Morrison." With Robert Stepto. *Massachusetts Review* 28 (Autumn 1977): 473–89.

_____. "Rootedness: The Ancestor as Foundation." In *Black Women Writers (1950–1980): A Critical Evaluation*. Edited by Mari Evans. Garden City, New York: Anchor Books, 1984.

Moses, Wilson J. *Black Messiahs and Uncle Toms: Social and Literary Manipulations of a Religious Myth*. University Park, Pennsylvania: Pennsylvania State University Press, 1982.

Murray, Albert. *The Omni-Americans: New Perspectives on Black Experience and Black Culture*. New York: Outerbridge and Dientsfrey, 1970.

_____. *The Train Whistle Guitar*. New York: McGraw-Hill, 1974.

_____. *Stomping the Blues*. New York: Vintage Books, 1976.

Nagendra, S. P. *The Concept of Ritual in Modern Sociological Theory*. New Delhi: The Academic Journals of India, 1971.

Neal, Larry. Introduction to *Jonah's Gourd Vine*. Philadelphia: Lippincott, 1972.

Odum, Howard. *The Negro and His Songs*. Chapel Hill, North Carolina: University of North Carolina Press, 1925.

Odum, Howard, and Guy B. Johnson. *Negro Workday Songs*. 1926. Reprint. New York: New Universities Press, 1969.

Oliver, Paul. *Blues Fell This Morning*. London: Cassell, 1960.

_____. *Aspects of the Blues Tradition*. London: Cassell, 1968.

Olmsted, Frederick L. *A Journey in the Seaboard States*. 1856. Cited in selection reprinted in *To Be a Slave*. Edited by Julius Lester. New York: Dell Publishing Co., 1968.

O'Meally, Robert G. "Riffs and Rituals in the Works of Ralph Ellison." In *Afro-American Literature: The Reconstruction of Instruction*. Edited by Dexter Fisher and Robert B. Stepto. New York: Modern Language Association, 1979.

Ostendorf, Berndt. *Black Literature in White America*. London: Harvester Press, 1982.

Oster, Harry. *Living Country Blues*. Detroit: Folklore Associates, 1969.

Owens, William. "Folklore of Southern Negroes." 1877. Reprinted in *The Negro and His Folklore in Nineteenth Century Periodicals*. Edited by Bruce Jackson. Austin, Texas: University of Texas Press, 1967.

Palmer, Robert. *Deep Blues: A Musical and Cultural History of the Mississippi Delta*. New York: Viking Press, 1981.

Payne, Ladell. *Black Novelists and the Southern Tradition*. Athens, Georgia: University of Georgia Press, 1981.

Pelton, Robert D. *The Trickster in West Africa: A Study in Mythic Irony and Sacred Delight*. Berkeley, California: University of California Press, 1980.

Plumpp, Sterling D. *Black Rituals*. Chicago: Third World Press, 1972.

Poussaint, Alvin F. *Why Blacks Kill Other Blacks*. New York: Emerson Hall Publishers, 1972.

Puckett, Newbell N. *Folk Beliefs of the Southern Negro*. Chapel Hill, North Carolina: University of North Carolina Press, 1926.

Quinn, Patrick J. "Ritual and the Definition of Space." In *Roots of Ritual*. Edited by James D. Shaugnessy. Grand Rapids, Michigan: William B. Ferdman's Publishing Co., 1973.

Radin, Paul. *The Trickster: A Study in American Indian Mythology*. London: Routledge and Kegan Paul, 1956.

Rattray, Ronald S. *Ashanti*. London: Oxford University Press, 1923.

_____. *Akan-Ashanti Folktales*. London: Oxford University Press, 1930.

Rawick, George P., ed. *The American Slave: A Composite Biography*. Westport, Connecticut: Greenwood Publishing, 1972.

Redding, Jay S. "Portrait against a Background." In *A Singer at Dawn: Reinterpretations of Paul Laurence Dunbar*. Edited by Jay Martin. New York: Dodd, Mead and Co., 1975.

Reed, Ishmael. *Mumbo Jumbo*. Garden City, New York: Doubleday and Co., Inc., 1972 (1978 Bard ed.).

_____. *The Last Days of Louisiana Red*. New York: Random House, Inc., 1974 (1976 Bard ed.).

Render, Sylvia Lyons. *Charles W. Chesnutt*. Boston: Twayne Publishers, 1980.

Robinson, Rob, and Meade L. Lewis. ("Mississippi Sheiks"). "The Preacher Must Get Some Sometime." Paramount 13028, November 1930. Lyrics cited in Paul Oliver, *Aspects of the Blues Tradition*. London: Cassell Ltd., 1968 (1970 ed.).

Rogers, J. A. "Jazz at Home." In *The New Negro*. Edited by Alain Locke. 1925. Reprint. New York: Atheneum Press, 1975.

Rosenberg, Bruce A. "The Formulaic Quality of Spontaneous Folk Sermons." *Journal of American Folklore* 83 (1970): 3–20.

Royster, Phillip K. "A Priest and a Witch against the Spiders and the Snakes: Scapegoating in Toni Morrison's *Sula*." *Umoja* 2:3 (Fall 1978).

Ruas, Charles. "Toni Morrison" *Conversations with American Writers*. New York: Alfred A. Knopf, 1985.

Sackheim, Eric. *The Blues Line: A Collection of Blues Lyrics*. New York: Grossman Publishers, 1969.

Sandiford, Keith A. "Paule Marshall's *Praisesong for the Widow*: The Reluctant Heiress, or Whose Life Is It Anyway." *Black American Literature Forum* 20:4 (Winter 1986): 371–92.

Sartre, Jean-Paul. "Black Orpheus." 1948. Reprinted in *The Black American Writer Volume II: Poetry and Drama*. Edited by C. W. E. Bigsby. Baltimore: Penguin Books, 1971.

Shange, Ntozake. *Sassafrass, Cypress and Indigo*. New York: St. Martin's Press, 1982.

Shapiro, Karl. "Boy-Man." 1953. Reprinted in *Karl Shapiro: Collected Poems 1940–1978*. New York: Random House, 1978.

Skorupski, John. *Symbol and Theory: A Philosophical Study of Theories of Religion in Social Anthropology*. Cambridge: Cambridge University Press, 1976.

Spillers, Hortense J. "Martin Luther King and the Style of the Black Folk Sermon." *Black Scholar* 3:1 (September 1971): 14–27.

_____. "*Chosen Place, Timeless People*: Some Figurations on the New World." In *Conjuring: Black Women, Fiction and Literary Tradition*. Edited by Marjorie Pryse and Hortense J. Spillers. Bloomington, Indiana: Indiana University Press, 1985.

Stewart, Jeffrey C., ed. *The Critical Temper of Alain Locke: A Selection of His Essays on Art and Culture*. New York: Garland Publishing, 1983.

Stuckey, Sterling. "Through the Prism of Folklore: The Black Ethos in Slavery." 1968. Reprinted in *New Black Voices*. Edited by Abraham Chapman. New York: New American Library, 1972.

Tate, Claudia, ed. *Black Women Writers at Work*. New York: Continuum, 1983.

Taylor, Mildred D. *Song of the Trees*. New York: Dial Press, 1975.

_____. *Roll of Thunder, Hear My Cry*. New York: Dial Press, 1977.

————. *Let the Circle Be Unbroken*. New York: Dial Press, 1981.

Titon, Jeff Todd. *Early Down Home Blues*. Chicago: University of Illinois Press, 1971.

Tsuruta, Dorothy Randall. "In Dialogue to Define Aesthetics: James Baldwin and Chinua Achebe" (at the 1981 African Literature Association Conference). *Black Scholar* 12:2(March–April 1981): 72–79.

Wadlington, Warwick. *The Confidence Game in American Literature*. Princeton, New Jersey: Princeton University Press, 1975.

Walker, Margaret. *How I Wrote Jubilee*. Chicago: Third World Press, 1972.

————. "Richard Wright." In *Richard Wright: Impressions and Perspectives*. Edited by David Ray and Robert Farnsworth. Ann Arbor, Michigan: University of Michigan Press, 1973.

————. " 'Poetry, History and Humanism', an Interview with Margaret Walker." By Charles H. Rowell. *Black World* 25:2 (December 1975): 4–17.

Wallace, Michèle. *Black Macho and the Myth of the Superwoman*. New York: Dial Press, 1979.

Washington, Joseph R., Jr. *Black Sects and Cults*. Garden City, New York: Doubleday and Co., 1972.

Washington, Mary Helen. Afterword to *Brown Girl, Brownstones*, by Paule Marshall. Old Westbury, New York: Feminist Press, 1981.

Weixlmann, Joe, and Chester J. Fotentot, eds. *Studies in Black American Literature Volume I: Black American Prose Theory*, Greenwood, Florida: Penekill Publishing Co., 1983.

————. *Studies in Black American Literature Volume II: Belief vs Theory in Black American Literature*. Greenwood, Florida: Penekill Publishing Co., 1986.

Wepman, Dennis, et al., eds. *The Life, the Lore and Folk Poetry of the Black Hustler*. University of Pennsylvania Press, 1976.

White, Walter, *Fire in the Flint*. New York: Alfred Knopf, 1924.

Wicker, Brian. "Ritual and Culture: Some Dimensions of the Problem Today." In *Roots of Ritual*. Edited by James Shaugnessy. Grand Rapids, Michigan: William B. Ferdman's Publishing Co., 1973.

Wiggins, William. "Jack Johnson as Bad Nigger: The Folklore of His Life." *Black Scholar* 2:5 (January 1971): 35–46.

Wilgus, D. K. "The Negro-White Spiritual." 1959. Reprinted in *Mother Wit from the Laughing Barrel*. Edited by Alan Dundes. Englewood Cliffs, New Jersey: Prentice-Hall, 1973.

Williams, Sherley Ann. *Give Birth to Brightness*. New York: Dial Press, 1972.

Willie, Charles V. *A New Look at Black Families*. New York: General Hall, 1976.

Winther, Per. "Imagery of Imprisonment in Ralph Ellison's *Invisible Man*." *Black American Literature Forum* 17:3 (Fall 1983): 115–19.

Wolfe, Bernard. "Uncle Remus and the Malevolent Rabbit." 1949. Reprinted in *Mother Wit from the Laughing Barrel*. Edited by Alan Dundes. Englewood Cliffs, New Jersey: Prentice-Hall, 1973.

Work, John. *American Negro Songs and Spirituals*. New York: Bonanza Books, 1940.

Wright, Richard. "Blueprint for Negro Writing." 1937. Reprinted in *The Black Aesthetic*. Edited by Addison Gayle, Jr. Garden City, New York: Anchor Books, 1972.

————. "Big Boy Leaves Home." In *Uncle Tom's Children*. New York: Harper and Row, 1940 (Perennial 1965 ed.).

————. "Fire and Cloud." In *Uncle Tom's Children*. New York: Harper and Row, 1940 (Perennial 1965 ed.).

————. "How Bigger Was Born." 1940. Reprinted in *Native Son*. New York: Harper Brothers' Perennial Classics, 1966.

————. "I Bite the Hand that Feeds Me." *Atlantic Monthly* 155 (June 1940): 826–28.

————. *Twelve Million Black Voices: A Folk History of the Negro in the United States*. 1941. Reprint. New York: Arno and The New York Times, 1969.

————. *Black Boy*. New York: Harper and Row, Publishers, 1944 (1966 Perennial Classics ed.).

————. *American Hunger*. New York: Harper and Row, Publishers, 1944 (1983 Colophon ed.).

————. *The Outsider*. New York: Harper and Row, 1953 (Perennial 1965 ed.).

————. *Black Power*. New York: Harper and Brothers. 1954.

————. *White Man, Listen*. Garden City, New York: Doubleday Anchor Books, 1957 (1964 ed.).

Wright, Sarah B. *This Child's Gonna Live*. New York: Delacorte Press, 1969.

Index

About the Author

H. NIGEL THOMAS is an assistant professor of American Literature, and is an associate editor of *Kola,* a literary magazine. He has published short fiction and poems in magazines and anthologies.